THE MOMENTUM SALES MODEL

How to achieve success in sales, exceed targets and generate explosive growth

TIM CASTLE

K
N
O
W
N

WWW.GET-KNOWN.CO.UK

Also by Tim Castle

THE ART OF NEGOTIATION
HOW TO GET WHAT YOU WANT (EVERY TIME)

TIM CASTLE
Author of BE THE LION and THE ART OF DECISION MAKING

Anyone can learn to become a good negotiator. Let me show you how. I became a professional negotiator at the age of 23, and within just 12 months, I was single-handedly negotiating $1,000,000 deals. In this book, I'll share insider tips as well as teach you how to master the fundamentals, set clear objectives, overcome obstacles (i.e. turn "no" into "yes") and build long-term relationships, whether you are negotiating for yourself or on behalf of your business. Ready to see what you can achieve?

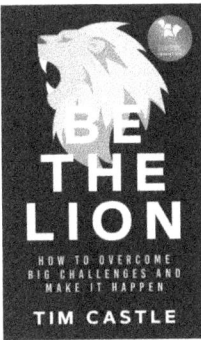

BE THE LION
HOW TO OVERCOME BIG CHALLENGES AND MAKE IT HAPPEN

TIM CASTLE

Want to achieve more without the stress and overwhelm? As an ambitious person, I inevitably have a lot on my plate. In just two years, I went through pretty much every life change you can imagine. I had to be the lion. I created new habits and thought patterns, and reconnected with my purpose to get sh!t done. LET ME SHOW YOU HOW TO SET THE BAR HIGH AND SUCCEED. Taking yourself to the next level and achieving huge success should be joyful. So let's have some fun...

THE ART OF DECISION MAKING

HOW TO MAKE EFFECTIVE DECISIONS UNDER PRESSURE

TIM CASTLE

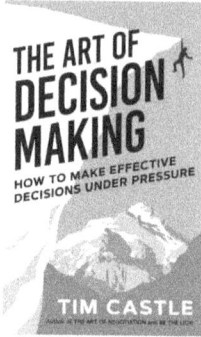

Making good decisions quickly is what marks out truly great leaders from the rest of us. Decision-making is one of the most sought-after skills today, but it is also one most of us have never been taught. Aged 19, I went off-piste snowboarding, way before I had the skills or experience to do so, and very quickly found myself hurtling towards the edge of a cliff face on sheet ice. Within minutes, I was literally hanging onto a boulder for dear life, with my legs dangling over the precipice. Every single decision I made over the next few hours was life or death. That day, my brain worked overtime to keep me alive.

After reading this book, you'll find making good decisions quick and easy and will no longer waste time stressing over them or avoid stepping up to make them.

Dedicated to you, the ambitious individual that seeks to better serve the world through sales, entrepreneurship and excellence.

Allow this book to change you, to help you operate with a higher standard and play full out. Step into that bigger vision of yourself and your life as if your success is guaranteed.

Never again shall your sales plateau, here's to your upward rise towards success, increased sales momentum and a life of freedom.

Pre-defined workouts for the mind. 66 Day Challenges you can take to LEVEL UP and elevate your life. Improve your ability to embrace stress, calm your worries, have a great day, every day. Available now on Google Store and App Store. Search *Level Up: Elevate Your Life*.

Hi, I'm Tim Castle – Author, Mindset Coach and Entrepreneur. This is my podcast where I sit down with courageous people doing inspirational things around the world. There is so much good in the world, so many amazing stories, each with their own valuable lessons, and I want to use this platform as a vehicle for change. Whether you are facing challenges right now, going through a tough time or on top of the world, we can all improve by sharing our story. My mission is to help others achieve their big goals, dreams and vision and become the best version of themselves.

This course will help you ingrain the principles and philosophies accelerating your development and results as a momentum seller. We go deep! If you're committed to your bigger, brighter future, jump onboard.

Contents

This Book Will

Whether you're new to sales, an old hat or at the beginning of a new adventure, either by joining a new company or starting a business, this book will help you to turbo charge your sales outcomes and create momentum.

The chief aim of this book is to systematically teach you how to develop momentum at all stages of the sales cycle, enabling you to take this skill with you anywhere you go.

In this book I'll go through each step of my Momentum Sales Model, which will transform you into becoming unstoppable in business development and sales. This model will work for you, whether you're the founder of a business in the early stages or part of a huge sales team in a multinational corporate. Each element of this 8-part model has been carefully and deliberately crafted to help you improve and maximise your full potential as a salesperson.

We'll start off by taking a look at your **mindset** and I'll help you to develop facets of your mental toughness and creativity, then we'll explore the **opportunity** and how to maximise it. Next, we'll tackle a big problem when it comes to sales momentum and that's **motivation,** and more importantly how to develop your persistence. Following this you'll be in prime position to fine tune your **energy,** enthusiasm and charisma to really get clients excited and emotionally connected to you and your offering. Once you're at this juncture, you're really starting to feel a wave of momentum behind you, but we aren't done yet, let's tweak that pitch so you nail it, and form winning habits that allow you to consistently keep **nailing the pitch**. One powerful habit that we'll focus on deeply is your **time management** so that you can be in front of prospects daily before 9am. In this new world, what it needs more from salespeople is **understanding**, so I'll show you how to weave it into your sales process without being taken advantage of. Finally, we'll develop the most important element – the habit of doing **more** than is required.

At the core of it, I'll show you how to create a magnetic field of momentum so strong that you'll have to fight clients away, which in and of itself is exactly the position you want to be in, giving you the flexibility to say "no" to business that doesn't fit your overall strategy.

When you reach this energetic level of momentum, you get to choose; you've earned the right to be selective and make choices that empower the future success of your business rather than scrabble around for loose change just to put food on the table and keep the lights on.

I'll teach you to make an impact in business so big that you'll be considered to have the Midas touch. It will be as if success rains down on you, everything you touch turns to sold and you'll be known for getting the job done and over-delivering on expectations.

We'll look at how to grow your authority and influence internally with co-workers and externally with clients, so you are seen as the go-to person in your business. This will shape how you go about your sales process, allowing you to influence strategically for the attainment of both your long-term and short-term goals. Ultimately, this will lead to building a culture of high performance that will set you apart from your competitors.

When you reach this stage, both you (your personal brand) and your business will take on a life of their own.

This book is intended to help you accelerate your growth, stand out from the crowd and, most importantly, put sales numbers on the board in a fun and repeatable way. This is the key: once you learn the Momentum Sales Model you can take it anywhere and repeat, repeat, repeat.

This book will take you from zero to your first million in sales and way beyond.

Once you experience success from the Momentum Sales Model, I hope that you will live it, love it and share it with others so they may benefit; that is my wish.

My aspiration for you is that it will change your life in unfathomable ways. I hope that it helps you create generational wealth, move your family from mediocre results to unbelievable outcomes. I want you to experience prosperity at the highest levels and live a life filled with grace, miracles and abundance. This is so that you can do more good in the world and enjoy the opportunity that working in sales presents.

I want that for you. I want you to experience the joy and the confidence of knowing that you can create momentum wherever you go, that you can truly put your dreams into action and you can, in a word, sell.

Let's begin this journey now.

Best,
Tim

.

Meet Your Sales Coach, Tim Castle

Tim Castle is:

- A loving husband and devoted dad to two boys, Levi and Rome. Being a role model for them and instilling the message that anything is possible is really important to him.

- A bestselling Author, Mindset Coach and Entrepreneur.

- A sought-after Sales and Negotiation Trainer for startups and corporates alike, involved at the grassroots level, working with founders, elite athletes and business moguls.

- A co-founder of Level Up: Elevate Your Life, a personal development app that helps you to develop positive daily habits through guided meditations and tasks.

- A co-founder of Get Gig Now, a hospitality-focused job site that matches your availability with the best roles at hotels, restaurants and coffee shops.

- A co-founder of Lion Up Health, a company focused on quality, transparency and great-tasting wellness products.

- The host of *The Tim Castle Show*, a podcast in which he interviews courageous people doing inspirational things around the world. Guests include Iron Cowboy James Lawrence, Glenn Sanford

(Founder eXp Realty and CEO of SUCCESS Magazine), Mental Toughness Trainer Steve Seibold and YouTuber Evan Carmichael.

- An investor in Web3 and Blockchain related projects.

- Passionate about wellbeing, success and self-improvement, life experiences and creating outstanding memories.

Tim Castle has:

- Sold multimillion dollar contracts to Fortune 500 clients around the world.

- Advised and built tech businesses across multiple regions, turning them into fast-growing entities, breaking records and executive expectations.

- Been a sales advisor to start-ups, preparing them to raise funds at investor pitch days, Angel and VC engagements.

- Helped both corporates and entrepreneur sales teams by teaching them how to sell using the Momentum Sales Model. Feedback from Tim's training:

> *"Tim's presentation was so much more personable than other sales strategies and the way he sets out his email hooks was really relevant to me at this stage of our sales cycle."*

> *"Best sales training I have attended – Tim really broke it down."*

"Tim is clearly passionate about sales and was able to very clearly articulate the steps that make a great sales strategy and execution. The best sales education I've ever had."

Find Tim on:

- Instagram @timjscastle

- Twitter @timjscastle

- Facebook @timjscastle

- Website www.timjscastle.com

Download the Momentum Sales Model free resources here:

My Philosophy: Believe it is possible

A quick word on my life philosophy before we begin.

For the past 15 years I have lived by the mantra *"believe it is possible,"* after negotiating my way into a top British university without a UCAS application. This changed my understanding of what's possible, and I haven't looked back since.

It is perhaps not surprising then that the first part of my career was spent as a professional negotiator, and the second half focused on driving business development and rapid expansion for companies in various counties across the globe.

As I move into the next stage of my career, I am now teaching what I have learnt, coaching go-getters and mentoring some of the world's largest corporates and most exciting start-ups. This is the point in my career that I feel it has all been building towards, and I am now directly able to help others achieve their big goals and become their best versions of themselves.

My *believe it is possible* philosophy has been a powerful driver for many of the most amazing experiences I have ever had. From publishing three bestselling books, with some of them going on to win awards and even get on to the reading list of celebrities and a prime minister, to advising some phenomenal founders and salespeople across the world, building startups and investing and hopefully making a difference.

If you get just one thing from this book, I want it to be this: go for it.

Sales and business development is about believing it is possible and forging a path where there was none before. It takes guts, imagination and foresight to walk this path. Therefore, if you want to maximise your sales, you need to get comfortable with being uncomfortable, doing things that others aren't, like cutting meetings short when they're not valuable, flying into a new market and seeing what you can make happen just with the belief that you can, and going against the grain.

You have to risk making the unpopular decision, for having a vision and holding on to it longer, harder and more persistently than anyone else, and, as Jeff Bezos says, be "willing to be misunderstood for long periods of time."

If you are ever facing doubts, remember the *believe it is possible* philosophy and truly know that a path exists – you just have to create it.

Prologue

I was sitting opposite the CEO of a large corporation.

"Tell me, Tim, what is it that you do?"

The answer was easy. "I create momentum."

The reason it was so easy to explain is because creating momentum has become part of the fabric of my identity. It's baked into the way I think, what I value, how I operate and the standard I hold myself and my sales team to. I live and breathe sales momentum.

The thrill of moving a company from zero to way past a million dollars and beyond is my motivation and the challenge I enjoy solving.

When you boil it down to the core ingredient, the secret sauce, the magic formula, when I go into a business or begin to build a business, my key objective, my goal, is to do one thing above all else – create momentum. This is what leads to success in sales and business development, and this is exactly what I'm going to teach you in this book.

This book will help you become a person who believes it is possible and doesn't hesitate to take action, knowing how to design and implement an effective sales plan that breaks records and opens many doors.

CHAPTER 1

Are you momentum negative or momentum positive?

Momentum definition:

"Momentum is the ability to create a wave of sales activity so big that it consistently flows into your business allowing you to maintain a healthy pipeline and multiply opportunities. It is a state reached through the initiation of a strategic process, setting in motion a series of effective sales rituals, performed daily, that require full discipline, complete ownership and absolute faith. It can be taught to anyone, but it is fully mastered by few."

– TIM CASTLE

MEET JOE

He's got a wife, a newborn baby (six months) and a two-year-old. He's renting an apartment whilst the renovations are being completed on his new house in a glamorous area of the city. He drives an Audi A4, enjoys long walks and BBQs.

Looking from the outside he's killing it; he's got everything he wants.

There's only one problem.

On the inside Joe's life is in turmoil. The pressure of a young family, the sleepless nights due to early morning nappy changes and bottle feeds, the bills mounting up, not just from the renovations but also from the holiday to the Maldives that still needs paying off.

If only there was a way to make some good money, he thought. Decent money that would fast track his goals and take the pressure off him a bit. A restart, a breath of air, a let-up, some form of relief.

He's been in his current sales role for nearly two years. Joe is well-liked and, despite a few niggles and disagreements with his boss, most of the time, work is alright.

The issue with work is he's been dealt a bad hand, as the patch of business he's been given doesn't consist of clients that want to spend money on the products he is selling. They either already have agreements in place with competitors, don't have enough money to start with or aren't ready to buy yet. Every which way you cut it, it's a struggle to get clients over the line and, even when they do make the decision, they tend to re-negotiate later or end up decreasing the size of the overall deal.

It feels like a downward death spiral; clients are stingy, life is getting more complicated – not to mention expensive – and the walls are closing in a bit.

Joe's Day

3.30AM	WAKE UP (GIVE FORMULA TO THE BABY)
3.45AM	QUICKLY WATCH THE FOOTY HIGHLIGHTS
4.15AM	BACK TO BED
8AM	WAKE UP, SHOWER, GET DRESSED, FEELING EXHAUSTED
9AM	NIP OUT FOR A COFFEE AND BAGEL FROM THE BAKERY
9.15AM	DIAL INTO THE SALES WHIP CALL (LATE), HEAR WHAT OTHERS IN THE TEAM ARE DOING
9.20AM	ASKED TO STAY BACK AFTER THE CALL BY THE BOSS
9.40AM	FINISH EXPLAINING TO THE BOSS THAT YOU'VE GOT IT UNDER CONTROL, YOU JUST NEED DECENT LEADS AND SOME SALES
9.45AM	SIT DOWN TO DO WORK, CHECK EMAILS, 32 UNREAD EMAILS
10AM	FOLLOW UP WITH OTHER SALES PEOPLE TO SEE IF THEY CAN MAKE SOME INTRODUCTIONS, NOT SURE WHY THEY DON'T HELP ME OUT MORE
10.15AM	BOSS CALLS AND ASKS TO BE TALKED THROUGH THE SALE PIPELINE, QUARTERLY PLAN, DETAILED EXPLANATION OF EVERY ACCOUNT, THEN HE ASKS FOR DAILY UPDATES GOING FORWARDS
10.45AM	GET ANOTHER COFFEE, SALES FIGURES DON'T LOOK GREAT, TIME TO HUSTLE, GOOD JOB I HAVE A CLIENT MEETING IN 15 MINUTES, MAYBE THIS WILL BRING SOME GOOD NEWS
10.59AM	EMAIL FROM CLEINT APOLOGISING FOR CANCELLING 11AM MEETING

11.05AM	COMMIT TO SEND OUT 120 PROSPECTING EMAILS USING STANDARD EMAIL TEMPLATE, AND SPEND NEXT FEW HOURS BLASTING ANYONE THAT COMES TO MIND
12PM	RECEIVE A BRIEF FROM POTENTIAL CLIENT REQUIRING A FAST TURN-AROUND
12.05PM	HAVE LUNCH, FEELING UNMOTIVATED, CLIENTS ALWAYS WANT THINGS 'URGENTLY'
3.15PM	ACHIEVE GOAL OF GETTING ALL 120 EMAILS OUT, KNACKERED BUT FEELING PRODUCTIVE
5PM	MEET FRIENDS FOR A QUICK BEER AND CHAT
6PM	COOK DINNER FOR KIDS
7PM	COOK DINNER AND EAT WITH WIFE
7.30PM	NETFLIX, SNACKS AND A COUPLE OF BEERS
11.30PM	BED

On a positive note, Joe wants to make a red hot go of it. Yet, it's hard to move the needle with clients that don't want to be moved, a boss who doesn't understand and a life that needs constant attention that takes him away from the business.

NOW MEET ERIC

He's also got a sales job, two kids, a wife who's made it big in TV and rents a house with a mortgage on another, which he leases out as a passive income stream. He's doing an MBA.

Eric knows that he's got a lot going on, but he also knows where he wants to get to. He's willing to make sacrifices now and invest in his future. He's a visionary and conducts his life through the mantra "either I win or I learn." This means that he's living in the present moment, not stressing about what he can't control but absolutely focused on changing what he can.

Eric has recently moved to a new job and wants to prove himself to the leaders of the business and make a name for himself internally. He's a fantastic networker and is always meeting interesting people and giving to others. He values family time, self-development and maximising his full potential. He sees life as a game and he's ready to play.

Eric's Day

3.30AM	WAKE UP (GIVE FORMULA TO THE BABY)
3.45AM	BACK TO BED
5AM	WAKE UP, MEDITATE, READ, JOURNAL, LISTEN TO 10 MINUTES OF THE MASTER HIMSELF, JIM ROHN, TO KICK THINGS OFF AND GET MIND RIGHT FOR ANOTHER AMAZING DAY AHEAD
5.30AM	TRAVEL TO THE GYM (LISTEN TO PODCAST ON WAY)
6AM	WORK OUT (LISTEN TO AN INSPIRATIONAL, ENTREPRENEURIAL PODCAST, OR PUMP UP MUSIC
7.15AM	WAKE KIDS, CUDDLE TIME, BREAKFAST, PLAY

7.45AM	MAKE A ROUGH PLAN FOR THE DAY, OUTLINE MAIN GOALS AND IDENTIFY WINDOWS OF TIME FOR PROSPECTING
7.55AM	FIRE OUT A FEW EMAILS TO CLIENTS TO GET THE BALL ROLLING, EMAIL OTHER DEPARTMENTS FOR REQUIRED INFO, PREPARE ANSWERS TO TRICKY QUESTIONS FOR MEETINGS LATER IN THE DAY
8.30AM	BEGIN DAY, HIT SEND ON 9 PROSPECTING EMAILS DRAFTED THE NIGHT BEFORE AND FOLLOW UP WITH CLIENTS WHO HAVE YET TO RESPOND, FEELING PUMPED FOR THE DAY!
8.59AM	DIAL INTO SALES CALL, ADD VALUE AND POSITIVITY WHERE POSSIBLE
9.15AM	GET CRACKING ON 3 BRIEFS THAT CAME IN LAST NIGHT, LIFE IS GOOD, LET'S DO THIS!
9.20AM	QUICK CALL WITH OTHER DEPARTMENTS TO CHECK IN, GET INTEL, GET ANSWERS
9.35AM	SEND OUT RESPONSE TO BRIEF 1
9.45AM	LOTS OF SALES TODAY IN THE COMPANY SYSTEM, MAKE NOTE TO CROSS CHECK AND TARGET SIMILAR CLIENTS IN THE SAME VERTICALS (LEVERAGE)
9.50AM	SEND A COUPLE OF WARM LEADS TO TEAMMATES IN THE SALES TEAM; WHAT GOES AROUND COMES AROUND
10.20AM	SEND OUT BRIEF 2 RESPONSE
10.30AM	MEETING WITH CLIENT, WE'RE REALLY ROLLING NOW
11AM	RECEIVE A LARGE BRIEF WITH QUICK TURNAROUND
11.50AM	QUICK CALL TO REPEAT CLIENT TO SEE WHAT'S COMING IN FOR THE QUARTER, INVITE THEM TO BREAKFAST ONE MORNING NEXT WEEK

12PM	WORK ON FAST TURNAROUND BRIEF, BETTER TO GET THIS BACK FIRST AND IMPRESS THE CLIENT (TAKES PRECEDENCE DUE TO TIME PRESSURE AND POTENTIAL REVENUE SIZE)
12.50PM	SEND OUT FAST TURNAROUND BRIEF, ASK FOR INTRODUCTIONS TO OTHERS IN CLIENT TEAM
1PM	LUNCH (WATCH TOM BILYEU'S IMPACT THEORY ON YOUTUBE WHILE EATING) LEARNERS ARE EARNERS
1.30PM	BACK AT IT, PREPARE FOR 3PM MEETING
2.15PM	WORK ON BRIEF 3, FEELING PUMPED!
2.45PM	SEND OUT BRIEF 3
2.55PM	QUICK CHECK-IN WITH ANOTHER DEPARTMENT TO ANSWER COUPLE OF QUESTIONS
3PM	MEETING WITH ANOTHER CLIENT
4.05PM	CLIENT CALLS UNEXPECTEDLY, QUICKLY ANSWER QUESTIONS RATHER THAN CALL BACK LATER
4.15PM	SEND OVER REQUIRED INFO TO CLIENT, IT'S A POTENTIAL OPPORTUNITY, NOTHING SOLID BUT COULD BE BIG
4.30PM	DRAFT UP AND SEND 10 HIGH QUALITY PROSPECTING EMAILS TO THE TYPE OF CLIENTS THAT ARE SPENDING WITH OTHERS IN THE TEAM
5.30PM	DRAFT UP A QUICK OUTLINE FOR THE DAY AHEAD
5.45PM	MEETING WITH ANOTHER CLIENT, BITE TO EAT AND DISCUSSION AROUND EXPANDING INTRODUCTIONS
6.30PM	WEEKLY CALL WITH SIDE HUSTLE, MOVING ENTREPRENEURIAL PROJECT FORWARD WITH OTHER GO-GETTERS

7.30PM	PUT KIDS TO BED
8PM	QUICK WALK AROUND THE BLOCK TO GET INTO NATURE
8.25PM	DRAFT UP A FEW EMAILS READY TO SEND OUT IN THE MORNING
8.45PM	READ SOME NON-FICTION PERSONAL GROWTH, MAYBE EVEN BE THE LION
9.15PM	BED

WHICH WOULD YOU RATHER BE?

Let's compare the two days.

Joe's day is a grind. The sales life is tough and being micro-managed by the boss is no fun. There's a boatload of missed deadlines and opportunities.

Ultimately, what we can see here is that there's no system or method of doing things and Joe's priorities are out of sync. Therefore when things need to move around it's hard to be flexible and know what to do next or how to best use the spare time when a client cancels.

There are elements of Joe doing the right things, but the sequence and intensity is wrong. In short, this is an attitude problem, most likely born out of someone who thinks they know everything there is to know about sales and isn't open to being coached or upgrading their belief system.

Joe has a fixed mindset around what he believes is possible; he feels like a victim not a winner and overcompensates with flawed short-term tactics. For example, sending out 120 emails blindly. Even though it's somewhat automated using a CRM system, it still takes its toll on his mental load and eats up valuable time that could be spent in front of clients.

Even though it seems easy enough, only having one tactic to operate by (the email blast) when rubber meets the road and big targets are looming is a stressful burden.

As a manager looking in at Joe, his flurry of activity could give the illusion of excellent work being done. However, not all action is the same. What do you think the open rate and response rate of his 120 emails would be? This is where the tactic will fall down because Joe hasn't invested his time where it matters most, by his clients' side, in their presence, influencing them, helping them and evangelising his product or services.

It's clear that Joe is on a perpetual road to nowhere. However, all is not lost, with a few shocks to the system, abrupt course corrections, tweaks and changes to his daily sales life and by implementing the frameworks and strategies in this book, we could see him making a noticeable impact in only a matter of weeks.

This would get his boss off his back and put some cold hard cash in his pocket, not only this, but life would become easier in general as success starts to mount. His profile within the organisation would change, other salespeople would trust him more and, as a result, he'd rise to the top as a team player.

In the game of sales, if you do the hard things, the sales become easier. This book will show you how to be less like Joe and more like Eric.

By contrast, sales just flow to Eric effortlessly. His day is grounded in rituals, processes and habits that enable his success, and allow him to make quick tactical decisions and adjustments when he needs to, whilst keeping his plan for the long-term vision of the business.

His sales games are both flexible and structured, it's got more ecstaticity and fun in it. He is seriously committed to the things that he knows will make him better as a person and add value to his life and others. He invests his time in self-improvement and self-growth because he knows this is what helps to separate him from the pack and create the life of his dreams. Eric has discipline and is willing to do the work.

He is committed to adding value to others and sharing useful information, he's constantly offering leads and opportunities to others in the sales team and is not concerned with how much they are making from it or what he can get out of it. This generous attitude goes full circle and he is often looped into email threads with lucrative sales clients.

He's well respected within the organisation by both leaders and peers, and as a result, he is trusted to operate how he sees fit. He consistently overachieves on his targets every month. This allows Eric to spend his time ahead of the curve focused on the months ahead and building the business rather than just focusing on the short term, chasing a monthly target and trying to keep the wolves from the door.

If you see yourself in either of these characters, Eric might sound too idealistic, impractical or just too much. If that's how you see it then I suggest taking a deeper look, asking yourself if you're ready to learn what the best do.

If you really want to excel, then you've got to make changes even if they are inconvenient, out of your norm or seem bizarre. **The purpose of this book is to grow your level of awareness and shift your paradigm around what it means to sell.** Of course, some of the momentum building tasks might seem odd, but that's because you're operating from your current state of awareness. Together we are going to change that!

WHAT DO I MEAN BY MOMENTUM SALES?

Quite simply, what I mean by Momentum Sales is the ability to create a wave of momentum so big through the repetition of the eight ideas described in the model, adopting a systematic approach towards prospects and clients that is repeatable.

More than this, it is a way of thinking that transforms how you sell, how your clients see you and experience doing business with you as well as how you see yourself. With Momentum Sales, you are an expert, a trusted advisor and you have the commitment and drive to help your clients find the right solutions and advance their business.

The beauty of my Momentum Sales Model is that you can take it anywhere. Once you have learned and implemented it and had the massive success with it, you will recognise that it is yours to keep. **It will become part of your identity.** No longer will you be someone who "might" hit targets, you are someone who has the ability to constantly overachieve on your targets. It's just part of who you are, and you will know intuitively what to do in any given sales situation to get the sale back on track, to motivate yourself to greater levels of action, prosperity and thinking.

The Momentum part of it is specifically focused on helping you break through your current patterns and thinking around sales so that you create a never-ending cycle of healthy opportunities that feed your pipeline. On top of this, it is about simultaneously increasing your close rate and learning how to build a business of incredible scale at speed.

Once you put the Momentum Sales Model into practice it multiplies. No longer are you wondering where your next client meeting will be or where the next big sale will come from. When you have the power of Momentum working for you, you will be attracting more and more, conquering new areas of business and expanding your potential. You will be a living, breathing, walking magnet for wealth, sales and abundance, you will work this formula and it will be ingrained in your identity.

This new way of living will become your identity, the Momentum Sales Model will raise your standards regarding what you expect of yourself. This means you won't copy others, you won't take their standard and hope for the best. You will set your own habits, rules and rituals that will guide your sales and open up vast quantities of wealth.

You won't fear spending money on investing in yourself, you will reinvest your commission cheques in improving your knowledge, skills and development. Because of this, and because you are focused, your social circle and your network will change. You will level up in all areas of your life. Mentors and people further along than you will appear in your life and, because you are ambitious, you will spot them and take advantage of the opportunity to learn from them. As a result, you will raise your own vibration, you will operate with a higher level of energy and, crucially, your belief in what's possible for you will change.

In Momentum Sales we are focused on looking for opportunities with asymmetric upside; imagine a snowball rolling down a mountainside – it starts off small, but as it goes it picks up more and more. It's the same with Momentum Sales.

This is what we are excited by as top producers: action that's effective and ever-growing. It's how you approach the opportunities and the energy you give off, that's how opportunities flow to you in abundance and you go from middle of the pack to the very top of the leader board. Once you're at the top, you might need to find yourself a new pack to run with. You constantly need to keep upgrading and pushing yourself. There's a certain 'gravitas' that having momentum has and knowing you can create it at will gives you unstoppable confidence. Think how that would feel, to know that you can walk into any business, any situation, any opportunity and start making progress. The Momentum Sales process allows you to turn any adversity, unlikely situation or potential opportunity to your full advantage and keep reaping the benefits to go bigger and help more people.

When you are in a state of sales momentum, everything you do adds value and brings you more business. Momentum brings incremental returns, the more you do, the more that comes back, the right areas of your sales funnel are fed at all stages. Sales gets easier and more enjoyable.

You have time to service your clients properly and ensure that they get the high quality of service they deserve and, as a result, you increase the likelihood that they will become loyal repeat customers and even expand into your new line of products as they become available. In a word, they become advocates and ambassadors for your brand, they are sold on YOU!

The reason they will expand their business with you is because trust is increased through your sales process – you delivered on your word and that's important. They know you care deeply for their business and, because you recommended the right products and services that made an impact and helped them achieve their internal goals, it goes a long way. When you reach this stage, you have a golden opportunity.

This is Momentum, not to be confused with taking action and being busy. There is a big distinction. There are many busy salespeople who are not spending their time correctly or least of all on the right things. They are busy doing non-needle moving activities that, whilst they look good to the company and tick the required boxes, don't help them to hit their targets, serve their clients' needs or make any real difference to their bank account.

Being busy is a loser's game. There comes a point in every salesperson's career where you need to take a risk and count on yourself. The current sales processes in play have been created for the masses, not the extraordinary, they help average salespeople get average results. Not enough to make real money but enough not to get fired. Where you want to play is in the field that is saved for the top 1%, the top of the accelerators, the 250% to target and above, consistently.

By backing yourself I mean knowing what is absolutely a waste of time and what's going to move the needle. Usually it's admin and reporting, using fragmented systems to track a few dollars that aren't even accurate.

Trust me, once you get 250% to target, people (meaning your boss) will leave you the eff alone! When you become a top producer for a company, then you gain respect; everyone will want to know how you do it and people will listen to your opinion. This is especially helpful when it comes to useless processes that slow salespeople down. When you reach the top, you will be able to help the business design more effective and efficient processes that will help other salespeople sell more instead of wasting their time on data entry admin-type tasks. There are far too many companies that expect success but, when you are looking at what the salespeople are required to do as a percentage of hours in their week, it's insane. It's not surprising that these companies fail to reach target, or only just make it by a hair's breadth.

Efficient sales processes are paramount and it's on you to back yourself, smash your target, prove that you are a beast and then help the business redesign how they do things.

It's the same if you are an entrepreneur working for yourself or a startup; the point is to be nimble and this will be your ultimate leverage. However, I see too many startups trying to be corporates, using tools and systems that slow them down and don't add value because they don't have the scale or workforce that they were designed for in the first place. There is no leverage.

Go out in the field and create a wave of momentum so big it takes your mission, company and vision into the stratosphere. You want to be the one who moved it to the next level, who changed the course of your history forever. It's great for the company and it's phenomenal for your brand.

WHAT HAPPENS WHEN YOU'RE IN A MOMENTUM STATE?

There is no better state – it's part joy, part anticipation and part deep unwavering inner confidence. You have faith overload.

Success to me is having the sales game down and implementing this model so that it all flows to you. Success in sales becomes part of your identity, it's what you do, and it starts with one thing above all else: building momentum.

When you know how to create momentum, it doesn't matter where you go, what job you take, what cards you are dealt, you will play that hand to inspire the most stubborn clients, you will lift your team's spirits and show them that it is possible. You will show them the way by your example. What you do speaks volumes. If you clock off early or arrive at the office late you are giving a signal. If you are on top of your game, killing it, people will take notice and you will raise the standards of your team.

Being able to create momentum is a fundamental skill that companies will pay big money for, because not everyone has it.

Think of being able to create momentum as future-proofing your career and your business. If you ever get stuck or find yourself in a tough spot, are made redundant, or want to move jobs, countries or industries, it requires you to create massive momentum.

This kind of momentum is special, it doesn't leave you depleted and hating your life but radiating all the goodness you have from within. When momentum starts to flow, it will affect all areas of your life and there's no limits to what can happen for you and where you can take it.

Momentum is the game-changer that can see you realise your dreams faster than you ever thought possible and make a difference in the world, along with providing for your family and being the person you have the potential to be.

How does it feel?

When you are in a momentum state you feel on top of the world; it's like everything you touch is a success, and you have an inner feeling that knows that it's because of you. There is a deep sense of conviction and you feel like you are buzzing, because in reality, you are, you are vibrating so highly. This leads me to my next point.

How do people treat you and react to you?

The right people are drawn to you when you have momentum; the exact situations, connections and opportunities that were once out of grasp suddenly fall into your lap. You will be surprised that it is happening, but it is all to do with your energetic state. I don't mean a hyped-up version of yourself that is loud and boisterous, I mean the vibration that you give off is one of abundance, joy and bliss. You feel blessed to have the opportunity to sell to your clients and grateful that you get to do this with your time. It's an honour and a privilege.

Another strange thing that happens when you have momentum is people respect you way more. This occurs because you respect yourself. Every day you are showing other people how to treat you by the standards you keep and how you operate. When you have momentum, you attract the best, things keep working out for you because of the mindset you apply and the confidence you radiate. It's an energetic state you carry with you. It's in the actions you take, the way you deliver your message and what you expect to happen.

This is a level of higher consciousness that only top sellers reach, they are fully aware and present and love the process of solving problems, putting together the pieces in new and innovative combinations to open new doors that lead to great things.

What happens to your targets?

Targets! You don't even focus on them anymore; you know you will fly right through them. It is a given. You are going higher than the company targets; you have your own mission and respect yourself for living at your standards and pace. Targets get left behind in the dust; you expect to overachieve with them, and they are merely a road sign, nothing more, because where you're going doesn't have a ceiling.

TYPES OF SALESPEOPLE WHO LACK MOMENTUM

Let's face it, in sales, whether you're working alone or as part of a team, there are a number of stereotypes of salespeople that you might encounter.

Let's be clear; the thing to recognise is, even though some of them might look or present themselves like they are top performers, they are not – the numbers and how they got them speak for themselves.

Let's have a quick look. I detail more about these characters in the free resource pack: **www.timjscastle.com/themomentumsalesmodel**

THE YO-YO-ER

This guy is everything but consistent, his attitude to sales is to blast out 180 emails in a day and then sit back and relax for the rest of the week, figuring that that should be enough to get the job done. Unfortunately, his attitude towards sales is the problem. He doesn't like being told what to do, thinks he knows better than the Sales Director.

THE EGO MANIAC

This guy won't let you in. He's in turmoil inside. He needs help big time, but his ego won't let him ask for it, be taught or go anywhere near how he really feels, especially when it comes to his sales ability. Deep down he knows this is *his* problem and no one can make him feel this way, but with his ego running the show he gets himself into many unnecessary disagreements and battles for superiority. He's insecure, yet it plays out as arrogance.

THE WORKHORSE

This salesperson is considered a top seller by the organisation, but the amount of work they put in to get there is unsustainable, which means they are not really a top seller. It is an illusion that will collapse like a house of cards, along with their self-esteem, when hard times come. They think in a linear manner (e.g. number of hours = sales revenue rather than exponentially e.g. leverage = sales revenue).

THE EXCUSE-MAKER

This salesperson has an excuse for everything. Instead of being a problem-solver, he defaults to accepting whatever his clients say and making excuses for low sales. He doesn't understand that sales is supposed to be full of challenges. He gets involved and wound up by office politics, gossip and drama.

Now we've debunked the salespeople that lack momentum, let's bust some myths as well.

SALES MYTHS (TO BUST BEFORE WE START)

These are the top misconceptions when it comes to sales that really mislead, derail and cause potentially great salespeople to spend their lives in the land of the mediocre, chasing their tail on a monthly basis instead of riding high on the wave of momentum.

Don't want that to be you? Then pay attention.

MYTH #1: IT'S ALL ABOUT FIGURES, TARGETS AND COMPETITORS

Obsessive focus directed towards your sales targets and competitors can take over the mission and the real point of becoming a top salesperson.

Let me be clear: the real objective is the journey and the person you become by operating at the best of your ability. That's it! How can you exceed the best of your ability? You can't, it's not possible.

Your goal is to become more, to do your absolute best, to raise your standards. You are in competition with yourself and yourself alone, not the other salespeople on the team.

Let me repeat this because all too often salespeople and businesses spend too much time focused on hitting a target rather than expanding their own growth and capability. **It's about the person you become**.

There is a freedom in knowing that you can take a situation and turn it around, that you can actually get pleasure from solving a challenging problem.

There's no fun in easy sales, no skill required and the reward isn't there because there is no test of your abilities. The reward comes from challenging and testing your creativity, your ability to navigate the sales process and doing what others think is impossible. You will prove them wrong!

MYTH #2: IT'S ABOUT MAKING THE SALE NO MATTER WHAT

Getting the sale at all costs is a recipe for being doomed to disaster. It will leave your conscience marred and heavy rather than clear and light. The client will find out that they have been "had" and your character will be questioned. Worst of all, you will question your own character. How you see yourself will diminish and that is not a place you want to be.

The standard that we as top sellers hold ourselves to is **doing what is right for the client at all times**. This means not pushing for the sale no matter what. We have guiding principles that we operate by, that keep us from ever getting into a situation where needs must.

Your commitment to do what is right for your client will radiate from your being. The very energy you give off will be a different vibration and your clients will recognise this. This helps them to buy from you.

As a result, they will see that you are different from other salespeople and begin to open up and divulge useful information that they do not share with everyone else. The walls will come down and rapport will be built. As a result, uncovering new information will allow you to get a more in-depth understanding of their problems and provide solutions that work. It also gives you a cracking network that you can tap into.

This feeds into my next point.

MYTH #3: IT'S OK TO GIVE CONCESSIONS IF THE SITUATION CALLS FOR IT

You should never *need* the sale too much because your pipeline should always be full of rich opportunities. You should be able to walk away from a bad sale, and that's one of the things that makes doing business with you attractive; you don't need it too much and you don't do business that's bad for your business.

Being too needy and desperate for the sale will repel the client and the sale. Just like in dating, if you are too clingy it suffocates the potential relationship. We've all seen it in movies: a guy falls in love with a girl, he becomes totally infatuated, he tries to do everything he can to please her and keep her happy. It's almost like he feels he doesn't deserve her and can't think of a world without her.

Long story short, the girl inevitably loses interest because it was too easy. She feels smothered and like she doesn't have to work for it, so she breaks off the relationship leaving the guy heart-broken and confused.

As we know, the guy really should have understood the dynamics at play here. It was bound to happen.

It's the same in sales; if you give clients everything, without them having to pay for it, it plants the seed that what you have isn't very valuable and your products are a dime a dozen.

Just like the guy with his broken heart, you'll be left wondering why the client suddenly overpays for a subpar product with your direct competitors. It's all to do with the perceived value.

A client wants to know they are getting something worth having and your need for the sale, your desperation to bend over backwards, is a warning signal to them that you might not have their best interests at heart.

If you focus purely on what's in it for you (e.g. making commission) it causes you to be blinded to what's really going on. Your client can sense when you are willing to take anything just to make the sale and it undermines your credibility. Once a client loses respect for you, they no longer see you as the expert, which is a challenging road to travel down.

When you're too desperate, the balance of power is shifted too much in the client's favour. It's not a healthy dynamic and makes for an uncomfortable ride.

The skill is noticing when you need the sale too much and when you are acting out of desperation not confidence.

The processes, strategies and Momentum Sales Model covered in this book will show you how you avoid being in that desperate position ever again. Like any good negotiation, the key is being willing and able to walk away from a bad deal.

On the other end of the spectrum, the opposite of desperately needing the sale and giving anything to secure it is being too pushy. This is a form of vulnerability that comes across as arrogance.

A confident seller knows that they have many more sales in the pipeline and so they don't need to force, strong arm or manipulate anyone into it to make the sale.

Please note, there is a big difference in being pushy and using the art of persuasion to confidently help your client to do the deal when you believe is right for them. Sometimes clients will need your confidence in order to make the decision.

We will cover this later on in the book, so watch out for this as it must be skilfully handled. Sometimes you will need to be direct in order to help your clients to move forward.

MYTH #4: IN A DIGITAL AGE, FACE TIME WITH CLIENTS ISN'T IMPORTANT

Spending all day attending to reports, spreadsheets, Slack notifications, emails and dashboards is a sure-fire way to lose.

It typically goes like this: your boss requires you to complete a spreadsheet, which is the same exact information you already entered into salesforce and two other documents, then you have a meeting to go through the spreadsheet, and then there's another document that you need to complete with the exact same information presented ever so slightly differently for another team, and so on and so on.

It's a tab fest of Google Sheets and data entry. Not quite the dream job you had in mind when you decided to start in sales.

I understand that the requirement to use some of these platforms might not be your choice and that you are seemingly caught in a web of glorified admin that's sucking the life out of you one notification email at a time.

But here's where the shift needs to take place. Instead of complaining, focus on creating time to be with your clients and offering solutions to streamline the admin. Often people just go along with the process because "it's what we do" or they don't want to rock the boat because it works to some degree.

Tools and technology are very powerful, and they are there to support, but it just can't be at the expense of the actions that are going to bring in the revenue – and that's human contact.

The way I see it, tech and data should tell you where to go hunt and how you are tracking it. It should guide your process so you can move quicker and with more impact.

Data capture is awesome and, as you'll see in this book, it will help you sell more not less. The point of this myth is that, just because you can conduct a meeting over Zoom, automate a client report or get the information you need over Slack, it doesn't mean you should.

What I have witnessed is, when a business misses their targets and is poorly run by an erratic boss, managers freak out and go into overdrive because they realise the buck stops with them (all too late) and fear losing their jobs. They then proceed to go on an insane rampage using every tool and system available to create maximum levels of micromanagement to "understand where the sales process is falling down."

This dictatorship saps any joy out of the sales process and the sales team loses their freedom, enthusiasm and drive. Any momentum is dispersed in a sea of admin. Salespeople become fatigued, start questioning their job, their boss and their mission. Ultimately, they start looking elsewhere.

All of this can be avoided if you as the sales manager understand what these tools and systems are designed for and take responsibility for tracking the right metrics so that you can spot the early signs of underperformance and optimise in real time.

Overkill of daily and weekly reports that need to be filled out leaves your sales team fixed to their desks instead of out building momentum with clients.

When there is more admin and red tape than actual client time, the very ingredient that can move the needle is reduced to a bare minimum. This is suffocating for a salesperson who is at the top of their game because they know that the key momentum driver is being limited.

In conjunction with increased admin on the salesperson's side, the level of automation that companies push for is actually creating another void that leads to ignorance.

Keeping clients at arm's length causes you to miss feedback and, before you know it, your client that you were relying upon to make payroll is gone. Yes, it's inefficient to do a face-to-face meeting but spending time with your customer is vital because it is in these conversations and these inefficiencies that the next product feature, improvement and deal can be found.

The main point is don't let technology and admin take you away from spending time with your clients. Instead, make sure you get a deeper understanding of their frustrations with your products.

To take an actionable step forward, we need to look at the cause. In this case, it's about securing more meetings with clients, and this means selling them on why they should meet with you in the first place.

To do this, you must be focused on the right metric, which is, time spent with clients. You should track this each week and commit to hitting a goal. This will help to increase awareness, so you'll gain a better understanding of where your product or service is weakest in the eyes of the customer.

This again takes work, so you have to protect this valuable time with your clients. If you let admin get in the way, your sales will suffer.

You might have witnessed this in your own organisation or fallen prey to it. As a result of ineffectual processes, micromanagement and increased internal admin, the salesperson often resorts to the weekly email blast to try to kill a few fish (land a few meetings) and once a few bite, they then take those meetings out of desperation because it's all they can get. They didn't use skill, they used dynamite.

Don't get me wrong, being desperate is a great place to be as it fuels your hunger to win, but if you are desperate because you aren't placing your focus on the right areas, you will never succeed.

The email blast strategy is weak as it fails to take into account whether the meeting will be worth your time and, as a result, poor quality meetings mean that more time is wasted and there is even more admin. The worst thing is the lack mindset that accompanies this type of behaviour. When you're struggling to get face time with your clients, you've got to take a look at what's taking your time on a daily basis and make some changes.

If not, the cycle will repeat itself and around and around you go in a downward spiral. Only this time it's worse; you'll have even less time available to spend on the thing that really matters – securing high-quality meetings with high-quality sales leads.

Now you know what sales shouldn't be, let me show you how it should work.

WELCOME TO THE NEW WAY...

This is the disruptive new way. I believe sales:

1. should be fun

2. should be full of surprise and delight for customers

3. should allow you to feel confident and in control.

1. Fun

Being stressed out by targets and having to explain under-performance is no fun. Getting caught up in admin, updating systems and records is no fun. Being micro-managed is no fun. Life for an under-performing salesperson is no fun, and that's not to mention the sales. But I believe it shouldn't be like that. I have a lot of fun exploring potential new clients, meeting them and navigating the challenges that pop up along the way.

For me, the fun comes from the fact I am so secure in the process, and confident that I will get results, that I can have freedom and fun with it.

If you follow the Momentum Sales Model the sales will come and, because you will be doing the work with the right attitude and energy, you can have fun because you have the flexibility created by success to enjoy the ride.

2. Surprise and delight

This is where you build a reputation and your brand on being someone who goes the extra mile for their clients; whether it's completing a project early or making a presentation more engaging, the ways in which you surprise and delight become your personal brand. This in turn helps you differentiate yourself from the crowd and other sellers. It gives clients who chose to work with you a joyful experience, so they are naturally inclined to refer you to their network and only come to you for any future business needs.

When you make client service a core element of your sales it speaks volumes about you.

3. Confident and in control

When you do sales right, it should build your self-confidence rather than diminish it. Far too often, I see salespeople afraid to take on challenges or bring their sales skills to the next level. When you keep the promises you make to yourself, you build self-confidence and, because you chose to follow this model to the letter and deliver on what you set out to do, you will feel more confident and in control.

When you feel confident and in control, you are actually more flexible and you feel able to have fun and surprise and delight your clients. This comes from the preparation and commitment to becoming the best in your field at what you do. You outwork the rest and focus on the right areas of the business that move it forward and secure the wins.

CHAPTER 2

Introduction to the Momentum Sales Model

WHERE DID THE MOMENTUM SALES MODEL COME FROM?

I was consistently over-performing. I say this not to brag but to give you some context as to what was going on in my life to make me realise that I must have a formula for what I was doing to produce exceptional results.

I was exceeding the expectations of the business and bringing in millions in revenue. The bosses pretty much left me alone to do my thing. This is where you want to be. When you do what others thought impossible, you gain new levels of trust and respect that put you in an advantageous position that you can build upon to go even harder. When you aren't caught up in the "normal" flow of business routines, of quarterly reports, internal management, reporting, you can use this extra time to gain even more momentum.

People kept asking how I did it, they would call, text, email, write or even stop me in the street for advice on sales and business development. This started happening a lot, and then a large start-up incubator approached me to run training sessions with their entrepreneurs and founders. Some of these folk didn't have a background in sales but really needed to secure investment and their first clients. I showed them how to do it. I really looked at what I do, and what others don't. I codified it into a simple model that can work for anyone. I started teaching it to others, and they got serious results.

One thing led to another, and more and more clients started asking me to train their sales and business development teams as word spread. It got to a point where I was inundated with requests.

I have a need inside to share my way of selling with others, to help raise the collective awareness of what it means to become world-class at sales, to have fun and sell more.

I have distilled everything that I do naturally into this model so that it can act as a blueprint for you to follow to get results quickly. You can start today and change your sales trajectory, radically.

Firstly, let me tell you that I wasn't born with an incredible sales gift. I learned the hard way.

I was once like you, tired of just getting by, making money, sometimes good money but never extraordinary, out of this world money, until the day that changed.

What changed? I hear you ask.

I changed.

I said enough is enough – I am going to become great at sales. As an expert, a highly skilled sales professional, I AM GOING TO LIVE AND BREATHE SALES. IT'S GOING TO BECOME PART OF WHO I AM. I HAVE WHAT IT TAKES.

I developed the Momentum Sales Model to help you accelerate your sales processes.

The key part of understanding how to create momentum is that you can't "hack it"– there are no shortcuts to this level of success. You need to get good at working the process. You might get lucky every once in a while, but for consistent sales where you are riding high and your commission cheques are snowballing – that kind of success only happens when you apply the model correctly.

WHO DOES IT WORK FOR?

What I want you to know is that it doesn't matter where you're at, you can apply this model and get results today. If you're new to sales or an old hand, the door is open to everyone. All you need to do is spend the time to read, digest and put into practice the steps that follow.

No matter what experience you have had, the bad habits you've formed, the failures you think are holding you back or the issues you tell yourself are stopping you from reaching the top level of success, this works.

Whether you've just been berated by your boss or have an inkling you're about to get fired, or you've just got complacent and performance has dipped, regardless of what's happened before, it can and will all change for you if you commit to learning these principles.

Working in sales gives you the opportunity to take control of your life, achieve your goals and become the person you aspire to be.

Great salespeople aren't always born, they're also made. We all have it in us. But I am specifically here to help those that want to take their business and their sales game to the next level.

HOW DOES IT WORK?

Throughout the model, I use the analogy of a steam train building up momentum. This is because George Stephenson, the guy who invented Stephenson's Rocket (the first steam engine), which now sits in the British Science Museum, was in my family a few generations ago and I think that's cool.

My parents were kind enough to include Stephenson as one of my middle names and, even though my grandad spelt it incorrectly (Stevenson) when filling out my birth certificate, cheers Grandad, it has always given me a sense of possibility to be connected to this great inventor in global history.

FIGURE 1: STEPHENSON'S ROCKET – DESIGNED BY GEORGE STEPHENSON AND HIS SON ROBERT

The reason why I love this metaphor for sales is, at first, a steam engine is stationary, this hulking great piece of iron is just plonked on the tracks, with all this potential but no momentum. That can be like when you start a new job or take over a new patch of business – it's dead still.

To get a steam engine moving it takes a HUGE amount of effort and hard work, large quantities of coal and human energy as well as a giant-ass fire, and that's just to get it rolling forward a couple of centimeters. That's like going from zero to one. Your first meaningful sale.

You've got to do all the heavy lifting. You've got to keep putting in all the elements in large amounts, feeding it with persistence to get this heavy lump of metal moving.

But there is a moment when everything changes, a transition from hardly moving to absolutely flying; once it picks up momentum, it's driving itself – it takes less fuel to do the same job, so it becomes easier and easier. Add more fuel and the train goes faster, the momentum compounds and, due to the amount of thrust it's built up, it's now operating in a state of net positive returns capturing enormous value. This is where you want to be with your sales process.

It's a force to be reckoned with, and no walls or barriers can stop it – it will crash right through them and just keep on going.

The momentum has built up to a point that it makes it literally unstoppable. That's what a steam engine does with momentum and that's what you'll do with the Momentum model applied to your sales operation.

Once you build up enough and catch that wave of momentum and it ripples throughout your business, the market and your clients, you become a market maker. Sales will flow in from all directions. These sales will encourage more sales and more clients to reach out, so the force of momentum around you and your business growth becomes exponential.

The beauty of the Momentum model is once you know how to apply it and you've experienced it in action and you've had a taste of its success, you never again fear making targets or creating new business. It will become a source of inspiration; you will feel confident and ready to take on the challenge.

When you know how to generate momentum from a standing start, you'll realise that you have changed. You've got momentum and you know how to create it. This is a truly empowering experience.

This is a big difference.

WHAT HAPPENS WHEN YOU WORK THE MOMENTUM SALES MODEL?

You set new standards for yourself and you play a bigger game. Every year, month and week, pushing yourself to expand and go bigger. Forcing yourself not to relax in comfort but to seek the crest of the wave of your sales ability.

You embrace your fullest potential as a salesperson and seek to deliver it every day, to serve your clients and push the limits. You operate at the boundaries of your capability, in motion and flow.

I love the Momentum Sales Model because of what it teaches you as a salesperson when you implement it and experience it working.

Never again will you believe limiting thoughts, because you know different; you won't fear change because you know what it can do if harnessed and, most importantly, you know that your ability to generate sales comes from within. It's in your control. It always has been and always will be.

That's why I'm so passionate about the Momentum Sales Model for sales because I know it can accelerate your business and what you believe is possible.

Let's dive into it in more detail.

THE ELEMENTS OF THE MOMENTUM SALES MODEL BROKEN DOWN

Simply put, it's made of eight core elements.

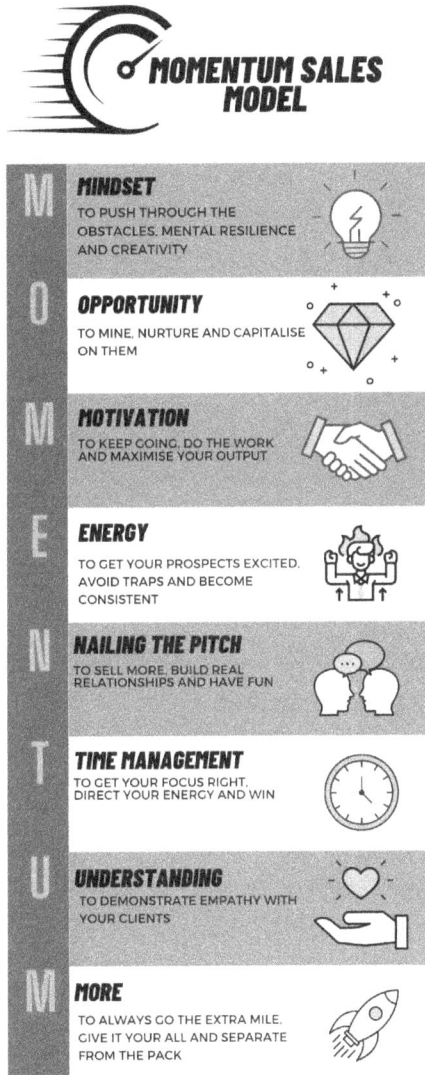

MOMENTUM SALES MODEL

M MINDSET
TO PUSH THROUGH THE OBSTACLES, MENTAL RESILIENCE AND CREATIVITY

O OPPORTUNITY
TO MINE, NURTURE AND CAPITALISE ON THEM

M MOTIVATION
TO KEEP GOING, DO THE WORK AND MAXIMISE YOUR OUTPUT

E ENERGY
TO GET YOUR PROSPECTS EXCITED, AVOID TRAPS AND BECOME CONSISTENT

N NAILING THE PITCH
TO SELL MORE, BUILD REAL RELATIONSHIPS AND HAVE FUN

T TIME MANAGEMENT
TO GET YOUR FOCUS RIGHT, DIRECT YOUR ENERGY AND WIN

U UNDERSTANDING
TO DEMONSTRATE EMPATHY WITH YOUR CLIENTS

M MORE
TO ALWAYS GO THE EXTRA MILE, GIVE IT YOUR ALL AND SEPARATE FROM THE PACK

FIGURE 2: THE 8 PARTS OF THE MOMENTUM SALES MODEL

Mindset – to push through the obstacles, mental resilience and creativity

Great leaders and success coaches know it's about focusing on what you can control. Your mind needs to become your biggest ally, your best friend. You can control the narrative you tell yourself about your past and, once you understand how powerful this is, you will become unstoppable.

I'm going to sharpen your mindset because it is critical to sales. Your mind is your greatest tool; it's something you can control, it informs your physiology, how you think about the future, it even helps you increase your vibrational energy to attract more positive people, experiences and sales to you in abundance.

Opportunities – to mine, nurture and capitalise on them

Opportunities come to those who go out and seize them. Opportunities are all around us, and once you've got your mindset right, the next stage is being aware of opportunities (especially those others can't see) and becoming a hunter.

I am going to turn you into an opportunity magnet and show you the exact strategies I use to magnetise sales, consistently over-achieve on targets and build influence at all levels.

Motivation – to keep going, do the work and maximise your output

World class salespeople stay motivated by connecting deeply with their *why*. They understand what's on the line and take time each day to focus in on it. They decide to be their best every day.

I'm going to show you how to stay motivated to do the things that others won't, so that you'll grow and develop your resilience and fan the flames of that burning desire you have to achieve. To rise to the top, you must be willing to push the peddle to the floor and accelerate. Here I will show you how to become a momentum building machine, an unstoppable force that is able to get moving even when you don't want to. This is an important transformational step.

Energy – to get your prospects excited, avoid traps and become consistent

Energy connects you to Universal Intelligence, to God, to your clients and to something greater than yourself. Tuning in and understanding how to use this force for good will not only be life changing for your sales numbers, but it will help you move through the world with more grace, joy and connectedness.

This might be the most important chapter in the whole book. I'm going to show you how you can use energy to achieve momentum flow as an opportunity seeker, a mindset warrior who is resilient and filled to the brim with motivation to go out and win for your clients.

Nailing the Pitch – to sell more, build real relationships and have fun

Nailing the pitch is about feeling authentic and learning how to have an absolute ball when pitching; it's about being yourself and loving the process so that your greatest self can shine through.

My goal is to help you fall in love with the opportunity to pitch by being prepared, knowing how to handle it like a boss when things go wrong and making the most of the precious time you have in front of your clients. This is where we overcome our fear of rejection and throw ourselves wholeheartedly into every sale. You'll learn how to infuse joy and fun into every meeting.

Time Management – to get your focus right, direct your energy and win

Successful days compound and, like sales, when you've got momentum it will feel like success is raining down on you everywhere you go. I'm going to teach you how to change your relationship with time because when you value it in a different way, what's possible for you will change. You will spend time on things that will move the needle in a huge way rather than living in a reactionary, stressed out, frantic approach that leaves you frazzled, drained of energy and constantly putting out fires.

Understanding – to demonstrate empathy with your clients

Here we are bringing the human element into the relationship with our clients. This is about making an effort to really, truly, sell to your clients how they want to be sold to, not how you want to be sold to. This is a big turning point for any salesperson. Your EQ is how you raise the bar in your sales game, and it takes you to a new level, a more inclusive, understanding state where you become a trusted partner for your clients.

It's about developing your EQ to the point that you are an expert in reading people, so that you have a spiritual awakening to a whole other dimension of sales.

Go all in on developing and demonstrating this skill and you'll experience a dramatic rise in your sales figures and also witness an unfathomable number of synchronicities, gifts from above and divine blessings.

More – to always go the extra mile, give it your all and separate from the pack

Finally, More is about doing more for your clients in terms of the value you bring, but it is also about doing more for yourself and how you show up each day so that you maintain consistently high standards that you keep raising.

This is about becoming objective about where you are right now and the level you are playing at, based on your current actions, and then committing to separate from the pack, to go the extra mile on every level. Sometimes, when we take a careful review of how much work we are actually doing, in reality, we can see the areas where we could be doing more. This stage is what takes you to mastery, it's where you go all in and become a momentum seller.

The Momentum Sales Model will allow you to consistently achieve world class standards whilst separating yourself from everyone else so you can reach the top of the leaderboard. By implementing this model you are saying to yourself that you're willing to be uncommon, to walk the road less traveled and go it alone in the pursuit of greatness.

I'll teach you the exact strategies to get ahead, so that you keep on turning the momentum up and being the hero in your own life, for your family, yourself and people around you who see you as a mentor.

Are you ready to dive in? Let's do this!

If you are serious about taking it to the next level, I have created a Momentum Sales checklist that you can download at **www.timjscastle.com/themomentumsalesmodel**. Keep this with you for at least the next two months to get yourself into the habit of thinking like a world class momentum seller. This is what those who really want to create prosperity do.

CHAPTER 3

Mindset – To push through the obstacles, maintain mental resilience and ooze creativity

"Don't focus on what you think you deserve.
Take aim on what you are willing to earn!"

– DAVID GOGGINS

INTRODUCTION

I've built up my sales career from nothing. I've literally had meetings early on in my career where I was so intimidated by the seniority of the people in the room, or underprepared for how to articulate the story, that the words just wouldn't come out. I was filled with anxieties over what the people in front of me thought of me, rather than focusing on telling the story. I was worried about being judged for my performance and, as such, my mindset wasn't working for me, but against me. This is not where you want to be; it's like having an inner critic pulling you back.

Over the years, and through the thousands of pitches, meetings and opportunities to sell, I have learned how to build a mindset that works for me. This mindset is sure of my gifts and talents, of what I am fully capable of and what I want to give to the world. It is my goal to help others achieve their big vision for their life, and I'm on a mission to fulfil it.

This is what I want for you: if you are someone that's struggling to love sales or holding yourself back from taking massive action when ideas flash into your mind, then I wrote this chapter especially for you. It is the first stage in the Momentum Sales Model that you need to master – you must be able to control your thoughts and not believe everything that you think so that you are surrounded with uplifting, beneficial and empowering thoughts that support your growth.

Let's be real, you need to get clear on what you will and won't allow to filter into your field of consciousness. This means not watching the news, cutting negative people from your life and reducing the pessimism and worry you experience. You need to stand guard like a warrior outside the doorway to your mind and police your thoughts and what you buy into. Positivity is the only way to live.

WHAT IS MINDSET?

It all starts here. A change in mindset can kick-start the most abundant chain of events. Mindset is about your attitude, having a deep connection with your own mental resilience, knowing that you have what it takes, that you will not stop, or let doubt take over.

You'll perhaps have heard people who claim to profess that optimists have their head in the clouds and pessimism is the only way to be. Maybe this is you. I want to address this head on and up front; world class salespeople are optimists, and studies have shown that optimism and longevity in life go hand in hand. Research has categorically proven that sales teams that operate with a positive outlook outperform those with a negative frame of mind.

I want you to adopt a mindset of optimism from this moment onwards, to be positive and to expect great things to happen with such frequency and abundance that negative, pessimistic people can't stand to be near you. Respond to pessimism with positivity, let it be your shield from the gremlins of lack that are trying to hold you back from the ultimate victory.

What if you woke up each day and told yourself that you live the most amazing life anyone has ever lived and money, sales and success are on their way to you right now – do you think you'd have a better shot of dominating than someone who just let doubts play on their mind?

I want you to have back-to-back multiple successful years, where you can be elevated in your finances, wellbeing and wealth building because you mastered the skills required to build a wave of momentum so big that it flooded your life with good.

I want that for you, for you to keep expanding your success and for each year you live to see you become a better version of yourself, a wiser, more confident being that will grace the world.

In this section – our foundational starting point, the block that we stack everything else on – the mindset of a champion salesperson is what we'll build.

HOW MINDSET HELPS BUILD SALES MOMENTUM

- Mindset will keep you going through the inevitable challenges on the road to sales success.

- You can take charge of your attitude and your mindset so that it works for you and boosts you when you need it most. Having the right mindset will actually make life and success a lot easier.

- Having a positive mindset will help you gain more self-confidence, you will respond to guidance, feeling resilient and strong.

- Having an entrepreneurial mindset is empowering because it forces you to take ownership and look for creative solutions to problems.

- Salespeople who operate from a positive outlook on life outperform everyone.

In sales, developing the mindset of an entrepreneur is key – both from the perspective of persistence, like Thomas Edison, and from the perspective of having a vision and sticking with it, like George Stephenson and the first steam engine. You need persistence and a big inspiring vision.

In order to reach the upper echelons of success, a world class salesperson must switch from seeing their day job as a 9-5 and treat their sales patch like they are CEO of their own mini-business.

This does two things; it teaches you to be accountable and take full responsibility and ownership for the outcomes and performance of the business unit and it also means you operate with an entrepreneurial mindset, looking for solutions instead of complaining about what's not right. This helps to reinforce a positive, optimistic mindset and helps you to become an action taker. You'll be surprised just how fast doors open for you when you stop complaining and start taking massive action.

In sales, when you join a big organisation with product marketing departments, business development people and account managers, you get spoiled. End of. The risk is that you lose that edge, that grit and hustle that allows you to continually push the envelope, take initiative and be solution-oriented. Never lose sight of what you personally can be doing to take initiative and move your business forward. Explore the ideas that pop up in your mind at 2am and take action on them right then and there.

As a startup entrepreneur there is no one coming to save you – you are the hat wearer, the head honcho and the assistant, the business development, sales and the marketing. It's all on you. Daunting as it is, it is real and the skills you'll learn in this environment are some of life's finest.

Take the mindset of an entrepreneur to EVERYTHING you do in sales; it will set you apart. When everyone else is complaining about a lack of resources, you're out there finding a way forward, making the connections and putting it together – you're building a business.

MINDSET OF AN ENTREPRENEUR – GEORGE STEPHENSON, FIRST STEAM ENGINE

FIGURE 3: ROBERT STEPHENSON (LEFT) AND GEORGE STEPHENSON (RIGHT)[1]

Just to circle back on my main man George Stephenson for a second, when he and his son Robert were on a mission back in 1829 to enter the Rocket (first viable steam engine ever built) into a competition, they had to overcome significant hurdles. This was particularly important as there was handsome prize money at stake (£500, which in today's money is around £56,000).

To get to the trials, they had to first dismantle the Rocket and take it on a huge trip by horse wagon to Carlisle and then steamboat to Liverpool, before reassembling the whole 4.3 tonnes ready for action on the other end.

---

1 https://www.railwaymuseum.org.uk/objects-and-stories/stephensons-rocket-rainhill-and-rise-locomotive

The event was held over nine days, more than 10,000 people showed up to witness the competing vehicles race down a 1.5-mile length of track ten times, each measured for speed, fuel and water consumption.

Rocket, as it was appropriately named, had a number of factors going for it due to its revolutionary design having a more efficient method of producing steam, more effective boiler to blast pipe exhaust, higher surface area, two big drive wheels and it was lighter to boot.

The Rocket team spent the day entertaining crowds that had turned out to witness this engineering marvel. They attached carriages enough to fit 30 people to the back of Rocket and gave rides up and down the track.

Long story short – Rocket won!

It was this combination of factors that made steam engine locomotive transport viable, and these features were incorporated into all trains going forward for the next 160 years!

Rocket was the only engine to perform flawlessly in the competition. Robert got the 500 pounds and snagged a contract from L&MR to build seven more engines. He made improvements as he went, and the railway loved it and bought 19 more! This guy had some serious momentum.

I want you to get that what I am giving you here is a roadmap for success in sales. We are reinventing the sales process, much like Stephenson's Rocket, by putting together a combination of factors in a revolutionary way.

However, it also happened because of the 'never give up' mindset of an entrepreneur. Here's a quote from Robert Stephenson on just how he felt about his mission.

*"Rely upon it, locomotives shall not be cowardly
given up. I will fight for them until the last.
They are worthy of a conflict."*

- ROBERT STEPHENSON

Having this mindset will make you more resilient, trustworthy and it will do wonders for your self-confidence. When you know how to create momentum and you combine that with a positive, solution-only mindset, there's not much in this world that can keep you from greatness. It's your destiny.

If you're with me, let's get to work.

1. LET'S TALK ABOUT HOW GREAT AND UNIQUE YOU ARE

YOU ROCK!

Firstly, I want to call out any "sales shame". Reframe your job in sales and recognise how important your role is. It is a privilege to serve the world as a salesperson. As a world class sales legend, remember that you are leading the world forward through your ability to creatively bring stories to life and help people connect the dots. If it wasn't for the skilful mastery of client handling, through the persistence and initiative of good salespeople, millions of ideas wouldn't happen at the scale we enjoy them today.

Ideas given to salespeople make the world turn. Without them innovation would never get funded, nor schools, hospitals, airlines, yachts, self-driving cars, rockets. The world needs salespeople – you perform an incredibly important function in helping life progress.

You are a visionary who is able to help others see the picture and make sense of it, even when you're scared, unsure and sometimes even running in the opposite direction.

Make sure you take time to remember that sales is an artform and there is an art to making a sale. You are the artist, and this is your painting, you're mixing up the colours so that other people may enjoy the fruits of your labour.

Don't let anyone dishearten you or tell you otherwise, sales require bucketloads of patience, enthusiasm and resilience. And you have all of these in droves.

BE YOURSELF, IT'S MAGIC!

In sales it doesn't always follow that what works for someone else will also work for you. It's fantastic to seek the wise council of those that have done what you want to achieve and then act upon what they have suggested. However, if you copy what others do and expect the same results, you may find the reason it works for them is because it's *them* doing it.

For example, if you pretend to act like the top seller in your organisation you will feel strange. Clients can sense that energy, and they can tell whether you are being yourself and you believe in what you are doing or if you're being fake.

This book talks you through what to do, but how you do it, well, that's all you baby! You've got to add your own flare to the recipe. Every Michelin star chef has their secret sauce, their way of cooking that inspires greatness.

Bring the essence of what makes you special into the room, share your talents when you sell with your clients.

It's time to release the fear of judgement from others. If you have an inspired idea of how to make a sale happen, whether it's sending a roast goose to your clients in Hong Kong because you know they love roast goose or taking them out for yoga, follow your instinct and do it in your way.

Don't worry about hearsay or listen too much to the opinions of others because once you find your groove no one can take that away from you, that's yours forever, your special sauce.

2. NOW LET'S BUILD YOUR MOMENTUM MINDSET

BE RESOURCEFUL – ADOPT THE MINDSET OF A PROBLEM-SOLVER

Sales belong to the resourceful, those that see solutions not problems. Whenever you are faced with an uphill battle, a curve ball, a difficult customer, be resourceful and do whatever you can to find a solution. Being resourceful and taking initiative are two of the most powerful weapons that a salesperson has in their arsenal. This gives you inner confidence. Imagine knowing at your core that whatever is thrown your way you can not only handle, but figure out, take responsibility for and turn into a success.

What does resourceful look like in sales?

- Doing more than you are paid for.

- Helping out others in different departments that ultimately help you get the deal done.

- Picking up the phone despite how you feel.

- Thinking four, five, six moves ahead, knowing the next play and figuring out a strategy for the different eventualities before they occur.

- Maintaining a state of optimism and mental toughness when others around you are going into meltdown.

- Seeing the possibility in a situation and doing whatever it takes to get the job done.

For me, I am a man of faith. God has taken me through some of the most difficult times and the most amazing experiences, and I rely on his guidance to go bigger each day. I'm not preaching to you but sharing what works and I know to be true. It wouldn't be authentic if I didn't share the actual process I go through that helps me.

Life is a collection of experiences; it's not worth it to spend a piece of your life surrounded by small thinkers, problem-centred, erratic complainers. Instead, when we realise that miracles, guidance and ideas can take us to the next level, we can detach from the feeling of being trapped and get moving.

Often, we can become trapped because our creative energy is zapped because we are giving our energy to the wrong things. This impacts how resourceful we can be.

When we limit how resourceful we are because we are focused on the wrong things, we hold ourselves back from the glory of victory.

Therefore, I encourage you to be open minded in sales. Give yourself time to think each day – schedule it in your diary, making it sacred time when no one or nothing can get in touch with you. Let your creative energies flow and explore the possibilities for your sales to spend time on doing the things that multiply your earnings, relationships, and prosperity.

PERSONAL STORY
What MMA taught me

Be grateful for the small things and the big things will take care of themselves.

After a busy week at work, conducting 11 external client meetings over four days, I was looking forward to Friday night. I had arranged to watch One Championship: Edge of Greatness, a Mixed Martial Arts (MMA) competition taking place at Singapore Stadium.

Over the previous six months I had been taking Muay Thai Kickboxing classes at Evolve MMA so this sport had well and truly entered my life.

It is important for salespeople to have an outlet to step away from the fast-paced nature of sales and focus on something completely different for an hour or so each day. I chose to try martial arts for the mental benefits, as it forced me to step away and take a break.

When you've got kicks and punches flying around in class, it forces you to be present. There's no phone calls, PowerPoints or spreadsheets there. It's game on!

The discipline and mental toughness required in martial arts can also be applied to sales and, trust me, when you have a few Thai Kickboxing World Champions leading the session, combined with the high tempo pace of the class, there is no alternative but to learn fast, be tenacious and dig in for the inevitable lactic acid build up.

To my surprise, I found that I could get through an entire class. In fact, I felt amazing. I even started to look forward to burning legs after kicking the bag repeatedly, alongside the pain, the suffering and the feeling of being completely exhausted. I was hooked; when I was in Evolve, I was locked in and in the zone, not thinking about work but being completely present.

A major brief came in during the afternoon, which was going to require me to work most of the weekend. I was also doing some consulting for a big global airline, and they needed a project turned around by Saturday, which again meant that my Friday night at the kickboxing event wasn't looking likely.

I weighed up the pros and cons and decided that after a hectic week filled with challenges, wins and progress, it felt right to go to the event, so I did.

By the time I finished up work and got down to the stadium I was a little late, so the preliminary rounds had already finished. I picked up my pre-ordered merchandise and headed to find my seat, feeling excited to watch the action and cheer on my favourite fighters.

Less than 30 seconds after sitting down I knew this wasn't going to work. Directly behind me, right in my earshot was a group of rowdy jokers out to let loose.

The issue was, because of the way the seats and rows were

positioned, I could hear every word they said. In fact, they had bored into the side of my skull like they were speaking through a megaphone.

I'm all for having a fun time but at that moment I just wanted to tune out and get super into the fight – not listen to the running commentary that was kindly being conducted by one of the guys to his friends. Every single move was being articulated and not even accurately.

It drove me mad.

It was excruciating and frustrating that I was giving up my valuable time to listen to this dude. I'd come by myself because I wanted to focus on the fight, I paid for an average seat (mistake), but the view of the ring was pretty good (win) and now this!

I thought it might stop but it continued, and I was also lucky enough to get his opinion on what he thought the fighter should do next, and next, and next. I couldn't take it.

I also knew that it was me that had the problem, not them. They had just as much of a right to be there as me.

I was acutely aware that I was giving up a few hours of my valuable time to come and relax into watching a few rounds of adrenaline pumping action and let my mind wander. These foghorns behind me had scuppered that plan. Without waiting to find out who my friends in the row behind thought was going to win the match, I stood up and walked back up the stairs to the top of the stadium.

Once there I was able to relax and began watching the fight in relative peace, but not more than another 30 seconds later did the attendant approach me and ask me to find my seat. It was a fair point but I just couldn't bring myself to explain the situation so I just moved further along the walkway hoping she would leave me alone.

Alas, she did not. She went and dobbed on me to another more senior staff member and I could see them walking over. I did not need this!

After a week of conversations, I wasn't ready for another one. All I was focused on was watching the fight in peace. Life had other plans.

Along they both came and asked me to go to my seat. I then took a deep breath and began to explain why I didn't want to do that, and I might as well go watch it online. To which they said they had no control over the people who sit around me. I explained that I wanted to focus on the fight without being disturbed and, of course, I understood that they couldn't control who was around me and how they wanted to watch the fight. I explained to them how this exact same situation happened before, when I came with my wife and we just couldn't get into it because the people behind were chatting nonsense that was not even related to the event.

I was resigned to the fact that I'd wasted my money and time and I should have known better, watching it online was perfect for my situation.

Then something happened.

The attendant asked for my ticket, I handed it to her, she

delved into her fanny pack and pulled out an array of tickets. She was palming through them at speed.

"Ah ha," she said, and handed me a new ticket. I gladly took it and thanked her for swapping my seat.

As I walked around the outer rim of the stadium, I could see that my new seat was in a block on the opposite side. When I neared the staircase to go down into the rows of seats below, it started to dawn on me that I was going to be going a long way down to get to row 9.

Low and behold, she had not only given me a new seat (solving my problem) but had also given me an upgrade to ring side! Now I was able to watch the fight up close and personal, and to top it off, I was sitting next to the sound guy, so there were no spectators around me.

This was a win, and if I'm honest, it was one I didn't see coming, or push for, which is very unusual for me.

The lesson I took from this was that, no matter the situation or the people you are dealing with, don't overlook the ability of others to do something for you... or their desire to help. Don't let the emotions you feel cloud your judgement of what's possible.

Upon review, I believe the thing that changed it was when I told the attendant the **story** about what happened last time when my wife and I came and the same thing happened. By doing this, I made it personal, and this transformed the nature of the exchange and the attendant could relate more to why I was not putting up with it and would rather watch at home online.

This moved her to make a decision to fix my problem. Notice, she always had the power to fix it, it was in her fanny pack, whether she was going to engage with that thought process so she could help was another matter.

What I will say is that I went into this small but meaningful situation resigned to the fact that nothing could be changed. I don't know if it was the result of a busy week or the pressure of the amount of work that I needed to get done or my pre-judgement of the event staff not having any power to change the status of my ticket, but I just hadn't given it any credit.

I had a fixed mindset. I didn't believe in a better outcome.

I know this might only be a trivial example, but it had a powerful takeaway that really stood out to me. The next time you're annoyed or frustrated in a situation, just remember the person you're talking to might have the power to turn it all around if they hear the magic words and they can relate.

The lesson is for you to release your fixed mindset. Tell your story and open up the door.

HAVE A WHITE BELT MINDSET AND SEE EVERYTHING AS AN OPPORTUNITY TO LEARN

Let me start this section by calling out the difference between a fixed and growth mindset. You are operating from a fixed mindset when you can't see the potential, when everything is as it is and is unlikely to change, especially when it comes to your skills and talents. You believe you've got what you've been given, and you don't focus on developing.

A growth mindset on the other hand is one of transformation, striving for greatness, and the pursuit of gaining more from your abilities. You believe that with enough focus, application and hard work you can change your talents and skills for the better. You can grow and improve.

In a nutshell, fixed means rigid and growth means improvement.

Now I want to talk about being a learner. Many of the greats, from Robin Sharma to Tom Bilyeu, all resolutely promote maintaining a growth mindset, no matter your station in life. If you haven't read Robin's *The 5am Club* or watched Tom in an interview on Impact Theory then please add these to your to do list for today, you won't regret it.

In fact, kill two birds with one stone and watch the episode of Impact Theory where Tom interviews Robin and take notes.[2]

Top salespeople embrace the white belt mindset with gusto. They're the ones asking questions, not fearing looking stupid, and taking an inquisitive and curious mind to each day.

They value growth and, in particular, they value themselves for having a growth mindset when it comes to solving problems and moving through the course of life's natural ebbs and flows. When you apply a growth mindset to sales, you see failure as a lesson not the end of the road. You understand that you can transform your key attributes through dedication and learning.

What's brilliant about this strategy is that, by placing value on your ability to learn rather than external factors like cars, money,

2 https://www.youtube.com/watch?v=i3_HQIUoM6E&t=2227s

fame and status (all things which can be taken away), you actually promote the thing that will make you improve.

Tom Bilyeu, legendary co-founder of Impact Theory and Quest Nutrition (which he sold for a pretty penny: $1 billion) calls this anti-fragile; he talks about this concept that the strength of something is defined by its breaking point. For example, steel is stronger than wood because it can take more pressure and strain before it breaks. But it still breaks. This is not anti-fragile.

However, something that is anti-fragile gets stronger the more you apply pressure, and being the learner is the epitome of anti-fragile. This is because the more you are shown your weak spots, the more you improve, because you derive your self-esteem from your ability to show up, learn and develop new skills. In the world of the learner, failure is not a bad thing – it simply points out where we need to improve.

That's pretty cool, right? If we only ever feel amazing when we are hitting or exceeding targets then, when tough times come along, as they always do, we will feel lousy at the exact moment when we need to be gaining strength and putting our all into taking bolder actions.

I want you to show up in your job as the learner, ask the dumb questions, be curious, push forward in pursuit of your greatest self and shift towards valuing your ability to improve, learn and grow.

Also, when you reach the top, if you get complacent in sales, it's a quick fall back down. Yet this strategy will counteract any complacency, as it will keep you searching for new deals, expanding your pipeline and always being on the lookout for opportunity.

THE BOUNTY OF AN ABUNDANCE MINDSET

When you have this mindset, you see the potential in everything, you are manifesting your dreams and experiencing the world as one giant magnet that attracts everything you desire to you. You aren't worried about the competition because there's more than enough to go around. If they win it does not mean you will have to do without, so you direct your energy towards faith and avoid negativity and doubt.

It's a state of higher consciousness reached by the world class salesperson that allows them to relax into the feeling that everything will work out as it should.

This is the opposite of a scarcity mindset, where you believe there is not enough to go around and have emotions like fear, doubt, anxiety, lack of clarity, hesitation, overthinking, small mindedness, judgement and hopelessness at a very impactful level.

These two energy states are worlds apart, and they sit on opposite sides of a spectrum. It's important that we monitor how we are showing up in life to practise the abundance mindset daily.

When you operate from an abundance mindset, you radiate a positive energy and vibrate at such a frequency that the world responds in the same way and reflects back to you that exact energetic vibration, often multiplied. In this space, you literally attract the things you most want. You are more open to opportunities than ever before, you feel courageous, confident, light, free and liberated, so ideas flow into your mind as if sent by God. The right people show up just when you need them, your life becomes magical, you are unafraid to be curious and can hold an enormous vision for your life. **Having an abundance mindset is one of the best things you could ever do for yourself, your family and your sales numbers.**

Here's how it works:

■ When you are free from worry, anxiety and doubt, it allows you to focus on solving higher value problems.

■ Focusing on solving higher value problems accelerates your prosperity as you make a greater impact upon the world.

■ People gravitate to those of the same energetic frequency. When you are abundant, you attract other world class individuals to yourself, so you are exposed to new ideas, opportunities and relationships.

Your capacity to earn is purely limited by your mindset. We live in prosperous times. You are a salesperson working in one of the most abundant, heavily resourced, flexible eras ever to have taken place.

This is YOUR time!

The mindset you apply on a daily basis to sales is the only thing either linking you to greatness or stopping you from reaching your full potential. The beliefs you carry around money and sales and the acquisition of both will dictate the ease at which they flow and stay in your life.

The sales industry is competitive. However, working in sales there is literally no cap on your ability to earn, there is no ceiling, and this is the beauty of it. If you can conceive of it, then it is possible. That is why, if you take an idea and plant the seed in the right energy, without second guessing it, you will succeed.

Even when you get rejections, or deals go south and you lose a sale, by responding to your clients with an abundance mindset you project confidence, stability and show that you are a trustworthy and reliable partner. **You literally draw future sales towards you by responding in this way.**

If you let your emotions take over and flip out because a client chose not to give you the sale, it demonstrates untrustworthiness and instability. Flipping out, getting mad, or feeling frustrated is easy, but they are all unproductive and not what top salespeople do.

Clients want to know you are there for the long haul and won't get jittery feet at the first hurdle. By sticking with it and asking yourself what you could have done better to win the sale you'll end up improving, and this is the magic of sales.

Here's where your abundance mindset needs to carry you through the learning process. When you allow the abundance to flow it enables you to engage with helpful thinking and actions.

It is inevitable that you will lose some sales, but that is it — some, not all — and this is what keeps you sharpening the saw, building the muscle of relentlessness and showing up again and again when all of the competition has given up.

What you must not lose focus on is just how capable you are, how much is within your control, to learn, to grow and to improve. You have the opportunity to show up every day with a rocking attitude and a mindset of possibility, and it is here where you will create the greatness of a sales superstar.

3. FAITH AND PURPOSE

TAP INTO YOUR VISION AND MISSION AND FIND YOUR 'WHY'

Having a purpose, a reason to go out and face rejection repeatedly, to push past the roadblocks and deal with the journey of selling at an elite level is 100x more effective than relying on willpower alone.

Every top salesperson has reached this level because they have a bigger vision driving them.

You need to have a vision so big and so powerful that it moves you to action even at your lowest moments. For you, your reason could be your son or daughter, your family, or it could be a situation or experience you lived through as a child and don't want to repeat. It could be your desire for a better life for your loved ones who are counting on you to make it happen. Whatever yours is, having this driving force behind you that will always get you up and out the door, striving, is what makes all the difference.

Whether it's to serve more, to leave a legacy, to provide generational wealth or to give your kids opportunities that you never had, this is where it changes for you. Once you find your *why* you will light a fire inside so powerful, so intense that nothing and no one can stop you from reaching your goal.

You need to know where you are going before you get there. You must be able to feel what it is like to have your bigger vision come to life. You should go out and touch it. Really experience what it would be like to live that life you dream of. This will help you make moves weeks, months and years ahead of when you are ready, or it even looks like it can happen for you.

YOUR PURPOSE ⟶ **ACCELERATED EXPLOSIVE GROWTH (ACTION)** ⟶ **MOMENTUM**

Man, I'm pumped just writing that! This is where it is at, this is where you change your life.

Sell yourself on what you are bringing to the world. The privilege and opportunity you have to be alive right now, selling the services you are selling to clients that need them.

Find your vision and dig deep, remember why you started and use this motivation to pull yourself out of your funk, to find the grit and determination to continue on.

It should become habitual and instinctive, you recognise you are going off course, especially at times when you feel unmotivated, depressed, sad or tired, and you course correct. This is the exact momentum that you use your creative imagination, intuition, and perception to increase your sales by several orders of magnitude. The biggest growth happens during the biggest struggles.

When these emotions occur, instead of letting them take charge and get the better of you, your reflexes must kick in and immediately bring forward your vision into your mind's eye.

PRO TIP

It must be something you truly want

If your purpose or vision for the future is not big enough, you won't be motivated to do what's required to level up. Spend some time figuring out what really matters to you, what would drive you to work Saturdays, evenings, early mornings, risking going out on a limb and taking gigantic leaps of faith. When you have this, you know nothing will stop you, and you just keep on going!

MY STORY ABOUT FAITH

Speaking of faith, I want to share with you the story about the miracle of the Chinese Bamboo Tree. This marvellous creation takes five years of constant nurturing, watering and care before anything will show above the surface. Growers must have patience and faith in the unseen.

Imagine that! For five years you've got to keep watering this patch of soil, just keeping the faith that what you are doing will take hold, making a difference and ensuring that you are going to see big results in the future.

It's just like this for you in pursuit of your big vision; when you invest in yourself and your personal development, you follow the process outlined in this book for explosive sales growth, there will be a period where it seems like nothing is happening. However, in reality, you are getting strong, developing from within, and then one day everything is revealed.

I'm not saying it will take five years as is the case with Chinese Bamboo but it might be a few weeks before the fruits of your hard labour begin to show and you will experience challenges and adversity that will require you to keep watering the seed and having the faith that what you are doing is making a difference.

In reality, with the Chinese Bamboo Tree what's happening is that it's growing an extensive root system below ground that can support its explosive growth once it is ready. In fact, this momentous little plant can grow up to 90 feet in five weeks once it breaks through the surface! However, it must have developed the root system below to support this growth beforehand.

Can you imagine that it has up to three feet a day in growth! If the grower pulls out his plant from the soil to check on it or gives up at any point during the five years, then he misses the remarkable trajectory and potential that was being prepared.

It's the same for you; you are the Chinese Bamboo Tree, so you are being prepared and the more you invest in building your root system, with daily self-improvement, small wins, overcoming adversity and putting in the work based on what I am sharing with you here in this book for gaining momentum, then the more you will see incredible success.

Keep nurturing, keep your faith strong, believe it is possible and don't lose heart when you don't see instant results. We've all been there, letting temporary emotions change our actions. When we get disheartened or have a bad day, we let that affect our performance and our belief in what's possible. As a result, we stop doing the things that will ensure our success.

By learning to control our thoughts and keeping tabs on our emotions and what they mean (e.g. the story we tell ourselves) we can push through the doubt, insecurities and disappointments.

Remember, everything, and I mean *everything*, is working in your favour, no matter how bad it is. Nothing is purely negative, there is always a positive. That's just the laws of the universe. Something that on the surface might seem like a complete failure or loss might actually be the biggest blessing in disguise. A lost sale might be saving you from an awful and destructive client, a lost job might be leading you to the biggest opportunity of your life.

It's when we let temporary defeat take over and give up on our plans or reduce our commitment to our vision that we do ourselves and our growth a massive disservice.

We must believe in ourselves and our greatness. You don't need a reason to give yourself a high five or a pat on the back. In fact, I want you to look at yourself right now in the mirror and repeat these words, "I am awesome and I am on a mission." Now give yourself a high five.

Get into the habit of praising yourself, being your own farmer, boosting your self-esteem and championing yourself just for sticking with the process and having faith that it will all work out.

Don't quit and go grow a different plant that's going to show results tomorrow, stick with it and invest for the long term. Once you learn the process outlined and become a momentum seller, then you can take this with you wherever you go, and you will no longer fear the path to building a business or taking over a hard patch of clients. You'll have a belief so deep in your ability, skills and persistence that it will provide you such self confidence that life will send all kinds of opportunities your way.

The next time you want to give up, or question if all the hard work you are putting in is actually working, I want you to think of the Chinese Bamboo Tree and keep on watering.

Look at the second to last sentence of my definition of momentum… it's right there: absolute faith!

MINI MOMENTUM BUILDER
Praise yourself

I want you to start praising yourself more for sticking with it and having faith in your bigger vision. To get closer to the life you want you need to step into it now, you need to celebrate the wins and make it habit, no matter how small. If good things are happening, be thankful for them. Book a meal out tonight somewhere you've always wanted to go, invite a friend or your partner and remember you deserve this and all the good that is on its way to you.

4. YOUR GO-TO DAILY OPERATING PRINCIPLES

HIGH STANDARDS

Do more than is required. As a top seller you treat your patch like it is your own business, you are an entrepreneur and nurture it as such. You aren't counting hours, or only doing the bare minimum to get the deal, you're doing your very best every time.

Just because you see others cutting corners or sending over subpar proposals doesn't mean you will. Make it your mission to always deliver to the best of your ability in anything that you do. Take pride in anything you send out with your name on it; it is your brand.

In sales your brand is your reputation, as Warren Buffett says, *"It takes 20 years to build a reputation, and five minutes to ruin it. If you think about that you'll do things differently."*

If you want to earn more money, have more wealth, then you must become more valuable. Once you put out more value to the market, do what others won't, the market will take notice and pay you more. It's an exchange.

Always keep investing in your own growth and development and never let it stop. This will enable you to keep increasing your value because your output and skillset will become more valuable. **If you want to attract success and wealth, become a person of value.**

Once you hold yourself to a high standard, all areas around you improve and, as a knock-on effect, you begin to notice attractive opportunities that would have previously passed you by. It's not just your wealth that improves, it impacts across all areas of life – your relationships improve, your health improves, your happiness improves. It is all linked, and it begins with holding yourself to account and to a high standard.

When you adopt a high standard of life, it becomes easier to also say "no" to the people and situations you know won't benefit you because you are on a mission to improve, to achieve your goals and to give it your all. You won't want to party every single weekend instead of working on your business and developing your mind.

You won't feel the need to watch mindless television shows or sleep in instead of reading books or taking courses in the early morning before work to improve. You won't resent the work you need to do to improve, your home will be full of new and interesting books, and the shape of how you orientate your life and what's important to you will shift.

How you direct your time and energy will also change. You'll hit the gym instead of sitting on the sofa with a pizza, you'll stop wasting time watching soap operas and focus on learning to build a website for your business and code. You'll hustle every night to find new clients and you'll take the time to invest back into yourself so that you can deliver more to the world.

What is important to you will change and as your focus changes so too will the people you hang out with – the people you aspire to be like, and the person you want to become.

It's this process of continuous improvement in pursuit of becoming better that will see you make monumental shifts to your income but also what you think is possible.

Do you think that I wanted to write out 45 tailored prospecting emails a day? No, but it taught me the principles of what works. Over time I became skilled and my response rate improved significantly. I studied copy and watched videos, anything I could get my hands on. I learnt everything I could about composition, timing and influence using emails.

I did the same with negotiations on email, over the phone and in person when working in corporate barter, and then read all I could over the years on negotiation strategy, psychology of persuasion and influence.

Over time these skills compound, and you start to see synergies that you can apply to accelerate successful outcomes. The more situations you have been in the quicker the lessons are learned and the more valuable you'll be.

Remember, this isn't about beating the next guy (although healthy competition is good). This is about beating who you were yesterday and who you want to be tomorrow. Be so good they can't ignore you. Raise your standards about what you will and won't accept in your life.

THINK BIG AND THEN THINK BIGGER AGAIN

There's tons of advice out there in sales and self-help entrepreneurship blogs, books and podcasts, all of them telling you to "think big". But what does that really mean in reality? I want to break this down as it's a pivotal point that is often underutilised when it comes to sales.

In order to get the full impact from thinking big you must first believe that your goal is possible and act in accordance with that level of awareness and consciousness.

If you have read any of my other books (*Be the Lion* or *The Art of Negotiation*), or come across my content or courses or heard me speak, you will know my mantra is "believe it is possible". As I mentioned at the beginning of the book, this has got me into some pretty incredible situations all by believing, having faith and then taking action.

The think big philosophy only works if you also act with the mindset of "it's possible". Half-heartedly going after your goal undermines the principle and therefore it doesn't happen. You are sabotaging the outcome before you even get started.

This happens, because if deep down inside you don't really believe it then you aren't committed to courageously taking the right actions with absolute faith. As a result, you don't step into the unknown and sadly you barely manage to move the needle.

For thinking big to really take effect, you must raise your level of conscious awareness; your energy must rise in line with that which you want. This is a 3-step process:

1. Start by thinking big.

2. Take massive action towards your goal through initiative and adjust as you go.

3. Have faith throughout and believe it is possible.

If you do this, you will experience extraordinary results but you must have all three elements and persist until it happens.

Thinking big is an energetic state, it's all about the energetic vibration you give off. When you think big and believe it is possible your energy changes and you can shift other people's mindsets and influence them to get onboard with your vision.

That's how you influence people. If you've got faith something will happen for you and you truly believe it, that level of confidence is supremely powerful. It can literally change the stars and open doors that didn't even exist previously.

You've got to believe it so much so that it is anchored to you, that it shakes you to the very core with energy, light and magnetism. Like a magnet, energy is attracted to energy of the same vibration. You literally attract the ideas, situations and people you want to you by the way you think.

For example, thinking big might be "I'm going to double my sales this month" – then ask, "do I believe this is possible?" Yes, because my pipeline is very healthy, and I've got x number of meetings coming up – in which case this is fine but it's not really requiring you to have all that much belief because the data points suggest you are going to make that type of leap upward.

However, if your goal was "I'm going to double my sales this month" then you're told to think bigger "I'm going to 10x my sales this month." That's when you ask yourself "Do I believe this?" – and the answer is "no". I've never done that and don't have anything set up that realistically enables me to think that it is achievable this month. It's just something I like the sound of saying. Then, this is where you need to get used to shifting your mindset into that of being a momentum seller who is thinking and acting from the vision of what they want. This is the critical point where you need to shift into a different emotional state.

When you doubt that it is possible, you cut off options. However, I am telling you that I've seen it happen – anything from 400% increases like $1 million sales months, when previously the seller was doing $200k, to other times where it might be 10x the sales in a very short space of time. When a seller is on fire and they are achieving these types of results you can see it coming through their actions before it appears in their sales revenue.

They walk different, talk different, there's a confidence and a deep inner knowing that shines through and you can tell they've got it. They believe it is possible and they're about to make it rain!

The reason it's difficult for most to do is because it seems out of the ordinary and they are too focused on external results (what's going on around them) rather than creating from within. You need to have faith, vision and imagination before you get the outcome, for it to happen. You've got to reprogram your mind away from thinking in logical linear steps and stop putting a cap on what's possible. There is no ceiling on what you can earn or achieve.

World class salespeople play in the realm way, way, above this.

It's a state of mind and action that produces incredible outcomes, an attitude most people can't fathom because the results seem highly unlikely and they've never experienced them before. In fact, they are so focused on what happens if they don't hit their target that, you guessed it, they don't hit their target. Rather than focusing on what they want and why it can happen, making sales come rain or shine, regardless of the environment or economic climate.

Now this might take you seeing someone else do it before you can believe it, which is why it is so important for you to align yourself and learn from the best salespeople you can. They will inspire you to think big and go after what you want without holding back for fear that if you charge "too much" then you will lose the sale. By hanging around these sales leaders they will raise your level of conscious awareness, and this will influence your subconscious mind and start to bring ideas and intuition into focus. From that point, as long as you take the action required, you'll start to move towards creating bigger results.

PRO TIP
Always seek the best

My recommendation is to find within your organisation the best of the best, seek them out and get to know them, become friends with them and learn how they operate, study the way they think about sales and targets, and you'll see that they aren't operating from a fear-based mindset.

By learning from those who have accomplished it, you'll see with

your own eyes that it is real. Once you see it, there's no going back.
Every action and every decision must go back to that question – is
what I am about to do growing my business, helping me achieve
my bigger vision? Does it help me grow as a person?

You must apply thinking big to your sales; when a client asks you how much you charge remove your self-imposed limitations, and really go big, focusing on the big money, big client opportunities. You need to become so focused on growth, every talk, every meeting, every action, every day needs to be pushing your business higher, bigger and further.

The average salesperson thinks of the maximum number they think the client would pay for a product, drops it down a few percent and then prays that they sign the deal.

It takes guts to tell a client that you need to charge more than the competition because of the value you offer and stick to it. It takes balls to strategically go after landing a huge account and commit a significant amount of your time and energy in pursuit of this goal at the expense of smaller amounts. It requires courage to know deep down that you have what it takes to upsell, cross-sell and provide more value than the next guy when the time arises. It is a skill, but it's one of the most important lessons you'll ever learn.

Top salespeople put the right solution on the table and then charge accordingly. They're not afraid to charge in line with the size of the problem they are solving and, because they think big and believe the client will pay, they achieve success.

When typical salespeople are challenged on price, they automatically resort to shaving 30% off the rate card to try to appease the client's wishes and undercut any competition. This is the easy way.

The problem with this strategy is that over time it becomes a race to the bottom. If your only winning tactic is to undercut the competition on dollars and cents, it will erode your margins and overall long-term business health.

It will make doing business unattractive and, worst of all, if you can't charge appropriately, it indicates that your client doesn't fully appreciate or understand the value of your offering and the problem you are solving for them. The very best don't undermine the value of the sale or their product by competing on price and, as such, tend to win more.

If you can articulate the cost your product is saving the client, and they see the need to commit to implementing your solution over the long-term, price becomes less of an issue.

When clients make price a major issue, it's either because you haven't helped them understand the size of the problem they face, or you can't really solve it to the extent that would warrant the cost you are charging.

Be sure to paint the full picture. What happens if they don't change? How will it affect their business in one, two and three years? Why is there a need for urgency? You must help them to see the reality.

To do that you need to understand the problem better than them, and you've got to share insights with them that even they didn't know! When you can do this, combined with your ease of talking about the subject of money and thinking big, you signal that you know you've got real value to offer and are the right company to work with. It's a winning combination.

Jack Ma, Steve Jobs, Elon Musk, all used think big strategies with their teams. Jack did this by doubling or even tripling targets and by moving the goal post further out to expand what his staff believed was possible. Naturally, his salespeople went for it, they thought bigger, and made bigger moves as a result.

The same goes for Jobs when he pushed developers to improve

the results achieved by the technology or to create something which they believed to be impossible. He would walk away and tell them to get on with it. By not accepting their third or fourth or even fifth attempts as the end of the road, he forced the team to keep battling with the problem long enough to solve it (sometimes way over a year).

Elon does his think big quite publicly – colonising Mars, a backup plan for Earth, electric cars – and because of this outward belief he actually draws the people, the opportunity and the money he needs to him to make it a reality.

Go make it happen, today, go forward from this point thinking big, and believing big. Seek out those who are doing it and know deep within that you too are capable of this level of success and more. This is not fiction; it is happening all around you right now and it's time for you to claim your spot at the top. There's a seat at the table with your name on it.

How can you apply Think Big to sales?

1. Set yourself bigger targets and push past any mental barriers.

2. Wrestle with problems longer and don't accept anything less than solved.

3. Make your intentions clear to others and back yourself and your team to make them happen.

4. Focus on cultivating a mentality that you won't stop until it is achieved, that it has to happen, that you will not give up.

5. When asked what your average size booking is, increase it and expand your horizons.

6. Increase your prices for a week on all new sales, just to demonstrate to yourself that it is possible.

7. When your mind knows that there is no option for you but the goals you have set, it will help you find a way of achieving them. Listen to your gut when big ideas appear as a result of this understanding.

THE NUMBER 1 RULE – THIS IDEA WILL MAGNIFY YOUR SALES LIKE NEVER BEFORE!

More than anything it is the power of **enthusiasm** that will transform your sales like nothing before or after; enthusiasm is infectious. It is the most potent form of energy and influence. By bringing enthusiasm with you daily into your sales meetings, pitches, calls, emails and interactions, you will overcome all manner of obstacles and your clients will love being around you and your anything is possible aura.

I can't tell you the number of times I have used the power of enthusiasm in my own sales to transform the outcome from a flat "no" to a "hell, yes".

This works whether you are communicating over email, on the phone, on text or in person – it works, if you work it. Be prepared for MASSIVE results, be prepared for colleagues to call you up after a meeting and thank you for your participation, for putting ideas out there, for getting the team going. Clients will buy into how you make them feel. Enthusiasm is like fuel – if you want to go faster just pour more on and watch it speed up.

PERSONAL STORY
The kitchen meeting that turned into my biggest sale

I remember one time I flew to the Philippines, checked into a hotel, ordered room service and decided to call it an early night. I arrived at the client's office bright and early the next morning ready for a meeting. Right away the client told me they needed to cut our one-hour meeting short. It's always a bit of a bummer when that happens, but not if you have enthusiasm and a love for the sales game. It was a test of my ability to recalibrate and ask myself "what is the good in this?"

I saw it as an opportunity. We sat down in the kitchen area of their office as there were no meeting rooms available and it was there, in that dimly lit kitchenette area, that I began to start the process of what would turn out to be the biggest sale I had made so far in the company.

Wow, I'm just starting to notice how many of my sales take place in random places!

If I had let the annoyance of chatting in a crappy kitchen and the meeting being cut short by 50% after travelling all the way there get the better of me I would have blown the opportunity that was staring me in the face.

Remember, when changes like this happen, nothing happens to the size of the opportunity; it is still there, waiting for you to grab it with both hands.

When meetings are cut short, get to the meat. I got right to it. I adjusted my pitch and reset for what was now going to be a 30-minute opportunity to communicate our value.

In fact, that was all that mattered. I didn't try to overwhelm the client with what we could do by fitting an hour's worth of conversation into the 30-minute slot. I didn't try to speak faster, or fantastically try to go through as much as possible.

All I did was focus intently on the client. What would serve them best right now?

I served the clients that were sitting in front of me. When they spoke, I listened and provided the most relevant information, examples and answers possible.

I didn't even present. I gave a passionate and humble overview of why I believed in what we were doing, and I believe that was the turning point. They could see that I was confident and knew what I was talking about. I wasn't overselling or underselling it – I was able to give them my honest view of where the products I was selling would be right for them and where they wouldn't.

It was this ability to adapt and redeploy my resources in a way that would best serve the new circumstance that won us the deal. That and consistent follow up over the coming weeks.

The lesson here is that enthusiasm will carry you through more ups and downs. It will help you stabilise the chopping and changing of circumstances and give you a rudder to focus on in stormy seas. By focusing on always seeing the opportunity you can't fail to do your best.

DEVELOP THE HABIT OF SELF-BELIEF

None of what I share with you in this book will matter if you don't do one thing. One thing above all else that **must** become part of your psyche, your daily habit, your operating system. Without this one thing you will not reach your full potential or maximise outcomes, and you'll also be left questioning your decisions and frustrated because you'll know you are meant for more.

Something inside of you, a voice, a fire, a yearning deep inside, knows that you are capable of achieving more. It knows that, if you really applied yourself, pushing yourself through the walls of your comfort zone, then you would have no choice but to achieve the greatness stored up inside you and, in the process, you would become more.

The habit I need you to develop on a conscious daily basis is the habit of believing in yourself. **You must believe in yourself**.

In sales and in life, this is everything. What if, starting today, you made a commitment to back yourself, to stop being so hard on yourself when things go wrong and instead put the failure down to learning? Then you could take the lesson and improve. How would that feel?

Instead of staying trapped in a cycle of self-doubt and negative thinking, mainly directed at how poorly you see yourself, let's make a commitment.

Today is the day that changes. From today onwards, you will get into the habit of reversing this destructive pattern, from here on out, all failures are lessons, they help you grow and succeed. A wise person knows that it is the obstacles and challenges that help them to overcome the biggest hurdles in life and develop character.

Now is the time to start believing in yourself. When you are working through this book and completing the tasks and putting the insights into action, I want you to come back to this simple but effective requirement. Make it part of how you go about life.

If doubt happens to creep in, snuff it out by flipping the switch – you are now a believing in yourself machine. You were born for greatness. Repeat these phrases to yourself whenever you feel unsure:

1. I was born to do great things.

2. Either I win or I learn.

3. Nothing and no one can hold me back.

4. Every day I am growing stronger and more resilient.

5. Now is the time to give it my all.

6. I believe in me.

7. I am here to give my all and deliver excellence.

8. Great things are coming my way.

9. I can do this, I will do it, I have done it.

10. This is my time to shine and I won't let anything get in my way.

11. I back myself 100%.

12. I am my biggest fan.

13. I am abundant and can make anything I put my mind to happen.

14. I am successful, valuable and inspire others by walking boldly.

15. I was put here for a purpose and I will lead, deliver and serve.

16. I trust myself 1% more each day.

17. I am courageous, persistent and on a mission.

18. I think and act as the person I want to become.

19. I love myself.

20. I am a winner.

21. I surround myself with other highly successful people.

22. I know that I can achieve anything I put my mind to.

23. I make decisions quickly and easily.

24. I do things that are uncomfortable because I know they allow me to grow.

25. I think from my heart.

26. I value myself and know that I am worthy of receiving in a big way.

27. I am in love with the lifestyle I am building.

28. I love who I am becoming.

29. I am focused on my own development.

30. I am here to put my God-given talents to their highest use.

31. I am focused on becoming the best version of myself.

32. I see opportunity all around me.

33. I see positivity and good everywhere I go.

34. I am creating my future.

35. I do what I say I am going to do.

Above all else, believe in yourself.

If you're reading this but thinking "well, I don't like myself very much, so how can I believe in myself?" This is where you need to start doing things to make yourself proud. Self-belief is made possible when you start making yourself proud.

You can do this by making your bed, cleaning the apartment, working out when you said you would. Once you start keeping the promises you make to yourself, even on a very small scale, it leads to bigger wins. You will start to feel better about yourself.

When we don't show integrity towards ourselves, and feel out of alignment, then it feels awful. Nothing really feels possible, so I get you, don't worry. Just focus on controlling the small things and putting one foot in front of the other. Even if it feels fake, still go through the statements above and whilst you are rebuilding the relationship you have with yourself you are priming your mind with the right thoughts.

By getting into the habit of striving for excellence you are telling the universe that you are ready, that you believe in yourself. Look out world, I am coming for you! I'm talking about taking confidence, ownership, responsibility into sales. You have a responsibility to share your product or services with clients, so work harder than you are paid for and wear many hats. To do this it may mean changing the way you think about how you spend your time and we'll get stuck into this a little later on. I'll give you tools and strategies so that you can work smarter and harder than yesterday.

That goes for how you allocate your time as well. This frame of mind might require you to hire a nanny, or a cleaner, to get an accountant or a gardener, as your time is about to become incredibly valuable and it can't be spent on tasks that aren't taking you close to your goal.

This doesn't mean working all hours of the day and night until you face burnout, that is not the way to maximise results. The way you need to do it is to spend as much time as you can on high-value activities, like spending time in front of your clients, taking the next right action, selling. Not logging expenses, doing life admin or preparing taxes – outsource the mundane so you can go out and be brilliant.

I believe in you, I know you have what it takes to get after it, to become a top seller, the very best you that you can be. You can become unstoppable, looking back in years to come and saying, "I did it".

There will be times when you want to give up in sales, when the road seems too tough, when it feels like nothing you are doing is working, but hear me now when I say you are on the right path – you *can* do this and you were born to be great! This is your time to shine. Together, let's take the next step and explore a little more about what they call the sales process.

PERSONAL STORY
When it's worth the risk

I was on a business trip to Hong Kong. I wanted to take full advantage of being one of the only salespeople flying into Hong Kong at the time of the political riots towards the end of 2019. I talk about this later on in the book, but I took a gamble with my outgoing flight and risked it for an additional client meeting.

I had a decision to make – take the midday meeting with a flight departing at 3pm and risk traffic delays and getting stuck in Hong Kong for another day or take the meeting and figure it out.

It might not seem like a big deal writing about it now, but when you're in a city with heightened political tension, and anything can kick off at any second, as a traveller in the city you are somewhat exposed with only a hotel room for cover.

Obviously, putting two meetings so closely together only a few hours before my flight out of Hong Kong was a risk, but so was being in Hong Kong in the first place.

I am not advocating putting yourself in danger for a sale, but I am advocating that you weigh up the information and take some calculated risks. After all, these risks are what will set you apart from the rest.

You continue on when others turn around. You will find a way to make it work, uncovering the solution to the problem in the same way you would fight to find your clients solutions to their problems.

The risk paid off. Two months later we got our first Nike booking and have continued to do amazing business with them ever since. Time and time again I have found that, by putting yourself in the path of success, by being in the fight, it pays off.

5. KEEPING YOUR MINDSET WHEN YOU NEED TO DIG DEEP

FIGHTING YOUR WAY THROUGH THE JUNGLE

Every once in a while, maybe once a week, maybe once a month, you will come to what looks like a roadblock. This bump in the road has the potential to derail the sale and put all your hard work to waste.

My strategy for dealing with this, to continue to push harder, to find the opportunity, to keep fighting through the jungle as I like to call it (the jungle being the mess of emails, calls, texts, conversations, unreasonable and unobtainable KPIs, razor sharp deadlines, no replies, losses and dead ends).

To be able to fight skilfully in the jungle, I practise in the real world. Once a week I will do something against the norm, like go for a run in the rain or just before a storm.

Yesterday, I went out for a fast-paced run. It was 1pm in the afternoon and the baking Singapore sun was mercilessly beating down.

Times like these reflect the journey in sales and entrepreneurship, when you are trying to create something from nothing and you need to find the grit deep inside to keep going and deliver your best.

One o'clock in the afternoon in Singapore is not the normal time for people to go running, but this is exactly what it's like when you've got to hustle in the jungle – you've got to fight for everything.

In sales, when you need to keep going, you need to keep prospecting, you need to keep doing that one more email, one more phone call or that one more client presentation that could close the deal that would mean your business takes off. It's the same thing, so I encourage you to go out there and not always do what the norm is.

Yes, it's nicer to run when it's not raining or the wind isn't blowing but every now and again you've got to **push yourself to show that you can**. That will mean that you need to go out into the storm, or into the heat of the day when you can feel the sun searing your skin. **You prove to yourself that you can do it.**

This is what it's like in business when you're fighting for your "whys", for your dreams to come alive, for the things that are pushing you further. Expanding yourself. This is exactly the jungle you've got to fight through, getting around the obstacles.

You won't see many other souls on the road and that's exactly the point; what you're doing is against the grain. To show you can, you move through the mud, the wind and the rain, and around the obstacles.

That's what builds the resilience muscle, but it's also what makes you do the work and do it differently because up there in your mind you know you can.

If you had to go run in that midday heat, you know you can – **you've proved it to yourself and it's knowing that you can do it that carries you through**. You've gone around the obstacles and made it happen.

That's the mentality you must apply to your sales, to your business, when you are faced by radio silence, or need to look harder to find the opportunity and deliver your best. Get out there and push yourself to do something against the grain. It's that mentality of knowing you can persist that helps you gain a competitive edge in your own mind.

Having the mental resilience and mental toughness to keep going through the times that are tough – when no one's getting back to you, where every email you send is hitting a deafening wall of silence and doesn't get a response – is key.

It starts to weigh you down, and you start to wonder: "am I doing the right thing?", "am I doing it right?", "is sales for me?" Then victim mode starts to creep in.

Doing things like this gets you away from victim and into warrior. Once a week, make sure you do something that's against the grain and apply that mentality to your business. It will pay dividends.

How to apply mental resilience to sales

1. Push yourself to do uncomfortable things and build mental resilience, the effect is magnified and trickles over into other areas of your life. Get out there and do the work daily.

2. Set challenges for yourself each day (e.g. "today, I will contact 40 potential clients and remind them how we're going to change the world together").

3. Make a list of all the items you must tick off today, order it by priority and commit to completing it. You build your self-confidence by doing the things you say you are going to do.

4. Email that big client that could change your sales trajectory – you know, the one that you are waiting for the right moment to make contact. Well, I've got news for you: the timing will never be just right and you risk waiting so long that they leave the company, change roles or, worse, die. Yes, I said die. Nothing is a given.

5. Get rejected. When you are in sales you need to be able to brush off criticism, objections and continue to move forward. Put yourself in that position on purpose and you will build strength and get more into the game. When that tipping point happens, and you realise the worst they can say is "no", it's all to play for. Remember your why. What matters most to you? A little rejection or achieving your bigger purpose?

What you'll find is that you get less affected by the rejection, or when a client brushes you off or doesn't respond with the enthusiasm that you expected to the proposal that you spent all weekend writing.

These little things that used to trip us up no longer have as much impact; they still happen but they don't stop your pursuit of going after your goals. You continue to push forward and sell.

It's how you wake up every single day and take your "A game" to the day, like setting bigger targets for yourself. This might mean you saying, "today I am going to send 40 prospecting emails and do 25 prospecting calls". If you normally send five or ten a day, and sometimes call a few people, then this is going to have a dramatic effect on your business.

But it's what happens next that is even more important than sending the emails and doing the business development work.

What happens if you send out 40 perfectly tailored emails, with case studies and links calibrated for the DiSC behavioural profiles (see the chapter on Understanding for DiSC), and then you put in your calls and you end the day feeling satisfied, thinking today was a good day?

You wake up the next day raring to go, but as the day progresses you realise no one is coming back to you. Even after doing all that action taking, still nothing?!

This **right here** is the moment you need to get the lion attitude to sales. You need to bring your warrior out and fight through the jungle to keep going, to persist even when the land is a barren wasteland, and it looks like water (the opportunity) will be hard to find anywhere. This is where your mental toughness kicks in and takes over.

You get back to it, and call all the clients you prospected yesterday, you find new clients to reach out to, you come up with creative and interesting ways to add value to your clients. You hit them with a "jolt" email*. You do whatever it takes, and because you've trained your mind to fight for your dreams, you don't disappear into victim mode, you don't give up and conclude that yesterday's hard work was a waste of time and you should just go back to living in mediocrity because it's easier. You have raised your internal standard.

Re-read this section "fighting your way through the jungle" every time you feel you have hit a brick wall or need to remember it. Read it once a day for a month before you begin your work and get it so ingrained in your psyche that it becomes second nature. This should be your default operating mode.

If someone asked you how you deal with difficult clients or tough sales – this should be your answer.

*A jolt email is a shorter email, more direct and to the point and intended to nudge the client or customer into taking some form of action.

Hi James,

Hope you're well?

Just following up on the above as it would be great to discuss this in a meeting.

Please let me know when you have availability in the next week.

Best, Tim

DEALING WITH LOSSES

Losses can be hard, but in sales they are inevitable. When they happen, they sting for a moment, or sometimes a little longer, but they don't signal it's the end of the road or your career in sales. The best way to deal with losses is all to do with how you respond both to your clients and to yourself.

Let's discuss an example to give this some context. Imagine it's a Saturday, you're out and about with your family doing some last-minute Christmas shopping. Spirits are high, the carol singers are out in force and Christmas trees adorn every nook and cranny of public space. You are waiting for your partner to finish browsing the last few racks of the year's must-have items, and you decide to grab your phone and check your work inbox. Not uncommon for you, but you are working on cutting down your mobile usage at weekends. To your surprise, you spot an email from a client you had been waiting for a response from in regard to a large sale. Now, before your brain can stop you, you've opened the email to discover that you haven't won the business.

Your eyes can't believe what you're reading. Your heart sinks and you think about all the work you've put into the pitch – all the early mornings, all the late nights, the sheer amount of sweat equity that you have invested into landing this client. You think of all the tiny, intricate details you found out for them, the back and forth for weeks, not to mention what a sale of this size would have done to your sales numbers.

Do you let the impact of this loss ruin the rest of the day with your family?

Do you respond immediately to the client in the moment expressing your upset and disdain at losing the sale?

How do you respond?

Well, actually, how you respond when losing a sale is EVERY-THING.

There's a right way and a wrong way. What I am going to share with you has the power to transform your sales business tenfold.

Firstly, the client probably agonised before sending the bad news to you, as no one wants to be the bearer of bad news, especially when you delivered a cracking pitch and deserved to win. The client also doesn't want to hear your sob story.

The way you respond will say a lot to your client and also subconsciously to yourself. How you respond to a loss actually has the power to affect all your other sales as it has to do with what you are telling yourself and your clients.

If you had hit your targets, you were absolutely smashing it, would this loss feel so bad?

Of course, it would still sting a bit and the opportunity not to expand your business further would be a shame, but how would you *feel*?

When we are in abundance, sales are through the roof, so a loss here and there doesn't feel so bad. This affects how we respond to our clients when we reply to the email telling them that we understand we haven't won the business.

What would a top seller do in this situation?

Well, for starters, they wouldn't take it personally.

They would probably do the exact opposite of a poor seller, who would express their annoyance in losing the sale, or not respond to the client at all. Either approach would only demonstrate that they were in fact the wrong partner for the client and that not winning the sale was the correct course of action.

How you handle yourself tells your clients everything they need to know about doing future business with you. When you respond, you need to be as courteous as if you had won the business – you are in it for the long game. You don't have to respond right away but how you respond is what matters. It can be in the moment, if you think you can bring the optimism, or take a day and respond on Monday.

Think about it from the client's perspective: would you rather get an email from a disgruntled, shirty seller who points out all the reasons why you are wrong for not choosing them and is upset about the money and time they wasted on the pitch? No. You'd avoid them like the plague in future and be thankful that this was an opportunity for them to reveal their true colours. When the pedal hits the metal in sales, you need to think of the longer-term future business.

A top seller operates from an abundance mindset, so they don't live or die by one sale. In fact, the losses drive them harder, and keep them motivated and hungry, like sharpening the saw. Without losses there is no game.

Sales professionals at the top of their game emanate success, whether it is through the language they use, when they write or speak, or the way they carry themselves. It flows through their being like an invisible force or energy that attracts more success to it.

Top salespeople don't go into victim mode or think "poor me". They think bigger, they expand their horizons and when they respond to clients, they do so with gratitude regardless of the outcome.

If you weren't worried about losing the sale, you would respond differently, more confidently, more humbly and as a result work more harmoniously with your clients. This is another factor that will help you to make a name for yourself, encouraging clients to work with you more frequently and ensuring you enjoy the process.

Key tips on how to respond to your client when you lose a sale

- Respond with grace.

- If you are deeply upset about the loss, then you are taking it too personally, and I recommend sleeping on it before you fire off an emotionally charged email that is driven by worry, which you will later regret.

- Thank them for the opportunity to do business together and for being included in the process.

- Talk about the future (not the past) – the conversation should be future focused, upbeat and optimistic.

- Be a person you would want to do business with.

- Have an abundance mindset – remember, this isn't your only deal.

- Respond as if you know many, many, sales are on their way to you. This was a loss, but it doesn't damage who you are and what you are capable of.

- Tell them that you are here for them and to reach out if needed (the funny thing about losses, sometimes they quickly turn into wins – clients change their minds, businesses need change, new budgets are unlocked). Always be hustling for the opportunity to win.

- Manage your emotions – this isn't about you. Show your clients respect and tell them that you understand their process and it was a pleasure to be involved.

- Don't come across desperate, don't beg. Be a professional with high standards – it didn't work out this time and that's OK!

- Send them a gift, and act like you won. I don't mean go crazy and start popping champagne, but I do mean that you should court your clients. The process is what you are in it for, that's the piece that matters, and you want your clients to involve you next time so be a partner that they can rely on at all times not just when you are winning.

- Ask questions that will help you prepare for next time (e.g. what can we do better next time? Was there anything else we could have done or you would have liked to have seen?).

Head on over to **www.timjscastle.com/themomentumsalesmodel** to download your free "Responding With Grace To A No Sale" email template and never have to worry again what to say.

Tips on keeping a Mindset of Abundance after a loss

1. Tell yourself that this leaves you open to focus on something bigger.

2. Find a way to see losing this sale as a blessing in disguise.

3. Tell yourself that you are a sales machine, there are plenty more sales on the way to you and that this one just wasn't meant to be.

4. Remember that you have plenty more in the pipeline and you're a top seller.

5. This is a sign that you're close to a breakthrough.

6. It's not personal, it's business and part of the game.

I would say that's a big one, don't take it personally. You didn't lose because you are a bad salesperson, sometimes sales don't happen because of a variety of factors that are often out of your control.

As a sales professional you also understand that losses are a part of the game, without them you wouldn't get stronger and you wouldn't become more resilient. Having and experiencing losses actually makes you tougher because you get a chance to prove to yourself that you can and will overcome it. This is great for sales and for your sales confidence. In fact, overcoming losses and dealing with them in a healthy way is beneficial to your sales game.

Losses can also be a blessing in disguise; was that sale the perfect sale, or would it have caused you a lot of stress? Does this free you up to focus on other clients more heavily? What is the silver lining? Once you find that, you connect with abundance and the experience of losing becomes a gaining experience, both from the perspective of valuable feedback from clients, the ability to direct your time elsewhere and the fact that this will only drive you to succeed greater. You get tougher the more you learn to roll with the punches.

How you handle losses says a lot about you. Carry positive energy into your next sales opportunity; don't linger or ruminate on what could have been, instead move forward with your head held high and your shoulders back.

WHAT TO DO WHEN YOU LOSE A SALE

I am writing this 17 minutes after losing a sale to a major client so that it's as raw, real and fresh as it can be.

I have a wound, and my pipeline has been injured. I needed this sale to come through in order to make commission. It took me by surprise as well because last Friday they seemed super pumped to do the deal and there was no mention of budget cuts.

Man, I am bummed.

What does this say about me as a salesperson?

What will my boss say?

Scenario 1:

I'm definitely going to get asked about it as I just brought it up in the 12pm Monday sales meeting. I made a big deal of it as well. I'm going to look stupid in front of the rest of the team and now I have a big hole to fill and only seven days to do it; that sale was a lifeline.

I was counting on it just to look good, to feel good. Man, I'm stunned. I'm going to go have a slice of pie and bury my head for a while.

Scenario 2:

I just lost a sale. It sucks. I wanted this client to buy with us, but they had an unforeseen budget cut. I guess that's a sign of the times and why I have so many plates spinning and I keep my pipeline full to the brim with healthy opportunities.

This is exactly why I put in the work and prepare on weekends, even when I don't want to. It's why I go the extra mile and make sure I don't take any sale for granted, no matter how fast and easy they come.

It's a shame, but I won't let it stop me. In fact, I am going to set aside some time this afternoon to conduct a mini post-sale loss review. Just to see if there's anything we could have done better.

Yes, that's what I'll do – I'll get something valuable out of it. I'll be courteous to the client and respond with positivity and cheer.

Which one of these camps do you think a Momentum salesperson falls into?

Clearly, it's the latter. It's easy to spot when it's written on paper, but why then is it so hard to do in reality?

It's similar to the financial advice that would help move people towards freedom. When times are tough, people contract, spending less and reducing expenses for fear of poverty, and when times are good, they spend frivolously, in large quantities with limited regard for the future.

In reality, the exact opposite would be beneficial. Spend more when times are bad to help create the momentum and innovation needed to secure golden opportunities and save more when the sun is shining to prepare for the bad times.

It takes discipline to save when everyone else is spending and flashing their latest toys around, likewise it takes courage to believe in yourself and spend when everyone else is contracting and acting from a place of scarcity, rather than making bold moves that will set them up for the future.

It's the same with how you respond when losing a sale. One way to respond is beneficial yet hard to do and the other is easy yet led by emotions.

Think about what Jim Rohn says about the seasons and Warren Buffett says about risk:

> *"Life and business is like the changing seasons. You cannot change the seasons, but you can change yourself. Therein lies the opportunity to live an extraordinary life—the opportunity to change yourself."*

– JIM ROHN

> *"Be fearful when others are greedy. Be greedy when others are fearful."*

– WARREN BUFFETT

The same mentality can be applied to sales.

When you have a failure, lose out on a sale and things don't go the way you planned, it's time to go harder, it's time to double the effort and the discipline whilst sticking to the plan. Because you have momentum, because you have been operating from this sales model, you won't be left short changed. You are futureproofed as your pipeline covers this loss and many more. You have more than enough, and you take action with a mindset of abundance at all times, even when you just lost a sale.

It's easy to copy other salespeople, to go drown your sorrows at the bar or eat junk, to make excuses about why you lost the sale, market, timing, budget, but what trumps all of that?

Having a process that you operate come rain or shine, day in and day out. Whether the opportunities and clients buy or whether they don't, you keep going, you stay the course, you have a big enough "why" and you aren't going to panic and pull the plug at the first signs of defeat.

Momentum will protect you from ever being in this position and let's just say, for argument's sake, that you do find yourself in this position, then you'll know exactly how to start over, how to create something from nothing.

You have the guide, the principles and process in this book on how to generate momentum from a stationary position, how to build it up into a frenzy of activity so large that you'll be forced to hire a team and expand.

It matters what you do next after losing a sale.

This is my step-by-step guide.

Steps to take after losing a sale

1. Email or talk to the client – service doesn't go out of the window just because they gave you bad news. Maintain your reputation and get back to them quickly and in the same upbeat manner that you would normally. After all, you anticipated this, you built this margin of safety into your model.

2. Conduct a review – is there anything you could have done better? Was there something extra you could have given the client that could have perhaps convinced them, sparked interest, or kept them moving forward?

3. Is it really off the table completely or can it be rescued? Will it come back on the table at a later point in time? What can you do to ensure that when it does, you will win the sale and potentially for more money?

4. How can you continue to build the relationship? Just considering the client and your future relationship will set you apart from the rest. Whilst everyone else is licking their wounds, you are gaining share, advancing the relationship with your client to discuss other future projects.

5. Project and maintain a mindset of abundance; the world is abundant not scarce, and you choose to see abundance.

6. Think: what is the benefit of this happening right now? Does it free you up to focus on something else? How can you harness this momentum to cover more ground and be more efficient? Who can they refer/introduce you to?

7. Remind yourself that you are a top seller, and this is why you do what you do. If it was easy then everyone would do it. This is an opportunity to get stronger, develop your character and resilience. It's an opportunity, not a loss. A gift, not a punishment.

Don't let the loss of a sale affect the rest of your day or seep into any of your communication, sap your energy, or take you off course. It is another distraction if you let it become one.

Put it behind you, learn from it and move forward. Be thankful for the opportunity to have so much business that you have a process in place that gives you the wiggle room for this natural occurrence in the game of sales.

Don't let losses distract you. Let them guide you.

PERSONAL STORY
Handling pressure

It was mid-November of 2019, the last quarter of the year, a chance to make headway into 2020 planning whilst soaking up some final wins of the year. I mentioned a few pages earlier I was in Hong Kong for business – it was at the height of the political protests and the city was experiencing tension. As a result, moving around the city became more dangerous and much more difficult. I had based myself on Hong Kong Island at the Park Hyatt Victoria Centric for the four-day trip.

I have a great respect for Hong Kong and its people. The way of life in Hong Kong – its culture and its energy – have really captured my heart.

It was Thursday morning, and I had decided I would make it my mission to see as many clients as possible. If they said "yes" to a meeting, I would be there, no matter what. By setting this criteria and standard as my goal, it meant that I naturally pushed harder to get meetings in the diary, but I also had to think outside of the box to make all my appointments given the challenges the situation at the time presented.

Taxis were in a complete grid lock and crossing from Hong Kong Island to Kowloon had become nearly impossible due to a tunnel closure and extensive traffic. Up until this point taxis and Ubers had been my main mode of getting around during previous visits to Hong Kong. The train was also not safe due to protesters.

This posed a challenge. I needed to think like a Hong Konger and travel by ferry to my meetings.

As I was running through the streets of Hong Kong to the ferry port, I knew I was making it happen. With the wind quite literally in my sails, I had a certain momentum behind me as I navigated from meeting to meeting.

This fact went down well with clients as I became more relatable and was seen to be making it work in a challenging climate. They also respected that I had made the trip to come see them. It was like we were in it together.

The key point that I want to focus on though is: when life

is moving fast it is much better to slow down your actions, think about your next steps and get it right.

Running through the bustling streets or down the centre of the road when it was clear of cars allowed me to speed up my journey and make it to the ferries I had to catch in order to get to my meetings on time.

Not listening to hearsay but instead fact checking for myself allowed me to make better decisions and stay one step ahead of the game. For example, I asked a taxi driver what was really going on and discovered that traffic was only blocking the tunnel in one direction meaning we could make it through the Eastern tunnel and into Kwun Tong by car. This saved me time initially. I got stuck in traffic the other side so paid the taxi driver, leapt out and started to run again. It was something like a movie. *The Pursuit of Happiness* with Will Smith comes to mind, but I was a little less on the verge of bankruptcy and there was no kid.

The relationships I fostered on this trip have stayed with me to this day. I have done business with these clients time and time again, even when they have moved companies, expanded teams and introduced me to more of their colleagues. Not only did managing my mindset during a heightened pressure situation, both externally and internally, lead to big business wins, but it also built my resilience, mental toughness and sales stamina. Sometimes you've got to go for it, just to stay in alignment with yourself. When it comes to mindset, let's just recap what we've learned so that you have a handy list to recall when you need a quick refresher.

MINDSET SUMMARY

- Live with a mindset of abundance and positivity – be that person who lights up a room and sees things from the optimistic viewpoint.

- Be the entrepreneurial type who is resourceful, persistent and takes initiative.

- Stay away from negative influences, control your environment and build your mental resilience; stand guard at the doorway to your mind and control what you feed it.

- Develop the mindset of a learner by being anti-fragile – either you win or you learn and your self-esteem is built on your ability to learn not win.

- Bring enthusiasm with you wherever you go. It is your #1 sales tool.

- Respond with grace to lost sales – how you respond is EVERYTHING!

- Know your why, your purpose for going for it, and recall it daily so you expand.

- Learn how to control your mind under pressure and think a few moves ahead, put yourself in situations to test and increase your capability, give yourself deadlines, goals, and create experiences that will ensure your growth.

CHAPTER 4

Opportunities – Mine, nurture and capitalise on them

"People, sensing my belief, wanted some of that belief for themselves. Belief, I decided. Belief is irresistible."

– PHIL KNIGHT, SHOE DOG

INTRODUCTION

Now that we've got your mindset primed and ready to go, the next building block is to focus on the opportunities that surround us. This chapter will set you up to be an opportunity magnet. I had to work to make this happen by learning how to aggressively nurture a pipeline so that it could support the full weight of my vision. That's when things really started to change.

Things to remember when going through this section and implementing it in your daily sales routine:

- Someone has to win, so it might as well be you!

- Mindset gets you halfway there, but you MUST execute when the idea strikes and the emotion is hot.

- Keep a list of daily priorities in the notes section of your phone. It is your ability to execute them that will dictate your success.

- If you want to be like everyone else, do what everyone else does; if you want to excel and live an extraordinary life, you've got to do what others aren't willing to do.

- Be prepared to be misunderstood and get comfortable with not needing to explain your actions to anyone. You don't need to justify why you've changed or what you are doing.

- If you can be, do and impact more, you must. It is your duty.

- Momentum is won or lost on your ability to take more action that is consistently effective every day.

- The real fight is against yourself: are you willing to get uncomfortable, make the sacrifices and do the work to reach uncommon excellence?

- It's all there for the taking – every day is a new opportunity to shine. Don't dwell on the past or fret about the future, be in the present moment.

- You won't ever give up on your big vision. It magnetizes you and propels you to action.

- Now is the time to get focused – not next month, next week or tomorrow, now!

WHAT OPPORTUNITIES EXIST?

If there was ever an area to focus on it's understanding how to prospect, qualify and accelerate opportunities. When I talk about opportunities, I am referring to sales.

There is a misconception in the corporate world that sales follow a standard, predictable path and if you follow their standardised process, it will all be OK Unfortunately, this is a one-dimensional view. A career in sales is electrifying and when you step fully into operating the Momentum Sales Model you'll start to see opportunities all around you. You'll go from a one-dimensional view of the sales process to a multidimensional view, where you're able to move at speed and in flow and alignment with all that's being sent your way.

An important point to make is that these opportunities were always there – it's just you weren't in the right head space to see them let alone activate them. Extraordinary salespeople are able to understand that there's a way to do things but it's not what the traditional sales cycle would have you believe. You need to work harder on prospecting high-quality opportunities and initial sales meetings than you currently are, and you have to add value early at all stages of the process. This means appreciating your clients, having high standards, doing more than is required to help them.

HOW OPPORTUNITIES BUILD SALES MOMENTUM

Prospecting and winning meetings with high-value clients is, in my view, the most underutilized part of sales in most organisations – if you want to make an impact, go out and get more meetings with desirable clients. Period!

The reason this area gets overlooked is because this is the area that requires consistency, persistence and discipline. It's hard to become a master. The pleasures of life can seep in and wipe away all your hard work within one to two weeks of laziness.

It will even be super boring at times; you will have to push yourself and hold yourself accountable, both at the times when you least want to but also at the times it would be so much easier not to, like when you want to stay in bed or scroll through Instagram. You need to be your own coach; the world class don't need any more motivation to get the job done, as they are their own biggest motivators.

The level of consistency you need to create exceptional results is hard to reach but, even if you just manage to double your current output, you will see results big enough to get you hooked and be a believer. You must ingrain the principle of consistency so that it becomes part of who you are. You are consistent, you do what you say you are going to do, and you find ways to take bold actions on a daily basis so you can expand your pipeline by adding value.

Surprise yourself with the magnitude and the speed at which you do this. The biggest driver of results is having a pipeline of attractive opportunities to work with. To get these you must cut the crap from your life (distractions) and focus on selling the first meeting with clients – not to be confused with your product. You need to sell them on why they should even meet with you in the first place.

In this section of the Momentum Sales Model, I will teach you:

- Why the traditional sales model is broken

- A different way to operate.

I want you to recognise that there is greatness inside of you, now I am going to give you the strategies and tools to unlock it.

Using your super-charged mindset of abundance and growth, you can go forth and dominate in this area of harvesting opportunities.

The door to your best life as the most incredible salesperson is open, the best meeting of your life awaits and we are going to make you have a highlight reel so fantastic that when you are 70 and sharing stories with your grandchildren they will be so filled with adventure, fun and wonder that they will put down their PlayStation 20 and marvel at your wisdom.

You will share your story with them on how you know when it's the right time to strike, how to thrive in sales, and how to make radically more money whilst also helping more people through the sale of high-quality products. Then you will explain how all of this got you where you are today.

This section is so important that it's going to affect your legacy and how your grandchildren see you and interact with you, before going on to affect multiple generations to come.

1. WHAT THEY TELL YOU THE SALES PROCESS IS

The most advanced companies in the world have spent millions of dollars on identifying the best practice steps to take to produce sales.

Simply put, the traditional sales process comprises of six linear stages, as outlined in the diagram below:

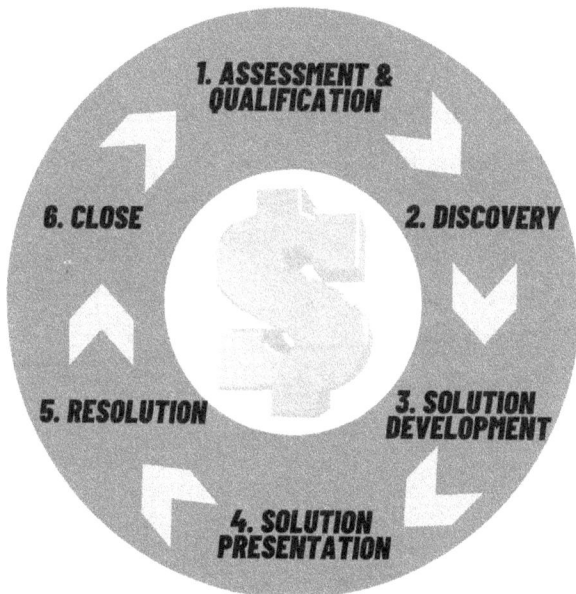

FIGURE 4: THE TRADITIONAL SALES PROCESS (LINEAR)

In order to move from one stage to the next, you must meet specific exit criteria.

For example, to move from Assessment & Qualification to Discovery, the salesperson must establish if the company they are trying to sell has a compelling need, or at least understands what happens if they do nothing. These are two key questions that define the exit criteria that must be satisfied before they can proceed to Stage 2.

The real question they are asking is "does the client actually have the money and the desire?"

If "yes" then box ticked, and they move on to Stage 2: Discovery. If it's "no" then it's "see you later", as this company fails to meet the criteria to move to Stage 2.

And let me be clear, I agree wholeheartedly for the need to have specific criteria for entry and exiting of each step. Having a specific set of objectives and a core purpose to each step, with neatly outlined process and defined areas of inquisition, provides rigor and standardisation.

Large organisations cling to this type of thinking as they see it as a way to move a salesforce in a specific direction and retain control. The issue it creates is that it leaves massive amounts of value on the table and doesn't provide the flexibility to really win hearts and minds. What I am about to show you is where and how you must *really* focus, and it is different to the above process.

Process is excellent and I am a huge fan of consistency and mastery, two areas that are indeed sharpened by process, which is what the above is.

On the surface this neatly outlined framework provides a roadmap to get from A to B and make it rain. Hey presto, you're going to become a multi-millionaire sales genius.

BUT, and here comes the main reason for this book, sales isn't always a straight line. This neatly packaged framework assumes that it's a smooth, linear process and all the information will always be given at the appropriate time. However, as any salesperson will tell you, you never get all the information, it won't be neatly presented and rarely do you receive it at the right time.

It also doesn't take into account that deals may skip steps, may not always provide clear exit criteria, and all the information needed to move forward nine times out of ten isn't provided. This sales cycle is just not the world we live in. As much as this is great for defining some of the key stops along the way, it doesn't tell you *how* to operate in the real world.

WHY THE OLD MODEL DOESN'T WORK

What happened at the start of the COVID-19 pandemic highlighted the cracks in the traditional approach. It was only the beginning and served as a warning to highlight an important (but often deprioritised) part of doing business, especially as companies grow and you move up the ladder. Flexibility.

If you want to survive, you must be flexible, adaptable and nimble. In fact, the same goes for your sales game. Businesses that were quick to adapt reallocated their resources, moved their business online and captured new streams of revenue.

Whilst this quick action helped them minimise the impact and move quickly into new areas or gain increased market share, it also did another thing: it underpinned the importance of strategy.

For example, in order to stay alive, Kyōten, a sushi restaurant in Chicago, adapted its price point to $600 per head and limited the total number of customers to two people only.

This created a new, previously unconceived opportunity. The adjustment in price point led to the ability for a couple to have a memorable and intimate dining experience together. Imagine being able to rent out the whole restaurant!

It also ensured that the restaurant kept their doors open and secured $600 a night. Rather than scrabbling to find customers, not knowing if they could afford to pay their chef and waiting staff, they reframed it, spent on marketing and now only needed to find two customers per night to make it a viable business model. The increased FOMO, extra PR and intrigue that was created as a result led to tables being snapped up weeks in advance. Pretty clever!

This is just one way in which something previously completely absurd ends up being a solution and given the context and consequences of not finding a way to make money, the alternative would have been dire.

Remember what I said earlier about going against the grain, not doing what everyone else is doing. If you act fast and with purpose, you'll take market share and thrive.

There are countless other examples – Virgin Airlines switched from commercial passenger to cargo-only travel almost overnight.

Luxury hotels, such as the Shangri-La, offered daycations and alternative solutions for work-from-home employees, thus tapping into a new market segment by offering a significantly lower price point use of their facilities during the day.

What's absolutely genius about this strategy is that, as well as capturing the hearts of customers, they were also there for their existing customers in a time of crisis. This led to increased brand loyalty whilst strengthening their dominant market position on two fronts simultaneously. It was short-term speed and innovation combined with influencing hearts and minds over the long term.

These are just a few examples of how "adapt or die" became a necessity in a radically short space of time and having the foresight and flexibility to rapidly implement a new plan and run with it became critical.

I'm guessing you know where I'm going with this after that build up, but the same goes for your sales career.

It should not be forgotten!

As you move through the ranks, you will be encouraged to use tried and tested methods of selling. Typically, the larger the organisation, the more red tape and the more processes there are to navigate, and with these layers comes complexity, rigidity and loss of speed. Everything we want to avoid!

Instead of staying nimble, the exact opposite happens: as a business grows in size, it finds it harder to move fast enough to win.

A sales team that is unable to move fast and build momentum finds that they have flimsy, unqualified pipelines and ineffective behaviours that ultimately sink the business.

At the corporate level, this is addressed by hours of product training each week. However, whilst this is important, it doesn't help you to get through the door, secure more opportunities and fill your pipeline so that it is overflowing. Likewise, on a personal level, using the old method of sales is risky because as soon as they fail to bring you the amount of business you need to meet targets, you're left all out of options and unsure why things went the way they did. You've got nothing left to try.

Normally, this leads the salesperson to develop an unhealthy relationship with sales that ends in burnout. They become a yoyo-er. Along the way they pick up a deep frustration with the organisation, have huge inconsistencies in effort and performance and that brings with it a host of unwanted attention from senior management and added stress.

In an effort to try to make the old system work, this type of salesperson ends up putting in incredible amounts of effort into intense yet misdirected bursts of ineffective activity.

Yes, a yoyo-er might land a big account every once in a while. They might even hit target every few months. However, when all is said and done, they know that they got lucky; it wasn't part of their sales process and that's a vulnerability that niggles away under the surface.

What's more, they are also well aware of the amount of stress and effort it took to hit that target, and because lucky timing played a big part, they aren't sure that they can pull it off again.

Low and behold, next month's targets are on the way and they have to pull it off again. However, this time the target is higher and the luck has run out! Around and around the process goes.

This in itself stirs up those feelings of vulnerability. They remain stuck because they can't ask for help for fear of looking stupid. They are trapped by their ego, which holds them back from learning from the best only to stay middle of the road and scraping by.

Inside, they are not really looking forward to the next quarter and feeling unappreciated and resentful towards the business because of all the stress and frustration they went through to produce those numbers.

It also makes it hard not to escape the boss's watchful eye, and they know they are being talked about in the weekly management meeting. It's hard to feel content in having done their best because, when all is said and done, they didn't.

Maybe you've seen this type of salesperson, maybe you recognise some of the traits in your own sales behaviour.

If so, don't freak out, that's what this is about – identifying where we don't want to be so we can move quickly towards a new reenergised way and start hitting our goals out of the park.

Let's jump in and find out a bit more about what the sales process really is.

2. WHAT IT REALLY IS

They say "*straight roads don't make for skilful drivers*", they being Paulo Coelho, world famous author of *The Alchemist,* and the sales process is no different. It's like a roller-coaster, some sales go quickly and are closed in a flash, seamlessly hitting all the check points and crossing the finish line like Lewis Hamilton. Others are more like a US/China trade deal, they stall, flip back and forth, get put on hold again, get the green light, inch forward, then get canned.

The traditional sales process and attitude towards winning sales assumes a linear relationship x + y = z, whereas sales is a journey and like any adventure it has its twists, turns, ups and downs. Now more so than ever. The key to all of this is learning how to take advantage of the twists and turns along the road and making them work for you so that you can advance and adjust as you go, always in motion. Waiting for things to be perfectly aligned, clear, and linear is unrealistic and not going to help you sell in today's business environment.

In sales, you need to be ready to face rejection, being prepared to play the long game, whilst having patience and resilience. You need to make the investment of time, money, thought, energy, and yourself to get to the finish line.

However, you being a super-achiever will summon the courage and stamina to persist where others wouldn't. You'll go the extra mile despite the changes and unexpected turns. It's the willingness and commitment to this higher standard of excellence in sales that will see you making it happen, time and time again.

Of course, there will be setbacks, failures and losses, that's the reality of the game, but you love the process of sales, and it is in the pursuit of this that your happiness lies. **And one fact is more powerful** than all others: if you learn to love the journey and not the outcome, you'll win every time.

Some of my favourite sales have been those that went back and forth, took huge amounts of work, had unexpected deadlines, all imposed at the last minute, and required me to think like an entrepreneur and out of the box.

The reason you will go on to win is because you persist in your mission to keep adding value through teaching, understanding and showing a willingness to keep solving problems for your clients. It's this commitment to implementing the building blocks of the Momentum Sales Model and sowing seeds of goodwill wherever you go that will transition you to world class.

How do I know this will happen? I don't, but if I had to bet, I would say that because you had the foresight to invest in yourself by purchasing this book, and you're committed to put it into action, you'll love the journey and therefore the process of generating sales.

By the end of this book, it is my goal to get you so intrinsically aligned to the attributes, characteristics and drivers that produce the right kind of sales, that you're going to be so insanely pumped with your newfound passion for sales that there will be no stopping you. Your clients will shift from seeing you as a cog in a machine to an asset, a must have, a valuable addition to the team.

ARE YOU READY? LET'S DO THIS AND GO MAKE IT RAIN! PROSPECTING: HOW TO GET A LEAD AND CONTACT THE RIGHT PERSON

In sales you want to aim to get as close to the "right" person as possible, like a missile hitting a target. Don't underestimate the months that can easily be wasted barking up the wrong tree, it is better to be ambitious and aim to get as close to the right people as possible rather than the wrong ones.

That's not to say there isn't importance in building influence across an organisation, but the best way is to focus in on that one person whose job will be made so much easier with your product in their hands. Get them on board and they can help you build a case.

The 6 prospecting steps outlined below might seem simple, but don't be fooled into thinking that just because they are simple, they are adhered to. Superstar salespeople are able to work all of the angles, day in day out; they bump into a client at the yoga studio, get a referral, send an email, make a phone call all whilst building their brand – and that's just one meeting for them. They are a wave of momentum, sweeping the floor with average salespeople and eating them for breakfast. What a top seller can get done in an hour is more than most achieve in a week. This is needle moving stuff and it compounds, day on day, week on week. In a word, they are effective – and it all starts with effective prospecting.

It takes discipline, resilience and commitment to focus your time on consistently getting in front of the right people but, boy, is it worth it. **This is an area of your sales game that you want to double down on by becoming an expert in being able to reach the right people.**

Below, I will outline the very best ways to do this in order of their effectiveness.

1. Referrals

Let's go right from the top. The absolute best way to go about contacting the right person is to get a referral. By piggybacking on someone else's introduction, you are acting on what's called "*borrowed credibility*" and the effect is five times as powerful as doing it by any other way.

What's interesting about this is how few people do it to get leads and meet new people of influence and power.

Did you know that 91% of customers say they'd give referrals and only 11% of salespeople ask for referrals? 11%! - Dale Carnegie.

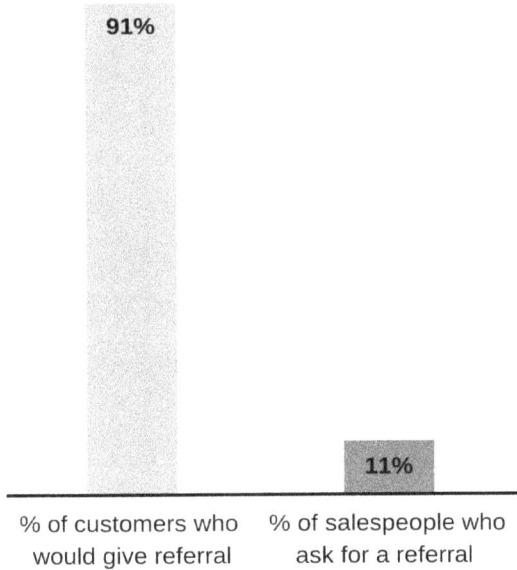

% of customers who   % of salespeople who
would give referral   ask for a referral

Customer willingness vs salespeople reluctance

FIGURE 5: WILLINGNESS OF CLIENTS TO GIVE REFERRALS VS SALESPEOPLE WHO ASK

That's astonishingly low! And a potential gold mine if you can work this into your daily habits.

You know what you should do right this second? Put down this book, pull out your phone and text someone you know in a senior leadership position and **ask** them, "do you know anyone working at XYZ company, would you mind introducing me?" See what they say.

MINI MOMENTUM BUILDER
Ask and you shall receive

Take action on this point now. It's not a game. I am interested to know what success rate you get and I want you to start getting into the habit of not over-thinking things so much that you never do them. Go for it now. Take a risk and ask. Then post a picture with the hashtag #momentumsales and tag me. This is going to be great!

Referrals are the accelerator. Just a causal "hey, you should meet this person" is sometimes all you need for the doors at your top target client to open and the wheels of success to start turning more quickly. **The thing is, it's all you; you have the power, all you have got to do is ask.**

Whilst we are on it, why don't we address the elephant in the room: why do so few people ask? Judgement and fear of rejection. Later on, I will give you some ways to combat rejection but, for now, if you sent the message, I am proud of you – you just took the next step to becoming the best salesperson you can be.

If you didn't send the message yet, what are you playing at?! Come on, consider this a warning! If you want to be a top seller, let's make it happen this instant! Whip out that phone and hit send.

2. Face to Face

Following referrals, the next best way to get in contact with the right person is to meet them face to face, either by bumping into them or strategically hanging out where they are likely to be. This is often most easily achieved by going to as many industry events and conferences as possible. However, you might need to manufacture some face-to-face meetings for yourself – you can't be waiting for the next big event to take place. Start hanging out at your client's favourite coffee shops, eat where they eat, work out where they work out and go the extra mile. Proximity is power!

The more effective action you take, the greater the opportunity to create an introduction.

I am telling you, only a very small percentage of salespeople do this consistently and people miss out if they don't. They lack the discipline and commitment of sticking to the right behaviours to deliver the results they want. They stop early before they get success because they don't think it's working. They let the present results control their thinking and their actions. It's sad but true.

By being seen at different events and being a familiar face at your clients' offices, the walls of the organisation start to come down. When you run in similar circles to the person you're trying to reach, and then you randomly connect at a conference, that mutual contact; the referencing of similar aspirations and a shared understanding for one another's business lifestyles will mean that you'll be bound to exchange business cards and arrange a meeting to assess the opportunity for you to do business together.

Start by making a commitment to ask for referrals in every meeting, making referrals your key driver of maintaining a healthy pipeline of meetings. Much like you don't need to wonder where your next sale is coming from; you never want to be wondering where your next meeting will be. Face-to-face meetings and referrals are like an infinite loop that will continue to become the foundation of your sales.

3. Email

Send a carefully crafted email, with a hook that piques interest, directly to the target contact. In the section ahead, I will show you how to craft a cold email using my cold email template that I developed and receives a 75% response rate upon the first contact.

Did you know that it takes on average eight cold call attempts to reach a prospect on the phone? Just think, how many people are giving up at the first or second try and how much business are they missing out on because of that?

Question: are you one of these people?

How many follow ups would you do before giving up?

Don't kid yourself! How many follow ups are you truly doing and where's your comfort zone?

Bullet-Proof Cold Email Template with 75%+ response rate

The cold email is much better if you have met in person face to face once before, even just in passing very briefly at a conference or in a client's reception. That way, you become a real person. It is why networking and events are SO important.

That said, you can still totally make a cold email work, and work well so that you are inundated with hot leads all wanting a piece of the action that you're selling.

Here's how you do it. Watch and learn, my friends, as this might just be the silver bullet to maximising your productivity when it comes to new business development. You need something that you can customise on the fly at speed yet still emphasises the salient points whilst building curiosity in the reader. It's time to go fishing.

The way to construct this email so that it is an instrument of mass sales and hits your objective of getting a response is to ensure that it contains all of the following elements. It establishes relatability, creditability and a request, whilst also explaining what's in it for the receiver and, throughout its entirety, promoting trust.

If you're a cold email ninja, then you'll find ways to inject all of these elements seamlessly into your creatively crafted and irresistible emails.

Here is an example below:

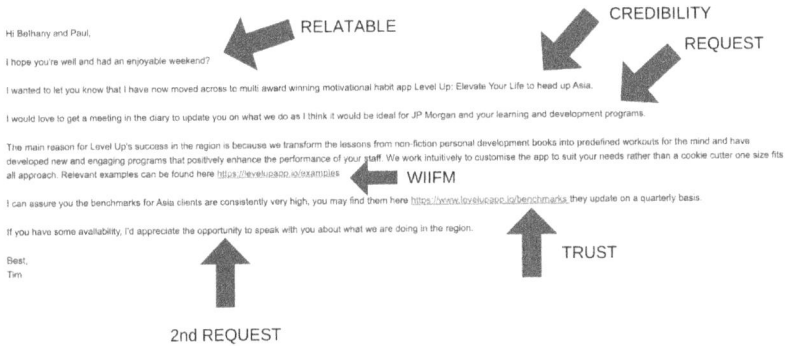

FIGURE 6: THE BULLET-PROOF EMAIL

As the sharp eyed amongst you will spot, there is an order to how you roll out these elements, and the order is very important. The goal is to answer the next question in the reader's mind. As they read, they should be taken on a journey that subtly answers the questions in their mind as they pop up in real time, as this reduces any anxiety and allows them to get closer. The emphasis placed on a single request (twice), first early on and then at the end, gently nudges them to respond.

This creates a number of questions in the reader's mind. Who is this person? What do they want? What's in it for me? Do I trust them? And sorry, what do they want again?

You'll also notice that I only focus on one ask. The email is focused on getting a meeting.

What you're aiming for here is like when you eat a chocolate fudge sundae; the more you eat, it just keeps getting better and better, so you don't stop until you've devoured the whole thing. You want the reader to finish the whole sundae and grasp exactly what you are wanting, make a decision and then reply.

MINI MOMENTUM BUILDER

Let's ramp up those high-quality meetings

Download my Bullet-Proof Cold Email Template with 75%+ response rate and fill in your specifics so you have this as your go-to. Just you watch your weekly meetings soar!
www.timjscastle.com/themomentumsalesmodel

Another example of an action provoking email is on the next page; this promotes a response by using a non-threatening, easy to answer question, followed by some useful information. Only use this for products and markets where you have actually seen a spike in demand. If used authentically, it will generate a flurry of activity for you. It's simple, inviting and easy to answer. Get ready to see the sales flow to you, this email slides right into the subconscious mind of the client and will drive valuable contacts for your business.

NON CONFRONTATIONAL AND INFORMATIVE QUESTION

Hi Alice,

Hope you're well?

I wanted to touch base with you to see if you'd be the best person at (add company) to talk about (add subject).

The reason I ask is that we've seen a spike in demand from (add country/state/region/area) in recent months for our (add product/service), partly due to covid restrictions easing but mainly due to the part that (add industry sector) can play in (add benefit).

We're working with a number of leading brands across (add country) and wanted to make sure you didn't miss out.

It would be great to catch up.

Best,
Tim

PROVIDES THE WHY, CONTEXT AND PROMOTES INTRIGUE

INSPIRES ACTION IN THE FORM OF A RESPONSE

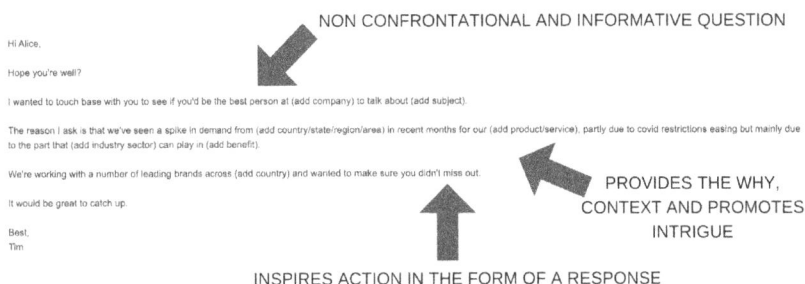

FIGURE 7: ACTION ORIENTED EMAIL TEMPLATE

Persistence, tenacity and determination are ridiculously important skills when it comes to follow up, cold email and phone attempts. Speaking of phones, let's dive into it…

4. Phone

When it comes to using your phone as a strategic sales weapon, it should be used to conduct checkup calls – not annoying "I want something from you" calls. Checkup calls are different.

You're not calling to hassle them about a sale, you're building the interaction and discussing some change in the business, some announcement, a new leader, a change in the market. Something other than "Can you give me money? I need to hit my sales target".

In a checkup call you are asking questions; you're calling a contact or an old colleague because you just saw on LinkedIn that they just got a promotion or moved companies. You are calling to check up and, in doing so, by having this kind of conversation oriented around the contact and what's going on for them, a valuable information exchange occurs.

The checkup call is an incredible way to stay front of mind whilst not being annoying. It keeps you at the forefront of market intelligence and doesn't have to take up too much time.

The information that is revealed during this discourse is priceless. Once you've finished asking questions about them, often the gesture is reciprocated, and guess what? New opportunities galore will be uncovered. I'm not only talking huge opportunities for sales, but finger on the pulse of the market type opportunities, information about your competitors, or who's up for a pitch, or information so juicy it can help you strategically target a new sector.

Make the "checkup" call part of your daily routine and watch how quickly your pipeline transforms. Now, it's over to you to go forth and multiply those sales figures.

5. Cold calls and cold meetings

Both of these have got to be skillfully handled, but they are worth doing if needs must. It's good to push yourself every once in a while. A cold meeting can be as awkward as walking in on someone on the toilet – yeah, that kind of awkward – if you don't know what you're doing and how to control the situation.

You are randomly invading the client's space, unannounced and taking up their time, therefore you need to make it look cool. Bring them a gift, make it look like you are dropping off this merchandise to all your clients in the area. Whatever you do, don't make it look desperate or else you could look like a teenager with a crush on the girl next door.

You get the idea: don't make it weird and it won't be. Explain why you're doing what you're doing and leave it at that. Let the other side then make the decision as to whether now is a good time for them to continue the conversation.

With cold calls, the philosophy is the same, but you've got to be even smoother as there are fewer data points to get feedback from. If you struggle with cold calls or even the thought of them, download my cold calls closer template and start crushing it.

PRO TIP
Do it now

Once you've secured the meeting, send the invite within five minutes! Leaving it too long and not acting whilst the opportunity is hot is a rookie mistake. You need to strike while the idea is fresh in your client's mind and subconsciously lock in their commitment. Leaving it for even a few hours has a detrimental effect.

You'll know when you are mastering the cold call when you feel comfortable **making the request,** for example "when are you available to catch up?". During the call, stay present, interested and engaged, really listen to what they are saying, and what they are not saying. Getting to the part where you make the request is your mission. However, you need to prepare the ground first, that's what you are doing in the early stages. To keep yourself from worrying, remember to approach this conversation like you would if they were a friend or a family member. You're here to add value.

You are leading this call, so you need to take control of how and when you present the request so that it is natural. As mentioned above, there will be a natural pause in the conversation when you need to act and clearly articulate what you want.

Things to note: Do you sense hesitation in their voice? Are they concerned? Are they too accepting, and just saying "yes" to get you off the phone? All this information is available to you if you understand how to read people verbally.

Often it is what they are not saying, or their tone of voice, the intonation, that momentary split-second pause while their mind is working out how to deflect or cover up, that gives you clues as to how they are really feeling. Focus your awareness on that idea.

If you sense something is off, address it, it's much better to have that conversation and get the elephant out there rather than hope for the best. Say something along the lines of "I get the sense that you're concerned about price" (or whatever it is you think they are worried about) and then let them answer, don't interrupt them – now it is your time to listen.

This is where (hopefully) they will open up and you'll be able to problem solve, moving the conversation into the zone of collaboration.

6. Your brand

My additional recommendation is to start building yourself as a brand. The world is full of noise and, to distinguish yourself in the future, you need to think strategically about yourself as a brand.

To do that you need to ask yourself these questions:

- What do you want people to think of you as the expert on?

- Why would they call you?

- What unique value/perspective/skill do you offer?

Start by having an opinion, speak out about it on your blog, on LinkedIn, at conferences. I understand being controversial is not the approach for everyone (but it really helps here), and that's OK. You need to be authentic. What interests you within sales or your industry? What would you like to have a juicy discussion about?

When building your brand, don't be afraid to push hard into

new unknown areas, for instance, productising your knowledge base. Offering an online or in-person course is a great way to go because it transitions you into the space of an expert, setting you instantly apart, and by its very nature it helps you differentiate yourself as a leader in your chosen space. Platforms like Teachable can help you get up and running in as little as 30 minutes.

What is stopping you from coaching, or packaging up your specific skills and experiences and consulting on the side? Why not start a podcast or become the expert on a topic of interest to you?

This is how you need to be thinking about your future. You could start a podcast within your industry and interview interesting heads of departments or leaders of companies you want to sell to. Not only is this a way for you to have fun and develop relationships with power players in your industry (which is an insane opportunity) but it is also your way of contributing, of making your industry better, of addressing key issues and debating what can be done.

This is just one creative way that you can stand out whilst building your brand. Once you take this step, don't be surprised if more opportunities come your way.

My goal for you is for you to be known for something, it doesn't have to be controversial, but put your two cents out there and have an opinion on things that you're deeply passionate about. If you do this, you'll see clients start to respect you in new and intriguing ways, so believe in yourself and become the authority. You'll know when you're getting somewhere when you have the right contacts seek you out and come to you for your specific skills, advice and expert opinion.

MINI MOMENTUM BUILDER
Action mode

Write down now in your phone or journal, or even in the margin of this page, any ideas that come to mind. I don't mind as long as it moves you forward. I want this book to be torn and tattered from overuse, with notes and highlighter all over it. When you've come up with your idea, make a commitment to make it a reality, post it up on social media and tag me @timjscastle and add #momentumsalesmodel. I love to see people taking action on their big goals and dreams and building their future. It brings joy to my heart to see you winning.

Here's a recap of what we've covered:

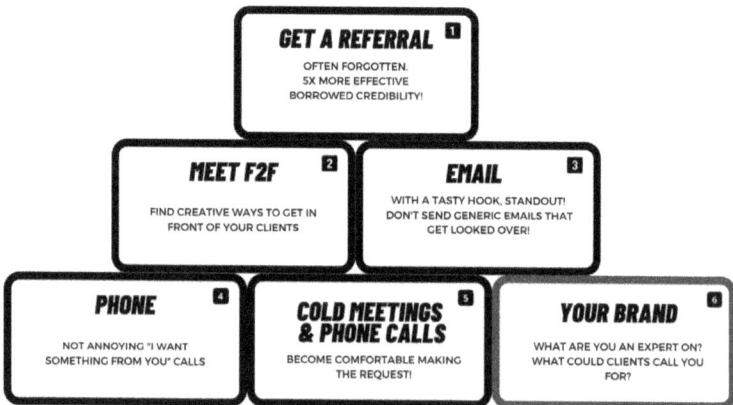

GET A REFERRAL [1]
OFTEN FORGOTTEN.
5X MORE EFFECTIVE
BORROWED CREDIBILITY!

MEET F2F [2]
FIND CREATIVE WAYS TO GET IN
FRONT OF YOUR CLIENTS

EMAIL [3]
WITH A TASTY HOOK, STANDOUT!
DON'T SEND GENERIC EMAILS THAT
GET LOOKED OVER!

PHONE [4]
NOT ANNOYING "I WANT
SOMETHING FROM YOU" CALLS

**COLD MEETINGS
& PHONE CALLS** [5]
BECOME COMFORTABLE MAKING
THE REQUEST!

YOUR BRAND [6]
WHAT ARE YOU AN EXPERT ON?
WHAT COULD CLIENTS CALL YOU
FOR?

FIGURE 8: PROSPECTING METHODS YOU NEED TO USE

PRO TIP
Watch and learn

The next time you are being sold to, look at how the salesperson is doing. This is one strategy to improve your sales: concentrate on what they do well and what they do poorly, as you are in the customer's shoes, notice how their comments, actions and behaviours either turn you off the sale or get you hooked.

GET A PEOPLE STRATEGY

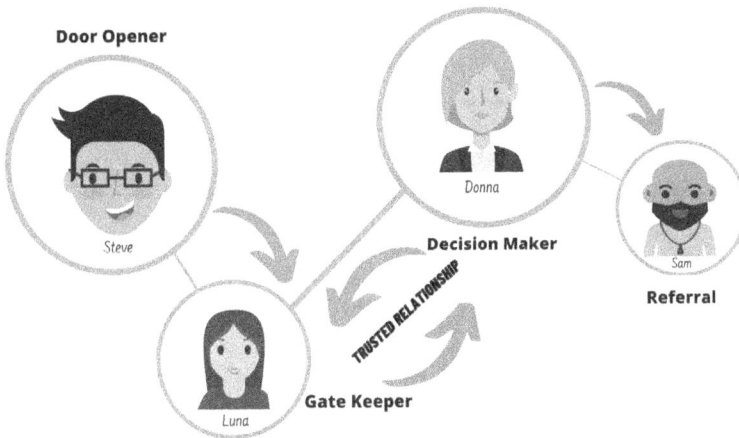

FIGURE 9: DEVELOP YOUR PEOPLE STRATEGY TO BUILD YOUR PIPELINE OF RELEVANT LEADS AND MEET THE RIGHT PEOPLE

Having a people strategy might sound like something out of a crime novel, but it is an integral part of account planning. It helps you know where you are going to go, and how you will allocate your time. After all, we each only have 1,440 minutes in a day, so it's paramount to your success to spend that time effectively.

When you witness a killer salesperson, someone who is really on a roll, they have explosive momentum because: 1) they figured out a people strategy and 2) they acted on it.

You need to start by asking yourself some questions about who it is you really want to influence.

Questions to ask yourself

- Who am I going to target within these organisations?

- Why am I going to target these specific decision makers?

- Why will they care?

- How can I help them?

- When will I target them?

- What do I want to happen?

- How can I add value to them?

As you can see from the diagram, it is hard to get to Donna and Sam if you fob off Steve and Luna. This stage of the process is about building opportunity and influence. Without lobbying Steve and taking him up on his offer for an introduction to Luna, you'll be stuck.

Door openers (Steve)

Often the simplest requests and introductions come from door openers. These are people that can move you into a sphere of influence
so that you can start lobbying gatekeepers like Luna. Door openers
are everywhere. They come in the form of receptionists, interns, new
hires and anyone on the periphery of who you want to reach.

In reality, they actually wield a huge level of power. They know
the inner workings of the company and key details about who you are
trying to make contact with. They also know information (or have the
ability to source it) that is highly valuable to you.

Make a mental note that from this day forward you will make
it a habit to befriend any door opener you meet. Better yet, write it
on your phone in the notes under "THINGS I AM GOING TO
START DOING". In fact, this should be your strategy for life, not
just in business; it's what makes the wheels turn just that bit faster.
It's what the best of the best do – they make door openers feel amazing, because they make them feel seen, heard and acknowledged.
This is a part that most people miss, they focus only on the decision
makers and miss the opportunity that's right in front of them. When
I negotiated my way into a top London University, I got a place on
the most popular course, two days before it started, without applying,
even when it was heavily oversubscribed. This was not because of
the decision maker but because of the receptionist at the Psychology
Department who armed me with key information that I could not
have known unless they wanted to share it. It was one of the door
openers that got me the opportunity.

I want you to take this strategy onboard, not just when it matters
for business but in your everyday life as well. At the height of the pandemic, I gave books away to staff at my local Starbucks in case they were
bored and wanted something to read due to low customer volume, and

to thank them for their excellent service. Now whenever I go, my coffee is ready before I even finish paying for it. **When you give you get, and you can give with a smile too; it doesn't have to be a physical product that makes someone's day.** Not to be ironic but you can even just hold the door open for a door opener – this would be a fantastic start – and then see how things miraculously change for you…

Gate keepers (Luna)

Luna is Donna's right-hand woman. She is her eyes and ears on the ground and a trusted adviser when she needs to make a quick decision but doesn't have all the information to hand. Luna, although not super senior, holds the keys to the kingdom in your eyes and should be your primary focus. By engaging in impeccable client serving with Luna, you begin to build a relationship and, due to your consistent professionalism, over delivery and the fact that you listen, it will only be a matter of time before Luna assists you in an introduction to Donna.

Of course, over the weeks leading up to the introduction, Luna will have also been dropping hints, subtly and maybe even unconsciously, to Donna, showing favourability towards your organisation and priming her for a meeting. Once you are through to Donna, you will have built a core of influence within your client's organisation; from the Steves to the Lunas of the world, you have been gracious, open and generous with your time and expertise. This is about to pay off big time. Can you see how you are starting to infiltrate and build a wave of enthusiasm from within the company?

Decision makers (Donna)

All this good favour will not go unnoticed by Donna who ultimately only wants to work with the best. You will of course have to begin a new relationship with Donna once you are introduced and will need to put in the legwork. It's not a given just because the lower ranks all like you.

You must tailor your approach, adapting it by using the information that Luna has given you. This is advantageous stuff that can help you tip the balance in your favour. Don't be afraid to ask Luna what Donna likes and doesn't like, what her thoughts are on your field and how best to approach the sale. If Luna is putting you forward and recommending you to Donna, then she wants you to win, so it's in her interest to give you the juicy and hard-to-come-by details (the inside scoop) that can help you win her over.

This is where you will flourish; you are now moving into the territory of a top seller, working the information to your advantage and closing the void between you being an outsider and becoming part of the furniture. You want to aim to feel familiar, like you "get" the culture and understand the challenges at a deep level that the company is trying to tackle. You go from pitcher (someone trying to sell me something) to trusted adviser and one of the crew, on the same team, an ally. This is a glorious space to be in, as sales will come pouring in and you will be able to harvest them.

Don't underestimate the power of door openers and gatekeepers – they are your ticket to freedom and maximising sales. Once you have gone through the ropes with Donna and she has approved you, then you're into the winner's circle, and the world is your oyster. Donna will refer you to other senior decision makers responsible for other bits of business internally, or perhaps even a sister company or other non-competing entity that may be useful to generate even more sales. This is where momentum really kicks up a notch. When you get to the referral stage, you are scaling your efforts and you have the most powerful method of sales influence working in your favour.

The point is that once you've got door openers, gatekeepers and senior decision makers going to bat for you, the doors to new business will well and truly open. Your job is to keep them open and keep opening doors until you make it all the way inside, to the heart of the company. You want every decision maker to understand the core value of your company and how you can add value to their business.

If done right, it's a virtuous cycle. The more contacts you make, the more business you do, and the more business you close, the more you are referred. As word spreads you get increased inbound leads that fill your pipeline with relevant opportunities

---

PRO TIP
What you track you get more of

The way you do this is by keeping a day book of all your interactions and break down where you are having success and track what actions you are actually taking. Day books are important because they will help you to see how much action you are actually taking and not what you just think you are taking. There is a difference, and when you really get started it can be easy to overestimate the number of key touch points you've made within a given week.

By tracking your progress, you keep this strategy front of mind and remain aware of the reality. Don't make the mistake of underestimating how much lobbying, networking, hustling on a daily basis you must do to get buyers to understand, remember and take notice of your business.

Lastly, door openers and gatekeepers can come in many forms, and these range from cleaning staff, security guards, receptionists, interns, mid-level managers, juniors through to influencers.

PERSONAL STORY
How to turn adversity into a gold mine

I'll give you a quick example just to clarify the point that receptionists are gatekeepers. I was once on a business trip to Bangkok and found myself at a client's offices. As I arrived on the client's floor and checked my email, I saw the client had emailed to ask if we could reschedule the meeting for tomorrow. As frustrating as it was, having travelled all the way across the city and allocated this meeting slot to the client, I knew that this also presented an opportunity.

I decided to use the time and the trip to the client's office to get to know the receptionist better. Over the course of the next 20 minutes, I explained what had happened and asked her questions about life at the agency.

She revealed some very key details about who looked after which client accounts, which ones were up for pitch and who I should try to get meetings with. She even went as far as to search their internal database for their email addresses to make sure I got the right people.

The lesson is that what could have been perceived as a frustrating wasted journey and an unproductive morning was transformed into a gold mine. Remember, you are a hunter! You are always thinking about how to expand your business and, when things don't work out as you planned, you pivot and recognise the situation for what it is, an opportunity.

THE 4A'S STRATEGY FOR ADVERSITY

Put the 4A's into practice the second adversity is experienced. This can be plans changing, people showing up late or cancelling, big deals falling through...

1. Adversity is experienced.

2. Generate Awareness as to what's going on around you and how you are showing up in the moment. Step back and ask yourself, "what is the opportunity that's right in front of me?"

3. Adapt the plan.

4. Take Action immediately on your idea and adjust if needed.

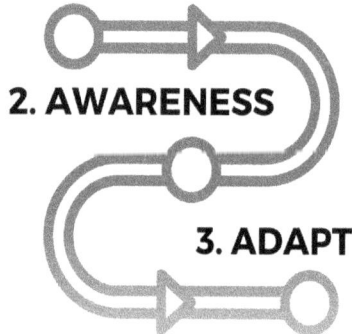

1. ADVERSITY

2. AWARENESS

3. ADAPT

4. ACTION

The trick with the 4A's strategy, **which will make it powerfully effective, is to remain open minded at all times and make sure you give your new plan of action time to show its benefits.** This is achieved by staying abundantly present, focusing solely on bringing joy, fun and positivity to the situation rather than anger, blame or judgement. When you do this, you invite positivity into your life and you'll be surprised what doors you can open. Oftentimes they are equal if not better ones.

Put the 4A's strategy into action the next time things don't pan out according to your original plan and challenge yourself to see what you can pull off. When you next experience a sudden setback or challenge, think 4A's!

What separates the winners from the average is winners don't get defeated, they get productive and use whatever is in their path to their advantage. You can go to the next level, take personal responsibility for the outcome and see the adversity in your path as an opportunity to manifest something even greater! You have this capacity within you!

Write down the 4A's strategy on a piece of card and pull it out the next time you need it, talking yourself through it step by step.

THE POWER OF KEEPING A DAY BOOK

A day book is a living document that helps you keep track of all the key details from the people you are meeting throughout each week. It's a buddy that taps you on the shoulder and says, "they, remember to message Simone (your client) 'good luck in the exam today'."

The major benefit is it helps you stay on top of your game, keep organised and track useful detail about your clients, like birthdays, interests, hobbies, favourite restaurants, ambitions and key KPIs for the year. It turns you into a rockstar with your clients – they will love you because it shows you care.

As the name suggests, it's to be used daily and should be open on your desktop for you to quickly reference on the fly with ease. You should be in and out of this thing more times a day than your Instagram, updating various elements throughout the day. If used correctly, it should feel like it's your most valuable document. A place where you can download all the interesting details about your clients and their concerns, likes, dislikes, preferences and intricacies you *think* you're going to remember (but actually forget) from your head into a structured and actionable file. It's a tool that helps you shine, stand out and be better for your clients.

A day book is back to basics account planning; I used this strategy when I came into a new business development role early on in my career and it worked like a dream! I focused on what drove sales and, by tracking all the calls and meetings I was having, with whom and when, I could double down on what worked. I was mapping out the road to success.

The above diagram represents one of my clients, an agency. This agency has multiple client accounts. It was currently producing zero revenue for us, and it was my job to bring it back up above the $1 million mark. As shown in the example above, I had a fairly broad coverage on my client, which gave me a detailed understanding of the briefing and sales cycle for each business unit and account at this client (the agency).

However, looking back eight years on, I can tell you it was a poor effort! You can see I was in this client's office not nearly enough. If I was to advise my younger self on how to get more sales out of these accounts, how to drive awareness, education and inspire the business to make more bookings with us, I would say this day book should have been a sea of blue and pink with no white space. My day book does not represent a world class salesperson. I show you this so you cannot kid yourself. You must find creative ways to meet with your clients, to practically live at their office or in the inbox, to open up

Name	Action	Client Patch	JULY				AUGUST				SEPT			
			WC 4TH	WC 11TH	WC 18TH	WC 26TH	WC 1ST	WC 9TH	WC 16TH	WC 22ND	WC 5TH	WC 12TH	WC 19TH	WC 26TH
Digital														
James Dawson	Catch up in for 14th July	Toshiba, Pizza Hut												
Sheila Harris	Invited to 101 bootcamp, emailed commercials	Head of Investment												
Danielle Koh	Met with Dani early June, will send brief	Royal Caribbean Cruises												
Max Trust	Meeting 8th Aug, go forward strategy	Innovation												
Brad Hill	Audi $20k Oct/Nov, no other briefs for now	Audi/VW/Banyan Tree/Accor												
Olivia Tsai	Prudential brief $200k, do direct deals	Prudential Insurance												
Pamela Tang	Just got back from holiday to USA	Disney/Harley Davidson/P&G												
Jude Davis	Emailed to introduce about Ikea, birthday in Sept	Ikea												
Rex Carson	Responding to $100k brief, 16th Nov, 31st Dec	Unilever												
Zeke W	Had a meeting, great guy, going to send booking	Lego												
Gemma Grace	Requested a coffee	KFC												
Paula Bucks	Had a meeting, took through offsiring, no briefs	Coinbase												
Judy Ong	Take to lunch to celebrate awards win	Head of Strategy (Global)												
David Lea														
Constance Wills														
Phil Farmagio		Cadburys												
Lucy Parks		Uber												
Megan Pierce	Moving off the business	Dairy Farm												
Mason Nectar	Had a meeting													
Oli Banks														
Angela Dawson		Coca Cola												
Amy Freddie		Amazon												
Harry Steel	Nothing for now.	SCJ												
Mark David														

Tracking against share rather than volume

Meeting
Phone/Email

FIGURE 10: MY ACTUAL DAY BOOK FROM 2015 (AMENDED FOR PRIVACY)

the channels of communication on exciting projects so that you are an integral part of their mission and front of mind.

FIGURE 11: WHAT TOO MUCH WHITE SPACE LOOKS LIKE

Back then I was learning how to become a sales master, but now with the eyes of experience on it, it stands out to me like a sore thumb. It is blindingly obvious. That is why having a mentor is important, someone who can call you out on things that might not be obvious to you. I am your mentor, having been there and experienced success and failure, I know that this is good (from the perspective of tracking my output) but falls below the level of activity needed to create a wave of momentum.

These days, I know how hard I can go. I can produce back-to-back weeks for a year, with upwards of 18 client facing meetings – it's part stamina, part strategy. If you're starting a new job in sales or looking to meet more people, set yourself this goal.

MINI MOMENTUM BUILDER
Momentum Meetings Challenge

I challenge you to do 90 meetings in the next 60 working days (that's 90 meetings in 12 weeks; this is around 7-8 high-value meetings a week).

This will build your resilience, stamina and network by learning how to develop your pipeline using the tools shared previously to sustain 7-8 high-quality meetings a week consistently for 12 weeks.

These are the kinds of ratios you need to be thinking about to make an impact as they allow you to develop influence and scale your business. This is where we become stronger than before, stronger in mindset, discipline and capacity.

As it was back then, eight years ago, luckily, the meetings, emails and phone calls that I did make happened to lead to sales. The critical thing to note here is there was room for improvement and the daybook gives you a visual representation of where that improvement should occur. Look at the amount of whitespace on this day book, all that missed – GO TIME! This is an area for improvement; it actually makes me cringe to share this with you, but I know it is important to highlight what is wrong so that you don't make the same mistakes, and if it can help you take your own business up a notch then it is worth it. Think of it like a simple tool for showing you who, what and where to work to get coverage.

When you are working to build influence throughout an organisation, the combination of targeting key strategic stakeholders and influencers first is a superb approach. As was the case in the example above, it is why I was able to make sales with what now looks to me as too few meetings. **I had targeted the right gatekeepers to get to the decision makers.**

A day book like this will also be incredibly helpful to you if you are taking over an account or client from another salesperson. If this relates to you and you are taking over a book of business from another salesperson right now, or opening a new area of the business, in a sense you are restarting the process and, by keeping tabs on your movements, you can keep yourself accountable.

Going back to basics allows you to reduce the overwhelm and take effective action. For example, when I started at another company leading sales for the Asia region, there was so much opportunity that I was really stumped as to where to start.

With so much business to go after, the danger is that you waste time on clients and accounts that aren't the right fit and lose months traveling down rabbit holes that lead nowhere.

Instead, by strategically targeting key people with access to decision makers and tracking your movements from day to day, you are laser focused and it becomes easier to spot where you are gaining traction.

From here, you can double down on these clients and get some early wins. This is especially helpful if you are new to the territory or if you are a startup. Having some credible early wins on your books facilitates more wins, giving you something to point to in meetings and helping you iron out processes.

There are more benefits to getting early wins than just making some revenue dollars, early quick wins help you to quickly identify problems, test strategies and give you a chance to get in and overdeliver. They put you on the map internally and as a business externally.

I strongly advocate the day book method because it is honest, simple to use, and visual, and by being visual, it allows you to see very quickly how much action you are taking and where. Most crucially, it tells you where you could be doing more.

MINI MOMENTUM BUILDER
Start a day book

Start a day book now and track who you email, call and meet, noting down any other valuable information and facts over the next three months, and see how this helps you to build up a profile of your clients. It's not widely or consistently done because it takes effort and people assume that they'll remember it all in their heads. Whilst this is true to an extent, when you're looking to become a sales superstar don't let a simple sheet stand between you and your goals.

Download your ultimate day book template at
www.timjscastle.com/themomentumsalesmodel

Identifying gate keepers:

When identifying gate keepers, my path to success is this: map out the client, put the key stakeholders into an excel spreadsheet or piece of paper and start by conducting this check list against each person:

- Have you met before?

- Do they have an in-depth knowledge of your product?

- Do they understand the field of business you are in, the specific area and why you are an important player?

- Have they spent money with you previously?

- How much budget do they have left until the end of your sales year?

- Is there an opportunity to cross sell?

- Bonus: Have they given you a referral?

Leadership Team

	Sam Wilson	Leon Hope	Jaye Maddison
Clients			
Met	✓		✓
Knowledge of (insert your company)			
Knowledge of programmatic (insert your specific area of the industry)			
Spent Previously			
Briefs remaining for the year			
Cross sell ATV/Dynamo (insert products/solutions)			

Directors

	David Li	Melody Goh	Simon Ng	Holly Price
Clients		Ikea	HCF	Amazon/Pepsi/Tesla
Met				✓
Knowledge of (insert your company)				✓
Knowledge of programmatic (insert your specific area of the industry)				✓
Spent Previously				
Briefs remaining for the year				
Cross sell ATV/Dynamo (insert products/solutions)				

Digital Team

	Sean Bancroft	Elouise Laughton	Paul Beeching	Emily McCarthy	Lola Sade	Jia Men
Clients	Deliveroo	McDonalds	Ferrari/ThaiAir	Visa	Ikea	Amazon
Met	✓			✓	✓	✓
Knowledge of (insert your company)	✓	✓	✓	✓	✓	✓
Knowledge of programmatic (insert your specific area of the industry)			✓	✓	✓	✓
Spent Previously		✓		✓		
Briefs remaining for the year		✓		✓		
Cross sell ATV/Dynamo (insert products/solutions)				✓		

SCREENSHOT OF MY ACTUAL DAY BOOK (NAMES HAVE BEEN CHANGED)

These are key questions because they help you sift through vast quantities of information in a direct way. These are closed questions, and therefore they push you to be specific and commit to an answer.

If the client contact in question doesn't have an in-depth knowledge of your product, don't lie to yourself, don't convince yourself that they do. Instead you should be honest and put them down as a no and note down that you need to spend more time getting them up to speed. In sales, you have to be the arbiter of quality control. If you don't, then you'll only be damaging yourself and your sales numbers.

Remember, in order to get on a client's radar, you need to get a person on the inside, an influencer. When you get six out of six ticks against the check list above it is quite possible that you might have an influencer on your hands, so look after them, take them out for a lunch and spend time getting to know what they care about, who they are, what matters to them and how you can help them. Surprise them, go the extra mile. Do the thing that no one has ever done for them before – be that person!

I am giving you my process because I know it works. You can see the value, and you have a clear way through the maze of your contacts to isolate those who will be critical for growing your business by helping them get what they want. It's time to get yourself ready for more sales. You can't help but win if you follow this method.

MINI MOMENTUM BUILDER
Influencer actions

Write down three influencers that you know in organisations you want to expand sales in.

1.

2.

3.

Now answer these questions:

- *How will you engage with them more frequently?*

- *How will you help them specifically?*

- *What do they care about in terms of life, values, outside of work, passions and hobbies?*

- *After today what is your next step to create better relationships with your influencers?*

QUALIFICATION

Qualification of your accounts in sales is do or die because it helps you to use your time effectively. Qualification helps you align new business opportunities with your strategic goals and therefore becomes the barometer of what you will and, more important, won't focus on. As your business grows and your strategy changes, so too will your qualification criteria shift but never the act itself.

BNTA (BUDGET, NEED, TIMING, AUTHORITY)

I was first introduced to this simple framework for qualification when I interviewed for a sales role at LinkedIn and I thought it was cool. Although things didn't end up working out with the position, I have used this framework ever since when I thought about the qualification of sales prospects.

Budget

Does your client, prospect or lead have the budget required for the product or service you are selling?

Logically, this is a sensible place to start with your qualification criteria because it informs your decision at the very basic level. Once you know the answer to this, you know whether you should proceed or not. Qualifying your leads like this, especially when you have a large amount (e.g. 100-3000) is important because it helps to direct your time to leads that could actually pay for what you're trying to sell to them.

When it comes to budget, it pays to stick to the facts and go after leads that fit the budget criteria you are looking for, rather than trying to convince a client who simply doesn't have the funds.

Need

Does the client have the need for the solution you are selling?

If they **do** have the need then you're in the game. This is super important to identify so that you don't waste time on opportunities where there isn't actually an opportunity. For instance, the client might just be window shopping, seeing what else is out there, but, in reality, they will never have the need or require what you offer. They may also be doing due diligence for a project further down the line. It is your job to uncover what type of opportunity you are dealing with and help your client understand what it is you can do for them and whether that meets their requirements. Understanding the need element of the criteria is a great approach for trust building.

PRO TIP
You are a valuable
person to know

When clients come to me with a need that I don't specialise in, rather than underdelivering by selling them a subpar solution that doesn't really fit their requirements, I will refer them to a best-in-class provider who can do the exact job they are looking for and overdeliver. This way I still add value to the client, who may one day be in the market for the solution that I am selling. On top of this, the partners that happily receive my referrals may reciprocate. There is a wonderful dynamic at play here, whereby best-in-class salespeople at different companies will refer clients and opportunities to each other because they know they aren't the right fit but want to help people they trust and assist their clients to make the right decision.

This is a sweet spot that is worth thinking about tapping into – rather than helping a competitor you are enabling your client to move forward and you become a valuable resource to both the client and your partners in the industry. As a brand, this behaviour helps you as a salesperson stand out and attain new levels of success because you are doing what is of greatest good for the industry. This is what world class salespeople do: they empower their network and build a reputation as a fixer and a person to know. In a world where everyone is ruthlessly focused on what's in it for them, or getting a referral, you will leapfrog the lot of them by giving in this way, plus it's a fabulous way to extend your network and demonstrate confidence.

Timing

Is it the right time for this client to spend, or do they work on a cyclical decision-making process?

By understanding your client's decision-making process, you are able to qualify them in terms of how urgent this opportunity is and provide them the appropriate level of client servicing. Understanding this also helps you to manage your time; you can go hard on deals that have a short shelf life and need to close fast and practise patience on deals that need a little more time to mature. The focus in that case would be to build influence through the key stakeholders of the organisation so that you can get close to understanding the real objectives of the company and sell in at that level. For sales that need more time, this is where you must practise your long game. This is about strategically manoeuvring through a company whilst continually adding value. The key is that you notice when they are ready and don't miss the boat, so you must be there with bells and whistles on and put in the same amount of effort without being complacent in order to make the sale. Timing is everything.

MINI MOMENTUM BUILDER
Your role as a resource

I want you to spend some time today to think about the following questions:

- *Where could you be referring your clients to new opportunities rather than just saying no to their business when it's not a direct fit?*

- *How could you implement this strategy and build your personal brand and reputation as a valuable resource?*

- *Where could you be adding more value in general? Identify a couple of situations where you could go the extra mile to help out.*

- *Who could you partner with to maximise this strategy in your lead qualification process?*

Authority

Do they have the authority to make the decision? Are you speaking to the decision maker or is there someone else you need to meet to get the sale?

Being clear on this helps you to align stakeholders so that you can get to all involved in the process and influence at the different levels. In large sales there may be 10-20 people needed to make a decision, in others the decision may be held with one or two key senior people. Understanding this part helps you to save time and understand the likely speed of the sale. If you're selling real estate, there could be one or two decision makers to influence, if you're selling a SaaS package to a large bank, there could be upwards of 15 different stakeholders you need to influence to secure the sale. This is why it's important to know who the key decision makers are as it informs you of the journey you need to take.

LEADS, PROSPECTS AND ACCOUNTS

Now you might be thinking you already know what these three categories are defined as, but I want to take a little time just to clarify as a refresher is always useful. Reason being, as your sales begin to skyrocket, and especially after implementing the lessons from this book, you'll need to stay focused on remembering which of your clients fit into which bucket.

This is so you can objectively qualify each opportunity and therefore maximise results.

1. A lead is a contact or piece of business that has the potential to become a prospect but has not yet been qualified.

2. A prospect is a qualified lead that fits your criteria for the types of clients you are looking to acquire and so it has the potential to become an account.

3. An account is a client you have already qualified and done real business with. An account may be considered existing in that you are frequently doing business with them or lapsed in that you have not transacted business for more than 12 months.

LEAD
ANY MARKET CONTACT
TO BE QUALIFIED
TO POTENTIALLY
BECOME A **PROSPECT**

PROSPECT
QUALIFIED LEADS WITH THE POTENTIAL
TO BECOME AN **ACCOUNT**

ACCOUNT
PROSPECTS YOU HAVE
WON AS **CLIENTS**

By understanding these three definitions properly, it gives you yet another framework to distil the noise and plethora of opportunities that will get flung your way in sales. It is important to rigorously understand the mechanics at play here because these three buckets help you to think clearly about how to structure your sales business as you grow and, most importantly, as the sales revenue grows.

An important distinction to make is that within Accounts there are two types. You've got live accounts, which are defined by the fact that they are actively spending with you in the last six months, and lapsed accounts, which have not spent in the last six months.

When you encounter an account that is considered to be lapsed, there are a number of reasons it could have ended up in this state.

A few include:

- It could have been the previous salesperson and how they were servicing the account.

- A key stakeholder at the client side may have left the business (this is super common).

- A new key decision maker may have joined the business.

- A new gatekeeper may have been introduced.

- The business may be in financial trouble and therefore no longer be a valid opportunity or be in a position to make decisions around purchasing right now.

- A competitor may have come along and offered them a better deal and stolen them away. You may have been outmanned and outgunned.

With lapsed business, it's important you find out the underlying reason why business and sales stopped and therefore you can figure out how to get it back on track and the next course of action.

Your skill in tactful questioning and reading emotional intelligence will strongly come into play when doing this investigative work. Just because they tell you that they aren't spending with you anymore because budgets are tight doesn't mean that it is actually the truth of the matter. The client may have decided to go with another competitor because they prefer certain things about the way they serviced them, or the business fit based on new criteria that you are able to provide but are unaware of.

Part of sales is retention. It is easier to cross sell and upsell to an existing client than it is to bring on a new one. With existing clients, they are already familiar with how you operate, trust has been established and you're already further down the road. Therefore, an upsell or the introduction of new products and services is somewhat anticipated, if not expected, and because of this it is considered.

PIPELINE MANAGEMENT

ACCOUNT PLANNING AND FORECASTING LIKE A BOSS

If you want your sales numbers to be on fire, then it's time to get serious about account planning. It will also help you to stand out internally as this is an area that most salespeople suck at. One of the areas I think gets most misunderstood by salespeople in terms of importance within a business is pipeline management and forecasting.

These are both crucial, without accurate pipeline management and revenue forecasting, key business decisions like expansion, hiring and client servicing become significantly more difficult. As salespeople it is our job to know our accounts, to keep track of economic and client movements, revenue pacing and anything that might impact the overall forecast from day to day, week to week and month to month. Demonstrating accountability and expertise for these tasks sets you apart as a leader. One way to think about it is that you should treat it as if it is your business. If you do in fact own the business then the diligence around updating this needs to be second to none.

Whether you plan and forecast using Google Sheets or work via a CRM platform like Salesforce, the main thing is you must do it consistently.

The reason accurate forecast is so important to a business is because it allows the C-Suite and Department Heads to make decisions on hiring or firing early enough before there is a crisis. Forecasting is a key skill of a sales machine.

Put it this way, if you aren't great at forecasting, the business will make unwise investments, it may hire more head count when they aren't actually required or lay people off when in fact they are very much needed. In the game of sales not providing an accurate (within 5-10%) forecast of your sales numbers each month is simply not acceptable for a top seller. People are counting on you to keep your forecasts up to date and provide them with notice as early as possible as to whether things are going well and, likewise, if the month or the quarter isn't looking too rosy for whatever reason.

It's outside the scope of this book but in the free resources pack you can find my Bottoms Up Account Planning Template forecasting tool and more details on how to nail it and stand out!

www.timjscastle.com/themomentumsalesmodel

3. ACCELERATION – TIME TO FEED THE FIRE

In order to gain massive momentum, you need to make a decision in your mind to step on the gas daily. There can be zero compromise. Momentum is easy to maintain once you've built it and much harder to get back once you've lost it. When you are on a winning streak you will win more, you'll be in the flow, on the top of your game and you will become dangerous.

To build momentum at the start, focus on the day ahead of you – the game is won one day at a time, repeatedly. Once you do the tasks outlined in this book for 14 days in a row, you'll see the first signs of the train moving out of the station.

Opportunities don't always come with a big neon flashing sign saying "opportunities this way" on them; sometimes it takes a bit of digging and creativity to recognise the gold that awaits.

You've got to get out of your comfort zone, so send that email, send that follow-up email, call, every three days. Get into the habit. A mindset shift needs to take place – **rather than think you're being annoying you need to shift to knowing with every ounce of your being that you've got something that is worth their time and valuable for them to listen to.**

Read the statement in bold again and let it sink in. As a world class salesperson, you aren't being annoying, you've got something very valuable to share.

Shift towards *What's In It For Them?* and you will reduce the anxiety around the actions you are taking (e.g. following up every three days when you don't get a response) and focus on the bigger opportunity to partner, collaborate and create value.

Ultimately, you are creating a partnership with your clients, and it **starts with you believing in yourself and why you are selling to them**. Without that, there is no habit, and without the habit of consistent follow-up, consistent opportunity hunting and excellent client servicing of your existing clients, there will be no business to thrive in.

You need to Prospect, Follow up, Influence, Prospect, Follow up, Influence, round and round, each opportunity at a different stage. You don't forget about them, you nurture them through the sales process and you WORK IT.

The only way you will know what's working is if you take time to analyse the trends, to look at the data and to ask the clients themselves. It's a big job, and not everyone is up for it, the mediocre get distracted by the latest must see show on Netflix, trending topics on Twitter and Instagram reels, they have an off switch that kicks in after 6pm. **You, my friend, are not mediocre, you're always on and ready for business. You have a sixth sense that's ready to take your sales game to the next level and you are there for your clients in a way that supports long term relationships to grow.**

This is my drafts inbox on Sunday night:

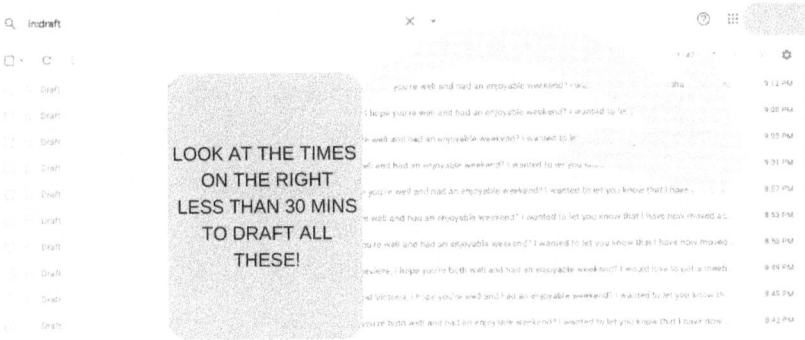

FIGURE 12: MY DRAFT EMAILS FOLDER

Look closely, notice the time on the right-hand side; this whole process only takes me 30 minutes, but the benefits are insane. These bad boys are ready to be sent out at 8.30am on Monday morning, come rain or shine. This is what it takes to move the needle and I promise you, if you do this every day, nurture, grow and have patience, your business and your sales muscles will expand.

The way to have a pipeline of new and existing business that is healthy or even overflowing with promising opportunities is to **take initiative**. Your pipeline is your responsibility, if it isn't looking up to scratch there's only one thing you must do: take, more, action!

DITCH THE DECK

If you are in a lull, the best way to reignite the flame is to meet face to face and the best way to meet isn't with a PowerPoint presentation in hand, it is actually to get them out to something more social where you can spend time bonding. Remember, *you* are your biggest asset and authentically connecting with clients is the chief aim. This is where you will grow your business beyond belief. When you start to put the needs of your clients first and really understand who they are as individuals, what makes them tick, what are their dreams and aspirations and how you can serve, it takes the relationship and your sales ability to a whole new level.

The fun part is finding new and interesting ways to connect with clients. This could be anything; I've seen all manner of activities work in sales, anything from a thoughtfully planned lunch to as extreme as sky diving or cage diving with sharks. I have witnessed both in my career in sales.

Time spent out of the office is valuable for two reasons:

1. It gives you an opportunity to talk for longer and more authentically. Sometimes the workplace can stifle conversations, whereas a different environment can increase trust building and the variety and breadth of conversation.

2. It helps you find out more about your client's objectives and who they are as a person. What's motivating them long term. Why do they do what they do?

PRO TIP
It's all about them, not you

When you are with your clients in these social settings focus the conversation on them, ask questions about their family and take an interest in them as people. Listen to their story, don't try to sell them on your product. This is often a point missed by mediocre salespeople, and you as a top sales professional won't make that mistake.

PERSONAL STORY
Party planner

I'll give you an example. I was planning a trip for my boss to fly into town, and due to this I had upped the ante on the number of lunches and dinners we were going to do, partly because his expense budget was bigger than mine and partly because I wanted him to have an awesome time and get to know a few of our newer clients.

Then, unexpectedly, there was an issue.

The next day I got a call. It was my boss. He told me the news he was going to postpone his trip to Singapore.

I now had a choice. I had two weeks of back-to-back meetings and client lunches and dinners planned across both Singapore and Malaysia. I had gone big and invited upwards of 30 people to some of these events.

In spite of all that was going on around me, rather than cancel the meetings and events I had spent so long organising, I decided to wait it out to see if the panic would die down and there might be a possibility to carry on regardless.

I took on the responsibility of keeping the plan the same. I would set expectations early with my clients and tell them that this wasn't the idea, but we were going to roll with it. After continuing with the two weeks of meetings, I learnt another lesson: act as if a senior executive is coming to town every week. By this I mean go bigger with your ideas and plan parties and larger lunches and dinners even if it is just you hosting. Bring in family and friends to help you organise it if needed. When you plan bigger, you act bigger.

I realised in that moment, that a new level to up the rate of meetings, the pace and the scale of initiative is very much in our hands, why not mentally say that my boss was coming to town every week?

What would you do differently if you were hosting your boss in your town for two weeks? Be honest.

Once you start thinking like this, move it up a notch, what about your CEO or even both your boss and your CEO?

Can you see what I am getting at?

The limitations of what is possible are only in our minds, and when you get used to a certain cadence or frequency of events you end up waiting too long to do them. This way of thinking even challenges the idea that you need a reason to host an event. What if you didn't need a reason like someone senior visiting from out of town. What if your mindset became how can I take this business to the next level every week?

Just get out there and host an impromptu pizza party or throw your one-year annual bash, even if it's just you on the team. Make it a thing and take ownership of your business like an entrepreneur. Remember, regardless of your budget, you can always do something, whether it is starting an annual picnic at the park, a bike ride, wakeboarding or a charity run. It doesn't need to cost money. You've got to get your thinking hat on and strike some deals. For example, you can pitch to a bar to host your party for a significant discount because of all the new clientele that will be exposed to their brand and, as a result, they will get more bookings. These things don't need to be expensive, just creative. You can also invite partners and ask them to sponsor certain elements of the party, lowering your bills. That said, sometimes, you've just got to go for it – even when hosting a party might seem expensive the payoff is in the networking and relationships that will be built as a result. Cost can then be a risk you've got to take to make it to the next level of your business. You've got to call in favours from your friends, ask around, get the local sports centre to do you a deal and run a sports day. The ways to create inter-action exist, and they are all possible, but it's on you to find a way to make it happen.

At some point, this is what happens to every successful salesperson, when you start treating your work like your business. Thinking like an entrepreneur, you go bigger; you don't wait for the perfect time, you just do it.

The timing will never be perfect, so you do need to bring clients along with you and swoop them up in a wave of energy and enthusiasm that is so encouraging and inspiring that they just want to hang out and connect with you. This is when you transform from an operator to an owner, and the two are very different mindsets.

It made me realise you don't need to wait for a big reason to put on multiple events in a week, you just need initiative and the guts to try. Now, you might be thinking, "I put on events all the time, and I do lunches too". If that is you, that's great!

MINI MOMENTUM BUILDER
Speak to their passions

Think about who your clients are and what they like to do with their spare time. These are indicators of activities they are more likely to say "yes" to. Now brainstorm some things you think they'd like to get some time off work to do. Is it golf, music, sports, travel, fashion – how can you bring these elements into your entertaining?

Now I want you to think harder about how you can really push the boat out and be inventive. What if you had events at the same venue every day for a week? What kind of deal could you negotiate with the owner, what kind of momentum could you drive?

Not only does this show you are listening deeply and that you care, but it also pushes you out of your comfort zone to learn new things. This in turn makes you a more interesting person to talk to and as a result you'll have lots to discuss when you are making small talk at that networking event you had to go to.

Lock it in now, if you see tickets to a show you know your clients will love, or a day at the races, or a concert. Anything to show you know your clients and you are thinking about them and are finding new and more creative ways to get to know them better that don't involve you showing them your presentation deck.

9 BEFORE 9AM PROSPECTING STRATEGY FOR SUCCESS IN SALES

Whatever happens, come rain or shine, I make sure I do my 9 before 9am. This one strategy has the power to radically change your sales career forever.

Every morning I reach out to 9 prospects, leads or clients by email, phone or in person before 9am to expand my business.

I am on a mission for more success, wins and prosperity than the day before. My mind is tuned into abundance, and I am only looking to improve on the day before. 9 before 9am is the key to growing your business.

Try it for yourself and watch your pipeline grow, new opportunities will reveal themselves in the form of doors opening that you never thought possible. A wealth of new opportunities will come into focus and you'll be ready to take action on them because you will have been looking for them and you'll recognise how they help you obtain your goal.

The reason this strategy is so vital to the success of maintaining a healthy pipeline is because in sales you must work the plan. To have the advantage you must maximise time and productivity.

This tool will allow you to keep a rigorous and aggressive approach to prospecting. I use this strategy daily. It is interwoven with writing my emails the night before and then sending them out at 8.30am each morning, as you saw in the earlier section on getting ready for sales overdrive.

Healthy pipelines don't happen by magic. Pipelines to be proud of happen where there is a relentless commitment to doing the work, pursuing excellence, aiming high and never giving up. If a salesperson has a dedication to these characteristics on a daily basis it means that they are approaching the job like a sales master.

One of my most prized tools for doing this is the 9 before 9am. This ritual gets me thinking more creatively. Not only does it keep my business front of mind with potential clients, broadening my sphere of influence and accelerating uptake, but **it psychologically primes me as the salesperson to be on the lookout for more opportunities for expansion throughout the day.**

Remember, it doesn't matter what you are looking at as a salesperson, a bad market, a challenging sales patch, or a disaster, what matters is what YOU see. Do you see opportunity, where others see none?

I find that by implementing my 9 before 9am strategy I am more aware, focused and ready to act with enthusiasm and inspired action. My aspirations are bigger, and I am more prepared for the day ahead with a sense of accomplishment under my belt; my day is already off to a flying start.

It's because of the 9 before 9am I find that the momentum I have created spills over into the rest of my day and I build more opportunities for expansion. Sometimes I am able to reach upwards of 50 different prospects and clients in a given day, but it all starts with a commitment to the 9 before 9am.

After three days, follow up on the emails where you didn't get a response. Three days is long enough not to be annoying, but short enough to still be relevant, not like an afterthought, or like you don't really care and are just winging it.

The three day timeline is also advantageous because it creates a habit and, trust me, once you get a habit around this type of follow up you'll see your sales game skyrocket.

THIS IS PROBABLY ONE OF THE MOST UNDERUTI-LISED PARTS OF SALES – YOU COULD CHANGE YOUR WHOLE SALES GAME RIGHT HERE. Read this part again and make sure it's deeply imbedded in your psyche and commit to shooting for stars and obtaining excellence in this area.

Remember, it might take eight, nine, or ten attempts before the client responds. This is not uncommon, nor should you take it as a sign that the client is not interested. **Keep going, keep believing in your product and the value you have to offer.** Keep following up every three days until you get a response.

This is where you need to remember that it is your duty to share this service with your client; it's of value to them, and you can help them overcome some of the challenges they are having. If this is not the case, then why are you contacting them? This is why qualification is so important. When you have serious impactful value to offer, be bold and go for it, don't let anything hold you back. Where you are chasing a meeting for a meeting's sake or to hit your company's weekly meeting target, then you need to think twice about why you're bothering.

Find companies that fit your criteria and, best of all, find clients that you *can* actually help. When you follow up, make sure you keep your message short, and offer more value than just requesting the meeting or the opportunity to pitch again. Share something, a case study, a stat, an article, a new product, a new offer, think about your client and why they might not have responded yet. They're busy, they're stressed, they have a million and one things to do and your email keeps coming into their already overly congested inbox. Make an impact and give value. This way you give them a reason to respond. By giving value first, you show that you aren't in it only to make the sale – you really care about your client's objectives and you're thinking about their best interests.

Somewhere between the second and the fourth email, people tend to get a little scared of sending another message out – it's like we've reached an imaginary threshold that cannot be crossed. Why is this? I believe it comes down to the fear of rejection and judgement; one and two emails are OK, but anything past that, well, you're being too pushy, impolite, and annoying.

But here's another way to think of it – you're there to help your clients do the best at whatever it is you do, you're the best in your field, an expert, and you know in your heart of hearts that what you have to offer the client will change their trajectory in a phenomenal way. The only problem is that they haven't heard about it yet. It is your responsibility to find a way to connect, therefore by taking this responsibility seriously and keeping your clients informed through the follow up that you do, you are actually performing best in class service. Because, trust me, it does sink in, and when the time comes, which it will, you'll be the first person they call and all that follow up and value adding will have paid off.

Of course, I must highlight that there is the odd curve ball, red herring and anomaly, every once in a while. You are bound to get a client that simply won't respond because they don't want to, but instead of telling you this they will just delete your emails and move on.

After two weeks of implementing this prospecting strategy, you'll be so inundated with client meetings that you won't even notice the radio silence from those not responding.

Remember, it is easier if you draft up the emails the night before. However, let me be clear that the goal is to get into the habit of being in front of 9 potential clients before 9am, meaning it can be in the form of email, a call, a coffee, a meeting. Whatever it is, you're about to put a rocket up your business and take it to the moon.

Try this one out tomorrow and see how it changes your perception of what's possible and notice how you feel good about creating momentum in your business, committing to a task and delivering on your promises to yourself.

Download my simple 9 for 9am template to help you define who you will target each day and then follow up with.

www.timjscastle.com/themomentumsalesmodel

4. DISCOVERY DONE RIGHT

Think of discovery as an opportunity to sell more and to build a meaningful relationship.

Discovery is like a second date; you've met once and decided there might be something half decent there, but you need to figure out if the chemistry is for real.

Discovery is where you uncover, probe and ask questions. Here is an excellent place to start lightly seeding the conversion with your benchmarks and results, nothing overtly direct but you should start influencing the narrative at this point and beginning to promote your products and services that might fit.

The benefit of the discovery of the sale is that you are exploring, uncovering new details and making friends. It's an awesome time to be excited about all the possibilities. This is a time to let your inner visionary come out to play, so don't limit what is possible, keep an open mind and shoot for the stars.

Discovery is one of my favourite stages of the sales because it's where the options live, you are selling without the formalities, quietly influencing, allowing the client space to open up and show you what they are thinking. When you let the client evolve an idea, see the potential and the bigger picture, they will often bring you in closer to their organisation and introduce you to more stakeholders. This is where the real magic happens.

Clients can sense when a sale is more important to you than it is to them. Don't be fooled by thinking you can pull the wool over their eyes. This is NOT the time to hard sell. This is the time for nurturing, letting the emotions rise, and with your confident sales manner, lead your clients through the maze, helping them understand where they want to go. This is an incredible skill and takes plenty of active listening, questions, and consideration.

Offer a brief solution description and the benefits your product or service has, seamlessly weaving in your value proposition and elevator pitch. Nothing hardcore, but you want them to start to understand why you are in the room and the value you bring.

An average salesperson can easily mess up discovery. The mistake most average salespeople make in discovery is they don't have the charisma, finesse and enthusiasm to really engage a client and get them to reveal what's really going on. As a result of not being able to discover anything of value, they panic and rush straight to pushing their products in an attempt to salvage a sale from the wreckage.

In reality, their mistake was not asking enough questions; as a result, the data they have to go on is limited and, in order to progress with the process, they make far too many assumptions.

Questions to ask in a discovery meeting

A great question before the start of every discovery meeting is to ask yourself "what is the purpose of this meeting?" By doing this consistently, you won't waste yours or the client's time. You'll be more likely to get the information you need, and you'll be seen as a professional because you'll have clarity over your goal.

Other great questions include:

■ I am so curious! How did that go?

■ Who do I need to meet down there, if you don't mind me asking?

■ It seems like you didn't like working with them, what happened?

■ Don't stop now, I need to know, what happened?

■ Tell me, what about this looks right to you?

■ Perhaps we could start with this, what is the best-case scenario for you?

■ I think we're getting at something here, what else can you tell me about…?

■ What did you like the most about what we just went through?

■ You're kidding, how did it turn out?

The formula is **Transition Statement + Question (or vice versa) = lands softer**, which makes your clients feel more comfortable and likely to open up with juicy details.

Don't necessarily always use straight open questions – How, What, When, Where, Why, Who – these can come across bluntly with some clients and your discovery session ends up more like an interrogation.

Especially a Why question. If you frame this in the wrong way, due to your tone of voice or speed and conjecture, it can sound like an accusation rather than a friend wanting to genuinely find out someone's decision-making process.

"Why did you make that choice? Why did you choose to go with that vendor?" Rather than "Can you share a little bit around how you made your decision or what factors led you to make that decision?" That approach is a lot softer and more inviting. It actually encourages reciprocity and free speech.

For example, if you say, "Why did you decide to give them the sale instead of us?" it is pointed, loaded and direct. This is a common question that salespeople ask and has a lot of potential value, but it is very damaging if it is not positioned delicately or reframed to something along the lines of the statements above or even simply "What made you choose them?" It's the "Why" that provokes negative emotion and causes the barriers of effective communication to cease.

The reason behind it is because when you frame something as "why" it has the potential to get the other side riled up because it's as if you are questioning their overall ability to make decisions, their rationale, and it puts them on the spot. This suggestion then brings up the defensive walls and reduces sharing.

Now you are somewhere you certainly don't want to be, you've flipped the conversation from a friendly discovery session to full on initiation of war! Especially if there's a more senior person in the room, like a boss, and the person you are asking the question to feels like they need to protect their decision, capabilities and integrity.

It pushes them into your competitor's camp more firmly. It solidifies in their mind that they did make the right decision and, as a result, you lose the momentum you've been building.

If you want to get a person's back up, ask them *why* they have made a decision, they will feel the need to defend it, and in doing so it will make the justifications stronger. In fact, you might even empower the decision by questioning it.

Therefore, in discovery it's best to use softeners and transition statements, as well as really focusing on keeping your body language open and tone of voice positive, upbeat and non-threatening.

This is where the *art* of sales really comes into play. I see this mistake all the time, where the salesperson knows that they are "supposed" to be asking deeply probing questions to uncover meaningful information; however, they fail to ask the questions in the right way.

Instead, they cause the client to close up, shut down and provide only surface level details to stop what they perceive to be an attack on their judgement or just downright rudeness.

You must set the scene for joint discovery, and you do that with your skill in being an expert communicator. Your body language, energy and tone all contribute to this harmonious exchange.

You'll also notice in some of the transition statements I am asking for permission. This is fantastic as, again, it helps the client feel more in control of the conversation, not like they are being pummeled for information and used.

The difference is massive.

It's where transactional focused salespeople lose out because the gold is in the empathetic, curiosity-driven approach that is able to draw out core details and keep the client sharing.

Remember the discovery meeting is a two-way street. Have you ever experienced when you met up with a friend and all they do is ask you question, after question, after question, and it feels like they want you to do all the work? Then, whenever you ask a question to them it's shut down pretty quickly, like you don't get any real meat on the bones?

Been there? OK great, you know what I am talking about. With all this talk of asking questions and being interested in your clients, you also need to share information as well. It's not a one-way street, so make sure to really listen and to engage with your clients, giving them your thrilling stories but not too much of them, offering interesting revelations but keeping them wanting more.

Just as with dating, you must increase your skill in the art of the conversation and intersperse your repertoire with the right questions, delivered in the *right* way to be natural and charismatic and helping the conversation flow.

Once you identify as a top salesperson and you have that identity there's no going back, you just see things differently and are willing to walk the road of continuous improvement to reach the highest levels of your capability possible.

Once you discover how to create momentum in your business, then everything changes, a world of possibility and adventure awaits. The only question is, do you have a purpose big enough to keep consistently implementing the blueprint outlined in this book, day after day, until you guarantee success?

In the next section of the Momentum Sales Model, we'll discuss how to keep going so that your output becomes a self-fulfilling prophecy and the momentum you generate multiplies all that it touches. After this, people are going to say you have the Midas touch. In reality, you know that it comes from awareness and putting these thoughts, actions and behaviours into practice on a daily basis.

OPPORTUNITY SUMMARY

- Momentum is won or lost on your ability to take more action that is consistently effective every day.

- If you act fast and with purpose, you'll take market share and thrive.

- If you learn to love the journey and not the outcome, you'll win every time.

- 91% of customers say they'd give referrals and only 11% of salespeople ask for referrals. 11%!

- Creating a bullet proof email and increasing the response rate is a sure-fire way to succeed.

- Your brand is a powerful tool that can generate awareness and open doors to empower your network.

- What you track, you will improve, keeping a day book helps to identify areas of opportunity and keeps you accountable.

- The Momentum Meetings Challenge builds stamina, character, and confidence. When you're inspired to serve you can make it happen. Your network will explode.

- When you face adversity remember the 4A's strategy.

- Always ask for referrals. Tattoo it on your hand until you don't forget!

- 9 before 9am will set you apart. You'll have the healthiest pipene in the country.

- Improving your discovery game will open up a whole new world. This is where most salespeople fail.

CHAPTER 5

Motivation – To keep going, do the work and maximise your output

"If you really want to cut through the noise, you're going to have to outperform everyone else."

– TOM BILYEU, Co-founder of Quest Nutrition & Impact Theory

INTRODUCTION

This is where the rubber meets the road. The techniques, tools and real talk in this section will help you to deal with overwhelm, finding extra gears to keep going when times get tough and increasing your ability to achieve goals.

I don't want to sugar coat it. Times will get tough. There will be days when putting in the work for future wins you can't see yet will feel like going to the dentist.

There will be times when what you are doing will feel horrendously monotonous and boring. However, the trick is to find ways to keep yourself having fun, to make it a game and to focus squarely on *why* you are doing it. You must focus on your why so that it is absorbed by every fibre of your being so that your bigger vision for your life is the thing you wake up thinking about and go to sleep at night dreaming about. You must surround yourself with A players, people that inspire you to go harder, do better and be more. EVERY DAMN DAY! And that requires one thing: motivation.

You may have heard some of these techniques before – in reality, it doesn't matter if you continue to hear about them a thousand times more if you don't put them into action and stick at it. Right through the moments when you want to quit, or when you feel uncomfortable or when you strike out and you're not making sales – right then is when your habits and rituals carry you through, when you need to have this stuff down so that it is on autopilot, and it is just how (insert your name) shows up for life!

WHAT IS MOTIVATION?

It is the driving force that keeps you working towards your goal, that burning desire inside that helps you overcome obstacles and become obsessive about your purpose. It's 1.18am and I'm still writing. I was up at 5am, why is that? It's because I am motivated to get this message out to you and finish this book that you have in your hands right now. (Also, it's partly because I ate a huge burrata as part of my celebratory birthday feast and now can't sleep, but that's beside the point – motivation, passion, desire is goals.)

In this chapter I will show you how to:

- Maximise your motivation

- Set effective goals and targets

- Reveal the formula for hitting targets every time

- Dig deep when times get tough

- Get a mentor.

HOW DOES MOTIVATION BUILD SALES MOMENTUM?

As salespeople it's what we do consistently that matters, day in and day out, and a lot of the time it will be you alone in the office before everyone else gets in. You have to get used to doing what everyone else isn't and thinking and doing things independently for yourself.

Other higher performers are doing this, they are motivated to be up at 4.30am completing their morning routine and getting primed for an epic day ahead – they are CONSISTENT and they are your goal, your inspiration, your mentors.

If you want to become one of them, you will put in the work and you will become known for how you operate. Your reputation will precede you and that will open doors you don't even know exist. New connections and people will come into your life and your network and give you access to opportunities that you dream of, and it can happen quickly with solid consistent grind.

This is where you become the hero of your own life. You recognise that no one but you is responsible for getting you to the top and, in pursuit of becoming a momentum salesperson, you will become the hero you were looking for all along.

You will start to love who you are and your life in sales. Sales, your identity, a person of integrity and a finisher will take on a new meaning in your life. The way you do things will change, pain won't keep you from the finish line, instead you will expect it and know how to handle it.

These principles will help you along the way. This is your journey, and I am here to help as I have travelled and continue to travel down this road myself – always learning, always ready.

Motivation will mean that no one and nothing will keep you from achieving your best.

Put yourself first and throw yourself into everything I am saying and you will come out on top.

Let's go!

1. MAXIMISING MOTIVATION

SET YOUR BIG PICTURE VISION

This is a must. World class salespeople engage with their big picture vision multiple times throughout the day, read any books by Bob Proctor, Steve Siebold, MJ Demarco, Napoleon Hill and other expert thinkers and entrepreneurs and you're going to find this theme time and time again.

Having a big picture vision motivates you to do things that other people won't. We covered your purpose and why in the Mindset chapter, but this is about keeping it front of mind. You need to make sure you absorb it, feel driven by it and are totally onboard with smashing the heck out of every day for it. Put up photos on your wall, save it as your home screen on your phone and laptop. You need to make sure you visualise it daily, many times, as this needs to be so ingrained in your subconscious that it's your identity. It just becomes who you are. I transferred my big picture vision on to a huge red A1 board that sits in my office daily so, as a result, I engage with it every day.

You might feel weird having a big board up in your house but, trust me, the discomfort you feel from having this displayed is a fraction of the discomfort you are going to feel if you get to the end of your life and know you left your full potential untouched. Remember, it is all about who you become on the journey. Whatever motivates you, whether that's an exotic sportscar, a huge mansion or the opportunity to set up your own charity. Keep it in front of you at all times and keep driving forward! Your vision has to be big enough that it excites you and scares you a little so that when it happens you will be transformed.

I find time to reengage with my bigger picture mission every single day. This often looks like sitting with my journal and reflecting on where I want to be in a year, two years and even five years ahead. This helps me plan a strategy and stay accountable, which informs what I should be doing daily.

Most people go after this thing they can get, but that is not enough. It doesn't inspire action. Instead, expand your vision to something that's really going to get you excited.

I had the good fortune of speaking with Mental Toughness Trainer and world-renowned speaker Steve Siebold when I was writing this book and I just *had* to include what he told me about the breath of fresh air you get when you have your first big break, as I couldn't agree more.

He said, "*Know that once you get to that first success you are going to take a breath of fresh air like you haven't breathed before, like you haven't been breathing in five minutes. That's the freshest breath that you'll ever take. All of a sudden you look in the mirror and see someone different and think, well, maybe I can pull this next one off because I pulled the last one off.*

"*It's why the first million is the hardest to make, because it's about belief more than the actual money.*"

Think about that for a second, you must have a desire so strong that it carries through all challenges. You must know in your heart that you can do it, that it will happen for you and your belief in this journey is what makes all the difference.

When you achieve your big vision, it changes you. The confidence you get from knowing you did it and the satisfaction is out of this world.

Steve is in the top 1% of highest earning speakers and has interviewed more than 1,300 millionaires over the past 37 years. I got up at 3.30am to talk with him and I recommend you take the time to listen to this conversation. You can find the gold on episode ten of my podcast, *The Tim Castle Show*. My advice, grab a pen and start making notes. Steve does not hold back in dropping insane value from the start! Just life changing!

Another technique I am dying to share with you is one from my mentor Ed Mylett. He came up with this idea of Possibility Projections as a way of motivating himself and I find it works for me to.

The idea is to project out into the future, to get really excited about it. If this sale comes through, what will that mean? If you hit target this quarter, what would that do? If you overachieve your annual goals in six months (personal and business) how would that transform the trajectory of your life?

The trick is to expand the possibility that you see, go as far out as you can, visualise and look at pictures of the car you want, the jet, the mansion with the pool, the villas around the world, the charities you run – all of it. Spend time absorbing these images of what you want and soak it up. Then work backwards from the future and figure out what you need to do to get there.

Boy, if there was ever a way to get me pumped this is it! It ties in so deeply with my motto "believe it is possible" and I love the way it keeps the limitations away and keeps me thinking about things that really excite me.

Here's a bonus, Bob Proctor would tell you to write what you want on a card and put it in your pocket. That way you will touch it every day and fuse mentally with the image of what you want. I want you to feel so electrified with motivation that you can generate it at a drop of a hat. The trick is to write your goal from the perspective that it has already happened, for example *"I'm so happy and grateful now that I earn $10 million a year"*.

GOAL SETTING

To hit the bull's eye, you must first know what you're aiming at daily. Each morning before I start work, I take 15 minutes to write out my goals for the day in my journal (which comes everywhere with me throughout the day). I suggest you do the same. I won't go into too much detail here, for proven strategies on goal setting check out *Be The Lion*, an award winning book I wrote that has helped thousands of ambitious people transform their lives.

By setting specific, actionable, time-oriented and detailed goals and then making it your mission to execute them, it allows you to stay in motion, to always be working towards your bigger vision and, as a result, there are many small wins to be celebrated along the way.

Every day before the sun rises, I'll go into my home office, sit down and pull out my journal. It's a beautiful time, as the first hour of my day is just for me. From there, I'll write my mission statement for the day and list out what I want to get done. These are tasks that I MUST do, no ifs, buts or maybes. This keeps me focused on spending my time on the highest value items rather than making it up as I go along.

Download my daily goal journal template at
www.timjscastle.com/themomentumsalesmodel

SETTING AND HITTING TARGETS (REFRAMING HOW YOU SEE TARGETS)

As salespeople, we love a challenge, as it keeps us hungry, motivated and poised for action at all times. Targets are a fantastic way to light a fire under your team and help drive the change you want for your business.

However, this is where I see so many businesses make mistakes. Any business that sets targets inappropriately without considering the market conditions and client patch will lose top talent because a real business works together with their salespeople to create tough but stimulating targets. If you work for yourself, I encourage you to think bigger – don't sell your dreams short by thinking small. Beliefs feed action!

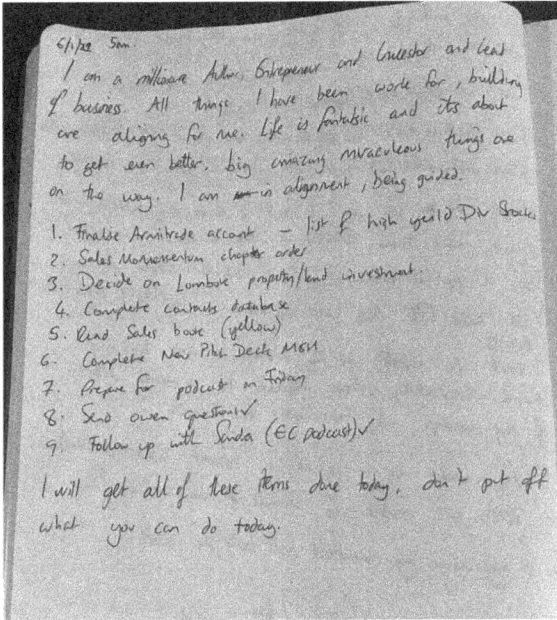

FIGURE 13: JOURNAL

If you find yourself in a position where your targets are forced on you without consultation, as many salespeople do, remember to have your own target in mind. For instance, your company might give you a target of $1.2 million in sales revenue for the year. However, you being you, a super star salesperson should be aiming for $2 million. Don't settle for less even if that goal is imposed by management, don't lower your standards to meet their target, **push yourself to go after what you truly think is possible.** The mentality you show up with every day dictates your outcomes. Just because your target is $1.2m don't let that cloud your judgement from what is really possible, push your mind just that bit further, stretch your imagination to its outer limits and be the salesperson you were born to become.

So much is decided in the mindset of what the salesperson expects to get, before any sales activity has even begun. **Let me repeat that: the salesperson's mentality will decide what is possible or not before they even begin to sell in market.**

The mind is the powerhouse of all activity and therefore sales mastery is formed in the mind before it is acted upon. If you believe that you will bring in more than your targets, then you are significantly more likely to do so than someone who has mentally prepared only to aim for the target.

If your personal aim is $2 million, you'll likely get to $2 million because you will take the action and behaviours required to achieve it. This will radiate from your person more obviously through your language, and more subtly in your unconscious thoughts and body language. To hit the mark, aim above the mark. You need to work with $2 million enthusiasm, which is different to $1.2 million enthusiasm. Do you think the salesperson who is on track to hit $1.2 million but only has a $1.2 million mentality will get out of bed early to meet with clients, or commit to 9 before 9am every day without fail?

A momentum seller will gladly rise early to take on the world, in prosperous times and in uncertain times. In fact, uncertainty causes the sales master to work with more flow and skill than ever before.

It is those who are unreasonable with the attainment of their goals and dreams who see them come into fruition.

Set your own standards for success and you will be happy in all ways. This is because the external doesn't control how you feel about yourself; you derive power from your internal expectations of yourself and therefore you know if you are giving it your all. That means, when you do business, whatever happens good or bad, it doesn't affect your self-esteem.

Plus, when you smash those company targets, you'll be rewarded with an accelerator for any dollar you bring in over your target. This is where sales masters can move rapidly towards their dreams with no ceiling above them. It's where the world class live and it's where you will be.

THE FORMULA FOR HITTING YOUR TARGETS

The best salespeople recognise that there is a formula that can help you hit your targets and, more often than not, overachieve them. This is where you play.

From this moment on, you recognise yourself as top of the leader board, the overachiever of targets. You decimate them, you break records, you strive to go above and beyond. This is what you associate with. No longer do you question whether targets will be met, you are all in.

To do this, work backwards from your monthly or quarterly target. You need to reverse engineer it.

For example, if your monthly sales target is $100,000 in revenue and your average sale amount is $10,000, you need to make ten sales a month to hit the target. Let's say for ease of maths in this instance that your close rate is one sale per three meetings, you therefore need to have 30 meetings that month to ensure you are taking enough *action* to hit your target.

TARGET $100,000
AVERAGE SALE $10,000
CLOSE RATE 1/3 OR 33%
NUMBER OF MEETINGS PER MONTH: 30
BUFFER: 20%
NUMBER OF MEETINGS PER MONTH: 36
NUMBER OF MEETINGS (5 DAY WEEK): 8.29
ACTION REQUIRED: 8 MEETINGS OR MORE A WEEK

**FIGURE 14: FORMULA TO SHOW NUMBER
OF MEETINGS TO HIT TARGET**

Note that I have included a buffer of 20% because we want to aim higher than the target in order to hit the target. This helps to account for sick days, mishaps, rescheduling, and drives the expectation to go above and beyond just average.

The drivers of this formula are close rate, average sale amount and number of meetings. If you improve any of these drivers, you are likely to overachieve your target. This is how you get leverage and exponential results. All top sales leaders know to focus on these metrics because they know that by increasing both close rate and average sale amount you can rocket to the moon.

Of course, it doesn't hurt to also maximise the number of inbound leads and referrals you are getting so your pipeline is in radically better shape as well.

You can see below, simply by improving one of the drivers it changes the outcome. This is how you overachieve targets – improve the drivers and keep your meetings per week consistently high.

TARGET $100,000
AVERAGE SALE $10,000
CLOSE RATE 1/2 OR 50%
NUMBER OF MEETINGS PER MONTH: 20
BUFFER: 20%
NUMBER OF MEETINGS PER MONTH: 24
NUMBER OF MEETINGS (5 DAY WEEK): 6
ACTION REQUIRED: 6 MEETINGS OR MORE A WEEK

**FIGURE 15: SHOWS HOW IMPROVING
CLOSE RATE CHANGES MEETINGS NEEDED**

Sales is both a people and a numbers game. What you are aiming for is strategically targeted accounts that have a high likelihood of conversion. You need to keep as many plates spinning as you can so that you can keep sales that are going to take a little longer still motivated and in the game for the next month whilst closing sales that are ready to land (that's the short game).

TARGET $100,000
AVERAGE SALE $25,000
CLOSE RATE 1/3 OR 33%
NUMBER OF MEETINGS PER MONTH: 12
BUFFER: 20%
NUMBER OF MEETINGS PER MONTH: 15
NUMBER OF MEETINGS (5 DAY WEEK): 3.75
ACTION REQUIRED: 4 MEETINGS OR MORE A WEEK

FIGURE 16: SHOWS HOW IMPROVING AVERAGE
SALE AMOUNT CHANGES MEETINGS NEEDED

In reality, you need to be playing short and long baby – all day, short and long. I am harvesting while I am planting more seeds. **Your ability to maximise sales comes down to reverse engineering what actions you need to take to hit the desired target.** It's about being disciplined, not having the market control you but controlling what you are responsible for – the amount of action you take in a day.

For instance, if you find that your close rate drops significantly to 1 in every 6 meetings leading to a sale (i.e., 50% less sales than the example above), you now know you'll need to double your number of meetings per week to get the same results as before.

Therefore, having your finger on the pulse of the market is important. Staying in touch with members of your team and trusting your gut about the market dynamics so that you know when it's time to step up your game and go extra hard is imperative for top sellers.

You can break this maths down further to inform your lead generation and prospecting efforts. Let's get busy...

If you require eight meetings per week, you now need to know how many emails, calls, interactions you need to make before you land an invitation to come in and sit down with a client.

Some deals happen fast, and some will test your patience. Therefore, let's assume that you need on average three attempts to get a meeting in the diary (this is very conservative as most statistics report it takes on average eight attempts to get in touch with a cold lead, but let's use three attempts for now because I imagine you at least know a few people you can sell to already).

This means that you need to be sending out at least 25 prospecting emails per week to sustain this kind of meeting schedule. That's purely from an outreach perspective, until your leads start to flow the other way and you have clients approaching you to come in and see them.

Why 25?

How did I arrive at that number? Well, if you need eight meetings a week, and it takes three attempts to land the meeting, and let's assume you follow up every three days, that means that over a 21.62 day period (normal average business days in a typical month) you need to send 107 emails to land 36 meetings (36 x 3 = 107).

The key driver here is the number of emails or calls it takes for you to land a meeting. In this case, we are assuming three attempts (e.g. you land a meeting every three times you send an email to request it).

The 36 meetings per month is calculated because you want to get eight meetings a week, then times this by the number of business weeks in a typical month, which is 4.345 (8 x 4.345 [average business weeks per month]= 36).

To get the daily rate you need to be reaching out to new clients to land new meetings; it's 107 (monthly emails) /21.62 (average business days per month) = 4.9 emails per day, rounded up this is, therefore, 25 emails per 5 days (4.9 x 5 = 25).

This assumes that you secure a meeting after three attempts with all prospects you reach out to, which we know doesn't happen. Therefore, you need to add on your own buffer to account for your prospecting to securing a meeting close rate.

Hence why my 9 before 9am strategy on top of your daily efforts puts you in a great position. If you follow what I am laying down, you can't help but win!

MINI MOMENTUM BUILDER
Do the maths

It sounds more complicated than it is, so don't worry if you aren't following. I have added a nifty Google Sheet to help you calculate your meetings per week and emails per week. If you go to www.timjscastle.com/themomentumsalesmodel you can download it for free and it will split out the key numbers you need.

Note – the level of activity will depend on the "coldness" and receptivity of your audience, so you will need to do the maths for yourself on the number of emails you must be sending per day. In my business, I may need to send anywhere from 7-20 emails to the same prospect before I get a response from a prospect. Use the spreadsheet to work out your numbers. If they are lukewarm then it drops to 2-3 emails before a response, and of course if they are friendly then 1-2 is typically the rate.

Weekly meetings calculator

Target Per Month	Average Sale Amount	Close Rate	Sales per month required (based on average sale amount and target)	Meetings Per Month	Meetings Per Week without Buffer	Buffer	Meetings Per Month	Meetings Per Week with Buffer
$100,000	$10,000	33%	10	30	7	20%	36	8

Key Drivers
Close Rate - the quickest way to increase your sales is either to increase the close rate or your average sale amount

Instructions
You only need to change column A, B and C - input your montly target, your average sale amount and your close rate

FIGURE 17: USE THIS CALCULATOR TO UNDERSTAND MEETINGS PER WEEK NEEDED TO HIT TARGET

Weekly prospecting emails calculator

Meetings Per Week	Meetings Per Month	Outreach attempts to land a meeting with one client	Outreach Per Attempts Month	Average Days per month	Average email outreach per day	Average email outreach per week required
8	36	3	107	21.62	5	25

Key Drivers
Roughly speaking, the number shown in column F is the number of meaningful well-constructed, curiosity inducing, action provoking taking emails need to go out from your inbox every day to the decision makers you want to sit down with
Instructions
Change column C to reflect the number of emails you typically send before you land a meeting with a desired prospect

**FIGURE 18: USE THIS CALCULATOR TO UNDERSTAND
PROSPECTING REQUIRED TO ACHIEVE MEETINGS TARGET**

For clarity, these are the key equations:

- Number of meetings per month required x number of attempts to get a meeting = number of emails you must send per month.

- Number of emails sent per month / business days in a month = number of emails per day that you must send to decision makers.

- Number of emails per day x number of working days in a week = number of emails per week you must send.

This is on top of all your normal emails nurturing clients that you have met with already, all your follow up, this is prospecting for new meetings.

This is where the consistency piece will play a large part in your ability to perform. It also means you've got a lot of work to do. You've got to feed the beast; this sales pipeline is going to need a fresh supply of decision makers to be targeted or else your five a day is going to dry up. **This means you've got to be out networking, but it also means that in every meeting you go to you've got to be probing for other people you can meet and therefore influence.**

At the end of every meeting, ask your clients, "Who else should I meet?" and "Can you introduce me?"

Get into the habit, it is SO easy to forget to do it, but also SO valuable for you. Just this one strategy alone could radically transform your sales.

Hopefully, by breaking it down to this level of granularity, you can see just how much you need to be doing in terms of outreach to hit your required levels of meetings with key decision makers to get enough exposure to exciting opportunities.

Prospecting for valuable opportunities and coming up with new ways to reach clients each day is what makes the difference – if you take nothing else from this book, take this!

If you get this formula right, and have massive momentum, you are doing your follow up consistently every three days as well as sending out five new prospecting emails or calls each day combined with requesting new introductions in client meetings to get a deeper infiltration and exposure across the organisation. Do all of that and **it will work**.

If you put in the work and you are committed to the formula it will get you insane levels of momentum, whether you can sustain that momentum, however, is on you.

The five a day email plan is a good target to start with. You might find that on some days you go over this, good for you, more power to you.

Here is where you can accelerate, and your new business development activities start to take on an automatic intuitive nature. You will find that you don't need to think about your prospecting activity because it will be natural and happen automatically at all times. You'll be hitting over the five a day with ease and, like any muscle, it will get stronger the more you practice.

Once you build strength in this area, you'll be able to set yourself challenges, "Right, today I am going to get 15 strong proactive momentum-driving emails out to my clients." This acts as a way to push yourself but also it literally makes you unstoppable, flexible and magnetically ready for sales.

When you go down this path, it's like you are attracting more and more success to yourself. I remember one time battling with the Kuala Lumpur traffic, hammering out email responses on my iPhone whilst giving directions to the cabbie in downtown rush hour.

If I hadn't have taught myself to act despite the distractions, time pressure, poor internet signal, obstacles like the bumpy road, and the noise, I might have been overwhelmed. But because I learned to fight through the jungle, I was prepared for anything. WHEN YOU REACH THIS LEVEL, YOU ARE DANGEROUS IN A GOOD WAY. Your enthusiasm for life and willingness to serve clients pulls more sales to you. You are a beacon.

WHEN IT IS TIME TO HUSTLE, DON'T LET DOUBTS HOLD YOU BACK

You know that feeling you get in the pit of your stomach? It can be from the knowing that you could be doing more to advance your sales performance or bring a certain outcome closer. There's that twang of nervous energy almost calling you, willing you into action, yearning for you to take a step forward and go for it with no regrets.

Well, that twang, butterflies, burning desire in the pit of your stomach is a sign. From now on I want you to recognise it for what it is: motivation. This is your internal guide, telling you to make it happen!

Let me give you an example so you are 100% clear on what I mean.

PERSONAL STORY
From an idea to speaking
to 100,000 people

One day I was at the office. It was a fairly normal day and I was having a cup of coffee brainstorming ways that I could get my message out there on a broader scale.

As you might know, my mission in life is "to help people go after their really big goals and become their best selves". Now, I had decided, it was time to really get the message out there, so I began where most searches begin – with Google.

My first book *The Art of Negotiation* was getting a lot of success and recognition, especially with students and ambitious go-getters wanting to advance their careers and score a promotion. In fact, the book had rocketed to number 1 in a few of the weekly bestseller charts.

This presented a huge opportunity. Go where it's hot! My rationale was, if something has momentum, it could lead to the bigger goal.

I decided to double down on using the traction the book was having in Singapore and Malaysia to try to get featured in an article by a large publication or, better yet, secure an interview on a few well-known podcasts. This strategy had been highlighted to me by American writer and entrepreneur, Derek Sivers. He told me doing 400+ podcast interviews was the way forward and untapped for authors looking to promote their work.

It didn't take long before I found a solution. Within a matter of minutes, I found myself on the homepage of Money FM 89.3, a business-focused radio station in Singapore.

Then something happened and the fire lit up inside. I saw that the show would be recording live from a shopping mall a few minutes away from where I was that day. In fact, they were already there.

This serendipitous moment presented a huge opportunity, as if on a plate, and produced the spark of an idea. When ideas like this flash into your mind, it is often the subconscious connecting with the conscious mind, and they should be acted on right away. This creative energy spreads so quickly that if you learn to tap into it and take action before you forget it, you know it's going to lead somewhere remarkable.

The idea I had was to go down there to where Money FM were live on air and try to talk my way onto the show. After all, wasn't this the opportunity I had been waiting for? A chance to go bigger and potentially speak to hundreds of thousands to help them achieve more success and invest in their own self-development.

It sounds simple, doesn't it? And, in reality, it is, relatively speaking. That is, until our heads get in the way and start talking us out if it, thinking of everything that could go wrong. "What if I get rejected?" or "what if they allow me on but I don't have anything relevant to say?" *What if? What if? What if?* When genius ideas begin to form, we must grab hold of them without letting fear stop them in their tracks.

It was only a few blocks away, and as I walked over and found the building, a sense of urgency and anticipation started to build. *Would I go through with it?* I began to question myself. You see, the thing with taking action is, if you get into the habit of taking it, continually pushing yourself to commit to taking the next right step, with no judgement and only lessons, then you can't lose – it is all an upside.

With this philosophy deeply instilled, I quietened the doubts that had started to take hold and remembered my mission. When you are doing it for something bigger than yourself, it can push you forwards.

I located the Money FM crew presenting from the lower ground floor in the centre of a shopping mall. As I got down there, I could see there were a few people dotted around sitting listening thoughtfully, but not as many as the crowds that I had dreamed up in my mind.

I spotted the host of the show (who I would later find out was Michelle Martin) and a guy stood off to the right-hand side of the set, and before I could talk myself out of it, my legs started walking (action taking muscle kicking in). Before I knew it, I was right up close with the guy. Now it was just me and him, looking at each other. I had no idea who he was or what he was doing. I hadn't planned this out. I was living in action mode. Action taking had got me this far, so I stuck out my hand to introduce myself and struck up conversation.

Pretty quickly after the pleasantries I got into my sales pitch. I was a local author, with a book that was going gangbusters on helping people with everyday negotiations, so could I come on the show?

There I was, I had rocked up to this live radio show and marched right into the heart of the action, centre stage, with all the onlookers gawking at me, and I had decided to pitch the guy right then and there to see if I could come on the show.

As luck, good fortune or universal master plannery would have it, this turned out to be the exact show that featured authors. They even had a section where they talked about business books!

My eyes, heart, stomach, and body lit up. That's exactly what you get when you follow your heart and don't let your head lead the way. Taking action and following your gut instinct leads to some miraculous places. It is an action-first mentality that will get you into these types of situations and put you front of centre for your own best life.

As it turned out, the guy was the producer of the show. He couldn't have been nicer and seemed really up for it, even though my pitch was made up on the spot (I didn't have any of my books on me or a business card). He seemed genuinely interested and took what I said at face value.

I managed to convince him that I had a book worth talking about, that was relevant and would suit the theme of the show. After a few minutes, Michelle jumped off the air for a quick song break and the producer waved her over to come speak to me. She was amazing, warm and upbeat and also seemed totally up for having me come into the studio and do an interview about negotiation and my books! *Could this really be happening? Was all that stood between me and speaking to a few hundred thousand people on the air waves just asking?*

We exchanged contact details and I walked away, elated. What I did next was probably even more important than what had just happened. I immediately followed up with a thank you email requesting a time to come into the studio and giving some more background information, just in case once I wasn't stood in front of them I seemed like a random lunatic and their enthusiasm started to fade. I wanted to build credibility and show my commitment to everything we had discussed. I also couriered over a few copies of my books to the studio that day for them to pre-read and also show them that I was for real.

That night I got an email back. This was really happening. We locked in a time for a few weeks down the track. The date was set and I was now going on the *Your Money* show on Money FM to help listeners with their negotiations.

In the space of a day, I had managed to change my fate from having a few followers in my audience to now being on the road and talking to hundreds of thousands. All because I took action on an idea and didn't let it slip through my fingers. I could have very easily reasoned that it was not possible to get on the show and held myself back or counted myself out.

It is the same in sales. When flashes of inspiration come

up on who to contact or who you can go pitch to, follow it through, take action and see where it leads. **These ideas, if acted upon, will set you apart from the competition and see you put yourself on the road to success.**

Of course, there are a few things that helped make this happen, like my book being at number one in the charts and actually having a product like a book in the first place to give credibility to my expert negotiator status. I am not sure it would have gone down so well if I had rocked up at a different time, when the producer was busy.

All these things played to my advantage. However, it was taking action and following my instincts that got the door of this opportunity wide open. If I hadn't have gone down there and then struck-up conversation with the producer, pitched myself and my mission to them with authenticity and a genuine passion to help, I guarantee it wouldn't have happened. It is the combination of making bold moves with a commitment to combining the elements you have in a certain way so that someone else can see what's in it for them and how their goals are met.

I wanted to help share my knowledge on negotiation tactics for everyday negotiations. That was the goal of my first book, to make people more successful in everyday negotiations, like pay rises, interviews and upgrades. Pitched in the right way, this spoke to the nature of the show and there was a real interest from both sides.

I do believe that we all have advantages that can be played, just like in cards. It's not the hand you get dealt but how you play it that matters. If you can practise taking action to actually get yourself the opportunity to pitch the idea, that's where the magic happens, and it has the ability to transform the seemingly improbable into being highly possible. It's a potent combination and one that I cannot overstate the importance of. Taking action on your ideas might be the most powerful message in this book!

Take it a step further, doing the radio show has opened up a wealth of opportunities and I was even asked back on air to talk about Momentum Sales and this very book!

My goal for you with this story is that you apply it to your own life. When you get those butterflies or that twang in your belly that says you could take it to the next level or put some crazy idea into motion, **act on it**. Don't let it go by in the haze of "what if?", actually make it happen and see where it takes you. For every one of these ideas that I try that works, there are others that don't. Sometimes I fall flat on my face, but it is the commitment to consistency in trying that sees, every once in a while, sunshine come through the clouds and provide the big break I was looking for.

I would also like to highlight that, if you are going to take action, then you should try to aim for those things that are really going to move the needle and build momentum, game changing events, things that could literally transform your business. This isn't about standing on the sidelines and then just moving one step along – instead, go for big, go for outrageous, and really push the boat out into the extremities of your mind as to what you think you could pull off, and then go for it my friends.

You are brilliant, and you are capable. Know that in your heart of hearts it is meant for you and that all that it takes is the persistence to keep going in spite of failure.

As Winston Churchill said, *"success is going from failure to failure without the loss of enthusiasm"* and *"success is not final, failure is not fatal; it is the courage to continue that counts"*.

How to apply this to sales

- Many industry sectors are seeing the rise of podcasts with companies and leaders taking the initiative to start industry-specific podcasts related to their field. Why not approach a few that are relevant to your industry and speak about a topic you know lots about? Not only will this increase exposure of your business and invite a flurry of hot new leads, but it will significantly raise your own personal brand.

- Write an eBook related to your specific industry, or a niche topic within your industry, and use this to host a launch party where you invite relevant speakers to discuss the topic in depth. You can then invite clients and prospective clients to the event. Tip – once you have an eBook you can also leverage this to go on shows.

- Approach your local business-focused radio station and pitch them to come on the airwaves – shows need content, and if you have an interesting viewpoint or expertise that can be applied to help listeners then there's a high possibility that the show may invite you on.

- Write to publications with your interesting story and ask to be featured or, better yet, ask to start a column.

■ Partner with one of your most valued clients and start up a podcast, or a prospective client that you would like to land. Going into partnership together will strengthen ties and also set you apart from the rest.

■ When it is time to hustle and you have that idea, be a self-starter and go make it happen. Don't wait until it is too late, so many incredible ideas go wasted because people either forget them or talk themselves out of doing them.

■ Sales come from finding new and creative ways to surprise your clients, so think about what they might need or want and get to work. Do your clients need a webinar on a specific topic? Could they use an open opportunity to learn? Could you initiate it and become the authority in upskilling clients on this challenging area?

■ Leave your clients in awe by understanding how they think and then delivering the goods. By going above and beyond to help alleviate your clients' pain points, you transition from a salesperson to an asset.

TRUST YOUR INTUITION

Learning to live by your instincts is a valuable skill. Sometimes you just get that feeling about a situation, person, or thing, you pick up on a vibe and you just know it's going to happen, or you can make it work.

Sales professionals who are at the top of their game know this and use their instinct and intuition to make decisions and judgements about the next right action to take daily. If I send this email written in this way then it will produce X outcome. If I say "yes" to taking this video call to a potentially large new client that starts in ten minutes,

I need to find a quiet spot to conduct the meeting, but I can do it. World class sellers trust themselves to be able to figure it out, to take a situation and, using their own intuition, find the solution.

Our gut is always telling us something, and the more you learn to listen to it the better off you'll be. And by listening to it I mean using your intuition to guide the actions you take, the words you say and the commitments you make.

If an interesting thought or fun way to generate sales comes into your head, regarding how you could promote your business in a new way, put it into motion and act on it, right then and there. Make the decision and move it forward. This is key. This takes you to the next level. No longer are you someone who just thinks about ideas, you are a person that puts them into motion and pays attention to how they affect your business.

1. First thing's first, when you have an idea, write it down.

2. Next, pick up the phone and figure out how to go about making it happen. Maybe you see an article that inspires you and decide to write to the editor and ask questions about how the writer got to write for this publication or, better yet, you set about writing an article you think aligns with their mission. Or perhaps you see that your favourite mentor/leader/coach is coming to town for an intimate speaking session, so you book your tickets right then and there. No thinking about "what ifs", this is all about making it happen and the more you get used to taking inspired action in this way, the more it will become your go-to habit for life. In turn, more opportunities will be drawn to you. You will spot new ways to make things happen and connect the dots in ways you never thought possible before.

Your intuition is constantly guiding you to the next right action. Make sure you put that wisdom to good use by following it, trusting it and taking aligned action.

CELEBRATE SMALL WINS EVERY DAY

You need to be your own generator of positivity and inspiration. As a sales leader, you must make it your mission to find the small wins in each day. This could be from a positive client meeting, a meeting you've been trying to land going in the diary, to a smile from the receptionist. **Go out of your way to notice and pay attention to the little pleasures in life.**

In sales, it is full on; if we are not careful, we can burn out because we are moving so fast we forget to keep tabs on what matters. To counteract this potential threat to your sales mastery, whatever the circumstances you are facing, you must find the good in each day and have fun.

PRO TIP
Connect with joy and
celebrate small wins

As a hunter going out in the wild each day, stay connected to what makes you fill up with joy. Play your favourite tunes before a big meeting, get pumped, and spread that happiness with others.

By taking notice and appreciating the small wins, you naturally make way for the big ones.

MINI MOMENTUM BUILDER
Keep a gratitude list

Keep a gratitude list in your phone's notes app or Notion, or in a notebook and review it frequently, once or twice a day. Make a conscious effort to keep it updated and pay attention to how much amazing stuff is actually happening to you and for you.

You have a roof over your head, a partner, a wife, a husband, a kid, a father, a mother, a sister, a brother, a friend, a dog, are breathing – whatever it is, don't discount it. If it wasn't there, all of a sudden you would notice and, if you find one day it isn't, be grateful for the fact that it was there at all.

The moment you shift to seeing your role in sales as a privilege to sell these awesome products to make your clients' lives just that bit better is a day you change the game and begin to step into your greatness as a salesperson.

Make that day, today!

Step forward and embrace the opportunity you have been given and go sell your heart out. I promise you; you'll feel a heck of a lot better about any situation, good or bad, when you are grateful for the privilege you have been given to be alive and selling right now.

2. FINDING EXTRA MOTIVATION GEARS WHEN TIMES GET TOUGH

DON'T PANIC WHEN THINGS GO WRONG

Nine times out of ten, everything will go without a hitch. Then there will be that one time that your computer freezes right before the start of a big sales pitch, or the client doesn't have the right adaptor for your laptop to be shared on their screen. (If it's the latter, it's your responsibility – remember that you're in the service industry. I am a major culprit with this one.)

The absolutely key thing if something like the above happens to you is to **remain calm**. If you remain composed and helpful, trying to solve the problem rather than getting stressed, it won't even matter, and it will be forgotten the moment the problem has been resolved.

However, if you kick up a fuss and get annoyed, that energy will enter the room and infiltrate the client's perception of your company and of you. The lesson here is just because you're annoyed doesn't mean that you should express annoyance in the room with the client. Handling yourself under pressure also shows the client that you can be trusted and that you are cool-headed when things don't go according to the plan (as happens in life). This is an opportunity to actually show your client you've got this.

PRO TIP
Have a backup USB

The strategy here is to have a backup USB with all the information on it so it can be handed to the client to put on their machine should any freak glitch strike your computer, and it also acts as a leave behind. It makes you look professional, prepared and ready for action. This will leave the client thinking that you are the kind of person they want to do business with. After all, you can handle this situation with grace, so it bodes well for how you'll handle the client's business when there are hiccups along the way.

If you make a mistake with a word or you fluff a sentence and the client notices and calls it out, embrace it. Firstly, only really awful clients are going to make you feel stupid for making a mistake and these aren't the kind you want to be doing business with anyway. If you mess up what you are trying to say, own it. You come across more professional for it and more human (the latter being the game changer). After all, we can all relate to being human and, if you're too polished, too robotic, it can also make it harder for clients to relate to you. What top salespeople do is aim for great without getting flustered when they miss the step every now and again.

PERSONAL STORY
Solve problems and win together

Another time I was thwarted by technology, I had flown in for a huge pitch. If I landed this account, it would have been the largest in the history of the company in Asia. When it was my time to go into the room and set up there was only one problem, my shiny new Apple MacBook wouldn't connect to the screen and the only adaptor available had been broken.

There I was sitting in a room full of people with my time to shine slowly ticking away. Talk about pressure! I was ready to go, but this stupid adaptor wouldn't work.

To begin solving this, I remembered my emotions in check. I wasn't going to let negative energy enter the room and take away from all the phenomenal work the team and I had been preparing. I came up with a two-pronged solution.

Fire up my personal laptop (which luckily had the correct port to fit the screen cable into) and start emailing files across to myself to be presented.

Whilst this was going on, the client rallied around to try to locate another adaptor and figure out why the connection wasn't working.

It might not sound like a massive deal now reading about it, but you know what it's like when you're pitching for business that could change the face of your business – you don't want simple things messing up your flow. If I had allowed my emotions to take hold, getting flustered or frustrated at this stage would have only made matters worse. Instead, I made a choice to engage the crowd. I encouraged them to open up the large box of cupcakes I had brought them and get stuck in.

In this instance, you aren't so much trying to distract from the situation as to not empower it. By acknowledging the situation and demonstrating that you're taking steps to handle it, whilst entertaining your clients, you are actually promoting skills of confidence, and that of a leader. It's like you're putting on a show and you're the only cast member; whatever happens you want the audience to feel like "you got this". Leadership!

The upshot was, one of the clients realised they had an adaptor at their desk and went off to fetch it. Within about five to six minutes, the ordeal was over and the result was that we all collectively felt like we had solved a problem together. The energy in the room was high and the pitch could begin.

Ultimately, if clients are having fun, engaged and the process in itself feels like a success then it will more often than not lead to good things. Hiccups and challenges are often how great relationships are formed because you have to get together and collaborate to solve it for the collective good. This in turn gets clients to bring down any walls and moves you closer to developing real, long-lasting relationships. Situations like this can be laughed about in the future and, if handled right, are a pivotal moment in sales for relationship building.

When the meeting is over, don't dwell on mistakes or rehash them with your client, that will only seek to undermine all the awesome work you've just done pulling it off. The end of the meeting is your chance to close it strong and leave a lasting impression that will override any early hiccups. The other thing is, the bigger deal you make the tech issue, the bigger it will be. When clients think back to the meeting, what they recall is down to you and what you focus their collective attention on.

Remember, there is always a way to turn a bad situation around and it comes from seeing the opportunity in the challenge.

Whilst we didn't win the deal, we did go on to win bigger campaigns from this monster of a client on a repeat basis, so overall the effect was incredible.

PERSONAL STORY

How I went from an abandoned building to 250% to target in under three hours

It was the first time I was doing business in Kuala Lumpur; I had lined up a stack of meetings and filled my diary to the brim. I was leveraging meetings I was having in Singapore to introduce me to their Malaysian counterparts based in KL.

There are a couple of advantages to this strategy, by doubling

up and seeing the same client in both locations simultaneously in the same week, your sales patter will be just that bit
slicker, because you'll have more contextually relevant client
details to discuss.

I had this nice flow of Malaysian introductions going, and
my diary was full. On one email exchange with a client, they
offered to invite more clients to their meeting and make it a
companywide pitch. Game on!

In my excitement, I forgot to do the one thing that is normally automatic, which was send a placeholder invite. I think I
figured since it was all on email confirming the dates and times
of the session, and I had been told that the whole company was
now invited, there could be no way it wasn't locked in.

Fast forward to the day of the meeting, I had spent a number
of hours in the days leading up to it preparing a tantalising
deck, filled with relevant examples and entertaining snippets
so it would appeal to everyone in the room.

My main goal was to use this opportunity as a launch pad
to get more people interested and thinking that we were the
best-in-class company at what we do, inspire them to want to
do business with us.

However, when I turned up at the address there was no one
there.

I had arrived about 20 minutes early so not wanting to appear
too annoying I hung out in the lobby of the building and
waited until five minutes before the meeting. I took the lift
up to the twentieth floor only to find the whole place was
completely abandoned. When I walked out into what should

have been a brightly lit, action centre, it had been replaced with a gloomy and cavernous wasteland. Sitting on a sofa ahead of me were two people, so I promptly walked across the large floor and introduced myself.

"Hello," I said, "I am Tim, I'm here for a meeting with Louise from Unilever." To my surprise, they looked confused.

I still hadn't got it yet. "There is no one here," they said.

"I see, well, where can I find them? I'm supposed to have a big meeting in a couple of minutes and the whole company is attending," I said.

To cut a long story short, it turns out the elevators in the building had been faulty and randomly plummeting or keeping people trapped inside (Yes, the ones I had just used to get up there and now needed to ride again to get out), so everyone had to be moved to another location on the other side of Kuala Lumpur.

This was a problem. I was supposed to present, in precisely one minute, to the whole company! This was my big opportunity, and I was on the other side of the city, still having to get back down from the twentieth floor without dying in the faulty elevators and my moment to shine was slipping away by the second.

You know when you travel all that way, with excitement and enthusiasm bursting at the seams, ready to tell the world about all the wonderful things your company can do for them and then there's some form of challenge? You know that experience?

It's hard not to get annoyed in these types of situations and start asking questions like "how could they have not told me that their offices had recently moved? The freakin' building is named after them?!"

I pinged off an email to Louise informing her what had just happened and that I would need about 40 minutes to cross town, but I was on my way.

Hopefully, she would understand and could divert the masses while I figured this out. My main goal here was to avoid starting with a bad first impression, giving the client all the details of how such an error could have taken place and also giving them an opportunity to continue rather than postpone.

Then I received an email back moments later that shocked me. Louise had completely forgotten that the all-company meeting was happening, due to the fact that a placeholder wasn't in her calendar, and on top of this she wasn't at the office and none of the company was waiting. On the one hand, I was relieved I wasn't keeping 100+ people waiting and on the other I was frustrated all my meeting prep and effort that morning had been for nought.

Or had it?

What I did next was where the magic happened. This is where I flipped the situation and put my 4A's strategy for adversity into action. Instead of asking the driver to turn around I decided to press on and go to the new office location anyway to see what I could make happen. After all, I had a valid reason to be there and could potentially see if Louise, feeling bad for forgetting our all-company meeting, might come in and meet me later.

This was a strategically advantageous decision; it demonstrated to the client that I was committed to them, and it maximised my chances of achieving what I set out to do.

As luck would have it (LUCK BEING STAYING RESOURCEFUL), Louise said she felt terrible for missing our meeting and understood that obviously I had expected to present to the whole company, therefore the least she could do was come into the office to meet me whilst I was in town.

She then gave me the name of her intern, Felicity, and told me to ask for her when I arrived at reception. I did as she said, and when I got to the front desk a beaming intern came out to greet me. She suggested we go grab a coffee downstairs and that I take her through what I had prepared to present while we waited for Louise to make it to the office.

After about 35 minutes of taking Felicity through the product offering, we wrapped up. Felicity then offered to take me back upstairs to see if anyone else was around that I could meet.

This was a door opening moment if ever there was one, at the time I didn't know how big, but I was about to find out. If we think about having a people strategy, Felicity was a door opener and boy did she over deliver!

****GAME CHANGER ALERT****

If this ever happens to you and you are offered the chance to *see* who else is about, follow it through and find out where it goes. For the next 45 minutes to an hour, I was paraded around office after office meeting more people face to face than I ever would during an entire company meeting. I was able to briefly pitch each team of clients individually for about five minutes before I moved on with Felicity leading the way to the next office full of clients ready to hear what I had to say.

It was a dream scenario.

I couldn't believe my luck (LUCK BEING STAYING PRESENT TO THE OPPORTUNITY IN FRONT OF ME). Felicity was literally opening the door to every single client office in the building, no matter the seniority. I must have met over 35-40 different people and given out and received the same amount in business cards.

My arrival in the building created a buzz as the floor to ceiling glass partitions between each of the offices were transparent and therefore other staff members soon became curious as to what was going down. Momentum was building, even before I got to the next office, the client knew I was coming and was intrigued. We were absolutely cranking the momentum.

As we made our way around the building, giving pitch after pitch, I knew this was good, I could feel it. You can just imagine my salesperson's smile, the kind you can't wipe off your face even if you tried. It was excellent!

In the space of just over 45 minutes, I had met everyone I possibly could need to meet in the organisation, from the top down to the bottom, Managing Director all the way to Assistant. Then Louise arrived and, after a few apologies and some small talk, we got down to business.

What had started out as a complete disaster, turned out to be the greatest round of meetings ever. I ended up being in the building for around three hours, met all the decision makers of each department responsible for millions of dollars in revenue and I was able to develop deeper relationships than if we had stuck to the original plan of holding a companywide meeting.

The individual five-minute pitches I had been giving at each stop allowed each client team to ask relevant questions to their patch of business without being intimidated. This moved the needle in an irreversible manner.

This is a perfect example of what I mean about the opportunity not always looking like you might first have imagined or hoped. I had wanted to do the all-company presentation and naturally would have thought this was the best option any day of the week over meeting the intern.

However, what transpired was even greater than I could have wished – the all-company presentation turned into a series of micro-meetings, quick fire elevator pitches and purposeful questions. It was like speed dating, and I was a match with everyone.

Out of this encounter, I picked up numerous clients and the biggest spenders in the whole of the continent. As a result of this, Malaysia quickly became the largest market and it started by turning an adversity into an advantage by being resourceful, taking initiative and never giving up.

Here's the lesson: don't give up at the first sign of trouble and always push to make the next best thing happen. Opportunities lie within the challenge.

If when I turned up at the old office I had given up and fired off an email just explaining that I was not in the right place and we should reschedule, none of the above would have ever remotely had a chance of happening. What a waste! This is also what 95% of sales-people would do.

By pushing for the next best thing to see where it went, the advantages began to stack on top of each other, each door opening to the next and so on. Like a series of dominos or a steam train gaining speed, momentum was well and truly in the house!

So, next time you are facing what you think is failure, see how far you can push it and find out where the adventure of being in sales may lead. You never know, it might just be the best option after all.

3. PRINCIPLES TO LIVE BY IN SALES

REJECTION IS ALL PAR FOR THE COURSE

Rejection, even the word sounds harsh. But it's not, it's the feelings we associate with it and the story that we tell ourselves, about ourselves, when we get rejected that hurts. In sales, you will get rejected every day. Use rejection to spur you on, to motivate you and make you hungrier, to fight harder, to keep going no matter what. Rejection is useful because it shows you what's not meant to be.

If you are someone who gets upset when things don't go the way you planned, you need to snap out of it. An excellent TED Talk to listen to is 100 Days of Rejection by Jia Jiang[3]. He speaks about his experience as a kid at school when the teacher decided to play a game whereby each child got a present if they could think of something nice to say to one of the other kids in the group.

As it turned out Jia was one of three kids that day that no one had anything nice to say about. That sucked, and he carried this fear of rejection with him from childhood all the way to adulthood. This continued until one day he realised he was absolutely petrified of rejection and that it stemmed back to his experience at school that day.

Jia Jiang then set himself the goal of overcoming this fear. To do this he came up with a plan, this involved him completing a rejection-inducing task each day and seeing what happened. On the first day Jia explains that he walked up to a complete stranger in the street and said, "can you lend me $100?"

Imagine that, just picking a stranger, walking up to them and

3 https://www.ted.com/talks/jia_jiang_what_i_learned_from_100_
days_of_rejection?language=en

asking for a loan. It's pretty uncomfortable even just thinking about it, let alone having the courage to do it and for Jia Jiang it was revolutionary. Forcing himself to push through the fear of being rejected by doing something that was clearly not in his comfort zone. You know what the most surprising thing was, the stranger said, "No, why?"

Jia Jiang remarks that after hearing these words he just ran away, but because he had recorded the interaction on his phone, he was able to watch it back at a later stage in the day and see that the guy had actually given him a golden opportunity. He had asked "why?" and that, my friends, is a game changer.

What Jia realised as he continued on with his mission each day was that if he just stayed with the rejection and didn't run away, the person doing the rejecting would often try to work out a solution.

He gives another example, where this time he improved upon his approach. He knocked on someone's door and asked, "Can I plant this flower in your garden?" The man replied, "No, man." This time Jia didn't run away, he stood there holding the flower and responded to the man, "Can I ask why not?" To his surprise, the man then gave an awesome explanation. It turned out he had a dog that would tear the flower to shreds if he planted it in the backyard, so the man offered a solution. He told Jia to go across the street and look for Connie who absolutely loves flowers. Off Jia went, with all his newfound conviction and did as the guy said – he went across the street in search of Connie who loves flowers. Connie let him plant the flower.

The way to deal with rejection is to get used to it so that when it happens in sales it doesn't make you angrier, we aren't talking about that type of motivation. As a future world class salesperson, it's about finding ways to use rejection to keep you motivated, to become better each day. Or as Napoleon Hill says, repeat this mantra to yourself every day: "I am becoming more successful every day in every way."

I love this so much I have it written up on the wall in my personal study so that I see it constantly.

In my early career, I was a professional negotiator working in the world of corporate barter brokering deals with publishers and some of the top Fortune 500 companies in both the UK and Australia.

What made this job fun was developing the hustle, the work ethic, the attitude to be able to face rejection, get up, brush yourself off, and carry on. Doing upwards of sometimes fifteen or twenty negotiations a day trains you to hear the word "no" and get rejected time and time again.

Similarly, the crucial part, as Jia found out, is that you build up a tolerance and learn to stay with the "no" and ask "why?" Suddenly, you aren't afraid of hearing "no" anymore, and you learn that it is all part of the course in striking a deal. The psychological term for it is called systematic desensitisation.

In Jia's case, his perception of rejection changed on day three of his rejection therapy training when he went into a Krispy Kreme donut shop and asked the person behind the counter to build him the five Olympic rings made out of donuts. An odd request for sure, and certainly not on the menu, but guess what happened... the guy behind the counter started taking notes and figuring out a way to make it happen. Jia had cracked it; he saw that by being prepared to face rejection and staying in the zone of rejection it was possible to get what you wanted.

This was a breakthrough moment for him, and it can be for you if you take the lesson here, which is, rejection is just the story that you apply to it. "I'm a bad salesperson", "I'm never going to sell anything", "they hate me", whatever and wherever your head goes when you get rejected. Learn to stay with the rejection longer and ask, "why not?" Get the other side talking and you'll see that you uncover valuable information that you can use to your advantage.

PERSISTENCE TO DO WHAT'S RIGHT, NOT WHAT'S EASY

As the top sales performer that you are about to become, there will be times when you don't want to put in the work, and I am not just talking about beating down doors here. I am talking about following up on what you said you were going to do in that meeting yesterday. Have you ever sent over the materials and answers to the questions your clients asked, as you half-heartedly said you would in the meeting?

There will be days when you get woken up at 4.30am for a conference call on the other side of the globe or by your neighbour's dog, or by your partner, but the thing that matters above all else here is that you don't drop your standards for excellence in sales just because you're tired.

"I'll do it later," becomes too late. It makes you look like you don't care about your clients and that you aren't a person of your word. This damages your integrity to your clients and with yourself. Do what's right, not what's easy. It's easy to stay in bed under the covers, it's easy to keep watching that cool new Netflix show, and it's not easy to force yourself to dig out all the answers to the client's tricky questions, think about how best to articulate your response and send it off at 10.37pm at night.

Now I want to tell you a story about Haikal Johari. He is the 44-year-old father of two and executive chef leading the charge at the Michelin star Alma Restaurant in Singapore.

He was a passionate superbike racer, then one day he suffered a huge crash in Pattaya, Thailand, and he was airlifted to NUH in Singapore. Haikal ended up paralysed from the neck down. He was given only a 3% chance of ever moving again.

For 10 months, he made small recoveries, first arms starting to move, then legs. He stuck with the rehabilitation for his kids, even though there were days when he didn't want to do it. All the while, his mind was at work, even though his body didn't move. He was thinking of ways to improve the restaurant, to innovate the menu. He managed to maintain his Michelin star whilst overcoming his disability. Being disabled would not stop him. He brought in a new chef and then oversaw all the orders, the service, the restaurant, the menu composition.

During covid-19 he was reminded of the health care workers that had helped him mentally to overcome the challenge of weaning off the breathing machine back in 2015 after his accident. He wanted to do something to help them, so he and his team set about directing their attention and the kitchen towards creating lunches for the nurses at NUH in Singapore. This is remarkable. This is inspiration. Not only did he turn his attention to how he could do more to help but he also managed to maintain the 1 Michelin star at the restaurant overseeing the operation from a wheelchair.

This is just one example that we are not bound by physical realities, that when the mind makes a commitment to strive for the best, to maintain high standards and not give up in the face of adversity, then we can do it, and you can do it!

"I told my team that the most important thing in life is to never give up. If you give up, you've already lost. We will try every avenue to find a solution, even if it means selling burgers. Even if we fail on one day, we will try again the next."

– EXECUTIVE CHEF HAIKAL JOHARI, ALMA SINGAPORE

MOTIVATION SUMMARY

- Staying motivated is your responsibility, no one else's, and that's great because you are in control of just how big you want to go.

- When you get disheartened or frustrated, remember the bigger picture, sell yourself on your dream – your big vision.

- Conduct possibility projections and visualisation.

- Set big audacious goals and write your journal daily.

- Complete your gratitude list daily.

- Hitting sales targets is a formula.

- Get a mentor and ask for their guidance.

- Keep your standards high, no matter what – there is no room for compromise.

- When you experience an adversity, pull out the 4A's strategy and get moving.

- Overwhelm dampens effectiveness, remember to focus 60% or more of your time on important non urgent tasks.

- Expect rejection and look for ways to achieve systematic desensitisation.

- Do what is right, not what is easy.

- You are doing a disservice to your clients by not telling them about your product or offering.

CHAPTER 6

Energy – To win more deals, accelerate your momentum and carry on when others would stop

"Enthusiasm is by far the highest paid quality on earth, probably because it is one of the rarest; yet it is one of the most contagious."

– FRANK BETTGER

INTRODUCTION

Now you've got your mindset, opportunities, and motivation right, you're dialled in. You're making fantastic progress towards becoming a revenue generating machine! The fact is you're prepared and ready for anything. It's safe to say there's a certain level of momentum that's now self-propelling – congratulations, you're moving!

The momentum train has left the station, you've gone from zero to one, but in order to go supersonic there's another component that you need above all else, and that is energy!

If you want to make the big bucks – I mean millions that will provide generational wealth for you and your family for decades to come – then developing awareness of your energetic state and how to direct it at will is a skill you must master. In fact, mastering energy can help you achieve anything you desire, whether that's more happiness, fulfilment, friendships, love, anything you put your mind to, not just sales.

Energy is so darn important and yet so underutilized in sales because it is little understood and not taught in schools. The average salesperson gets thrown off by negative client meetings. They derail themselves just as they are beginning to make progress, and this is one of the biggest causes of failure in sales. They repeat this cycle and can't understand why, just as they seem to be developing momentum, it all goes wrong.

Sales energy relates to the amount of enthusiasm, abundance, positivity, faith and passion you are able to infuse in your interactions. It doesn't matter how the interaction occurs, it can be over video, on the phone, via email, in a message, what's crucial is how you show up.

Energy aids your ability to influence and develop inspired plans and ideas that will carry you upwards towards success. Those in the top 1% know that careful management of their energetic state is paramount to achievement. It's a way of living for them, their identity.

Energetic transfer is one big way to influence people, whether that's a large client, your team or even yourself.

Let's dive in and find out more about the thing that's going to send your sales meteoric.

WHAT IS ENERGY?

There are a couple of different ways we can think about energy when it comes to sales, the first is having energy, as in feeling physically and mentally ready to take on each new day. Energy as in kilojoules, nutrition and alertness to produce gumption, get up and go, a sense of urgency, determination to succeed no matter what and the ingenuity to go into battle and fight for your dreams.

The second is energy as a frequency that's vibrational, the energy you put out into the world. This is energy you radiate and give off to those around you and what you attract as a result. It is your energetic state.

This chapter will focus less on the cultivation of energy, in the sense of eating well and having enough sleep, and more on getting on the right vibrational frequency of what you want so that you magnetise sales, attract them to you and experience the abundance.

The first principle you must get to grips with is that all energy vibrates on frequencies. Match your energy with the frequency of the outcome you want and, hey presto, it will begin to manifest. It's as simple as that. Match the frequency with the outcome and it can't help but happen. This is how you attract what you want! They literally don't teach this stuff, but they should!

There are levels of frequencies, and all frequencies are connected to the next in an infinite number. In order to move upwards you must raise the level of your energetic vibration. Sounds simple, right? It is. But you need to be able to do it surrounded by rude clients, people that piss you off, annoying colleagues, bad bosses, traffic jams, computer crashes, screaming kids, the news (and we all know how cheerful that is!) etc.

Staying connected to the frequency of the lifestyle you want can be a mission at first but over time you will become more adept at aligning and raising your own vibration to the level of your biggest dreams. This is where the magic happens!

Why don't salespeople do this already? Why aren't more people talking about this? Why isn't this taught in schools if it is so important? Great questions. The reason is the majority of people are unaware that this power to create what they want on the outside in reality exists within them.

That's why this chapter on energy is vitally important for you to understand. When you operate at a higher vibration, you'll experience less pain in your body, you'll be more at peace, have more clarity and experience greater love.

Levels of energy, levels of frequency.

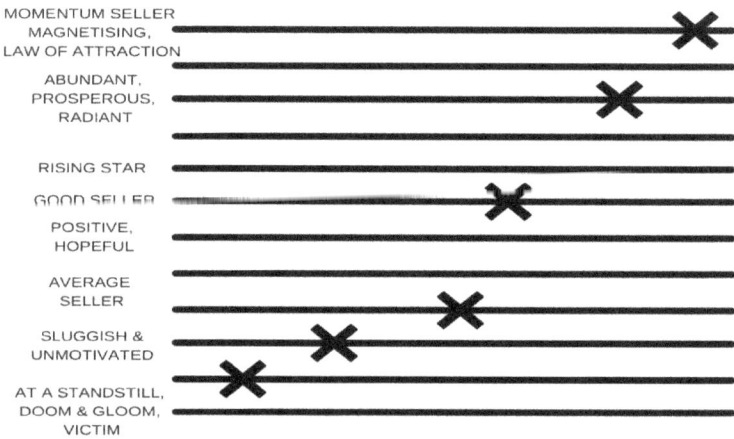

FIGURE 19: INFINITE NUMBER OF FREQUENCIES

Think back to different times in your life, these were just different levels of frequency expressed by the results that you were getting.

254

Everything is energy, just in different states. This is going back to science class but think about solid, liquid and gas. The Apple Mac I am using to write this book, the table, the chair, water, clouds, sand, the oak tree, light, it is all energy, moving at different vibrational speeds.

These invisible frequencies can either vibrate at a high, medium or a low level on a spectrum and this affects the state of the object. For example, water can be solid, liquid or gas, what changes is its level of energetic vibration.

In a steam engine, water vibrating at a high level, called steam, is forced into a small cylinder and used to drive the turbine, creating momentum. This is focused energy.

The thing is, energy is forever changing form, it is transmuting, to use a Napoleon Hill phrase. And it's the same for you, you are changing, and so will your results when you get on the right frequency and stay on it.

To this end, you have to change what you believe is possible and then start acting like the person you want to become. Again, it sounds simple, but we are fickle creatures, we don't adapt to change without a fight. Your habits and routines are ingrained in you, your natural tendencies, upbringing and mindset all control what you are doing right now and the results you are getting. Therefore, it makes sense that in order to change what you are getting on the outside you must first change what's within.

By changing your thoughts, the way you think about possibility, about optimism, about sales, then you change your behaviours.

The way this happens is your conscious mind can accept or reject any thought you give it. You have the power to choose, when you choose thoughts that empower you, that take you up rather than down and **you repeat them**, you imprint them on your subconscious mind. This is important because your subconscious is connected to infinite intelligence (if you don't know what this is, read *Think and Grow Rich*, Napoleon explains it).

Your subconscious mind will believe whatever you feed it, bad or good. Therefore, you must guard your mind and protect it from anything that's not good. It also means that if you start acting and living from a place in the future (i.e. a future you, the person you want to become), then your subconscious mind won't know the difference and it will think you've already achieved everything you set out to do. Living and acting from this place is key.

Say your goal is to become a millionaire, to sell the most in your company's history and to have the most impact you can on the world, when you make decisions and take action from this place, as if it has already happened, your subconscious mind already believes you have achieved it. The actions you take will be aligned with those of that person, the future you, and because you will be operating on that frequency, you will therefore get those results.

All of this is to say energy is very powerful and deserves your attention, research and continual study.

In the following sections, we'll address the things that can trip you up around getting you off track when it comes to energy, and I'll show you some ways to raise your energetic vibration so that you can improve the results you are getting in your life.

Don't panic if this all sounds a little strange. Trust me, it's the law of attraction and this is the way it works. I also happen to believe in God; therefore, when we talk about infinite intelligence and universal power, I am referring to Him. Being connected to a higher power like this, to source energy and training yourself to move through the world as an energetic being, a spiritual being, you will see things that you didn't see before. Opportunities, ideas, plans to show you the way to achieve your big goal will then appear. This is part of the process, when your subconscious mind has become so ingrained with what you want that you desire it, you've mixed your wants with emotion and created a burning desire to have it, your mind with infinite intelligence will produce the means to get there.

This is why it's hard for people to grasp because they go from "I am here, and I want to be there. How will I get there?" But the thing is that you don't need to worry about the "*how*", all you need to do is create the deep desire and have faith that it is possible for you to have it. Which you know it is because you can imagine it and, as Napoleon says, "whatever your mind can conceive and believe it can achieve." This is what he means: you've got to know you can have it, believe it is possible, before the means of getting it will be revealed, and then take action all the time with faith, persistence, purpose.

HOW DOES ENERGY BUILD SALES MOMENTUM?

As discussed, energy is transferable, it can be passed from person to person, colleague to colleague, from salesperson to client and your mind to your energetic state. Think of it like an invisible aura that floats around you; everyone has their own bubble and the higher the energetic vibration the more influential and magnetic it is to other bubbles of a similar likeness.

Much like in sales, the world class know the powerful effects of energy. They understand that in order to win deal after deal, their energetic state has more to do with the outcome than almost anything else.

The sale is won or lost by the energetic vibration you put out into the world. You must match the energetic frequency of the outcome you want.

Let me ask you this, have you ever come across a nervous sales-person? How did you know they were nervous?

The answer is, you could feel it, the energy was off. Despite the stumbling of words and the awkward silences, the most powerful sign you received, whether you knew it or not, was that their energetic vibration was off.

In contrast, a world class salesperson can raise their energetic vibration at will. They are able to meet the opportunity with the enthusiasm it demands and focus their attention on you, the client.

In doing this, they confidently walk you through their product or service with composure. You feel like you are whisked away on a jour-ney, the conversation flows naturally, in an efficient manner that still manages to transfer their belief, feelings and passion for the offering to you, the client. A world class salesperson *gives* the client their attention.

As a client in the presence of a world class salesperson, your ener-getic vibration is also changed; it rises to meet the salesperson, you get inspired, and you feel alive. Just like a chemical reaction in the lab, you absorb and are influenced by their vibration and begin to imagine the possibilities. This is where a transformation takes place and the power of momentum truly takes hold as you both move up levels together.

Yes, the conviction to do this is underpinned by solid preparation, in-depth product knowledge and the skill of the salesperson (due to repetition and experience) to present in a succinct manner, but the thing surrounding all of this is their energetic state that allows them to think clearly and adapt on the fly.

When your energy is right, as a momentum seller you can intu-itively adapt the conversation at will and the client becomes swept away in the magnetism of it all, in relation to their specific needs.

Penny drop moments will happen as if planned, they will see and believe in your conviction, and this will in turn influence their own. Clients can feel your genuine enthusiasm and belief in the product you are selling and whilst they know that your goal is to sell, they feel confident that you wouldn't be recommending it to them if you didn't feel it was the absolute best solution for them. Most of all, clients can feel your commitment to them, to help them solve problems and work through the questions, challenges and situation at hand with them.

This is where you win more deals than you know what to do with, where you're so busy that you're working double over time just because you're filling out order sheets. This is where you become a perpetual winner, here you really become dangerous (in a good way).

When you understand the role that energy plays in winning business and you can direct its power at will, boy you'll have transformed into a sales gun.

This means dialing up what you think is possible and becoming way more optimistic about life and your sales business. **To sell more, close more deals and to actually change the minds of others, you need to sell yourself on your product, your attitude and your passion for never giving up. You have to believe that it can happen for you.**

Any salesperson that does not understand the vital part that energy plays in making the sale is destined for underperformance and never fully achieving what they are truly capable of. You have got to get yourself in sync with your mission, motivated, vibrating in a high energetic state every day so that you are bursting at the seams to go sell.

The ability to generate a high energetic state and bucket loads of enthusiasm under all circumstances, every day, even when you don't feel like it, is what separates the very top salespeople from all the rest of the pack.

At the very top, winners are separated by millimeters not miles. The difference between masterful handling of clients that precedes securing game-changing deals that radically change your life and the life of your family and falling short and losing the deal is all in the details – and energy has EVERYTHING to do with it.

It's not something you can wish you had without study and repetition, to consistently drum up enthusiasm, to add positivity to your clients' lives and lift them up, even when you aren't feeling like it or aren't a fan of them, is a skill. It's a muscle that you can train, and train it you must.

Think of raising your level of energy and operating at a high frequency with enthusiasm as your mental gym, and we are going to work out every day from now on!

It's what makes all the difference and it's what will transform your life as a salesperson. Here you will build your legacy and have magical experiences that you'll look back on when it's all over and be thankful that you lived life this way. You will flourish! Think of any salesperson you admire. Whether it's from a TV show or within your own company, think about what they do differently. They are able to generate enthusiasm in such vast quantities, under pressure and in times of great stress and difficulty as well as when everything is going right. They can perform this feat come rain or shine. They plant seeds in the spring and reap in the autumn, regardless of how they feel.

Guys and girls, this is the chapter about something most sales books don't tell you. This is the detail you need to absorb to become a walking, talking magnet for sales.

In this chapter I will show you how to:

■ Take on new challenges

■ Change your vibration

- Understand the cycle of giving

- Protect your energy and say "no"

- Stay focused and create Momentum Moments

- Deal with competitors

- Stay consistent and committed to the mission

- Raise your identity

- Understand the power of intention.

Sustained Momentum relies on energy. When energy is focused, it transforms states and becomes the fuel that burns to produce momentum. You can do everything right but if you miss energy, you won't reach full speed and who wants that?! **Not us, we're here to break sales records, create a name for ourselves and build businesses that change the world for the better.** I want this for you so badly. I want you to experience the shift in your sales process, to feel what it's like to become the top seller in your team, company and industry, and to then surpass your wildest dreams where your only competition is you.

Think about it this way. Just as with the body, if you fail to give yourself any fuel (e.g. food) you'll eventually stop moving; it's the same in sales; starve your sales process of energy (inspired action) and your engine will run out of steam and the sale will go cold.

This applies to you as much as it does to the buyer. They will run out of steam because you are failing to pass it on to them because you don't have any.

You might be going through the motions, but the way in which you speak, your attitude, and the way you carry yourself will all tell a different story, which has an effect on the buyer and causes them not to buy.

Energy is highly contagious. That's why in Napoleon Hill's masterpiece *Think and Grow Rich* he talks about thoughts as vibrations, you can literally transfer thought energy into its physical equivalent by being on the same energy wavelength as another person. Because you are both in sync, ideas and inspired action flows, your belief gets stronger, and with persistence and faith, the outcome is produced in reality.

It's the same in sales – you must feed your prospects with your energy and enthusiasm.

Likewise, energy conservation is paramount. You must know where to direct your energy and protect it from anyone or anything that seeks to steal it. Get yourself in a high energy state, even when your drafting emails, when you're prospecting and building out strategies – these tasks should be conducted from a place of openness, higher consciousness and positivity.

We'll discuss it all, so come on, my friend, let's begin.

USE YOUR DESIRE TO PUSH YOURSELF TO TAKE ON NEW CHALLENGES

When you have a burning desire to achieve new levels of success you can use this to drive you to take on new challenges. Rather than focusing on how you might come across, what could go wrong, what you are afraid of, you use your desire to take action in ways you normally wouldn't.

This could be speaking on stage to thousands of people at a conference or webinar. **When ideas and plans come to you about how to achieve your goals, you use the desire you have within to push forward and take hold of them.** Fear, old habit patterns and doubts, will try to stop you but you know that your desire is too strong not to go for it. It's the way forward, these plans have been given to you as a result of your desire, so believe that it is possible and now is the time for you to take inspired action.

In order to centre yourself to do things that scare you, get quiet, take deep breaths and connect with the visualisation of how you want your life to be. Sit quietly in this state, focused only on how it is to live within your vision. What's your ideal lifestyle like? Who is the person you want to become? Can you feel your higher faculties starting to rise, your confidence starting to grow? When you connect with a higher plane of thought you move away from fear and towards the light.

You need to touch your dream and do whatever it takes to shift your identity towards being someone who does the things you are being guided to do. If you don't, you're not in alignment, if you do, then you'll see the momentum that it creates in your life. You will see how your life changes.

When I first became a bestselling author, it required an identity change. It didn't happen right away but over time I loved seeing myself as an author and doing what authors do. This came from giving talks at book launches, signings, interviews with the press, at first it was all unusual for me, of course, because I hadn't had these types of experiences before, but then as I stepped into this new world, it became my world. The firsts became seconds, thirds, and so on. I expanded my world and my vision became closer. I was taking the steps necessary to live the life that I wanted.

It's the same in sales – the more you take the steps, the closer you get and eventually your vision is just your life.

Don't hold yourself back, if it creates upward momentum in all areas of your life, it doesn't matter what it takes to make the shift to achieve this level of thinking. You might:

■ Invest in a new sales strategy, marketing plan, mentor or idea

■ Have breakfast at a nice restaurant

■ Spend time in luxurious surroundings at a spa, massage or hotel retreat

- Do things that scare you

- Push yourself to take on things you don't think you'll be able to do

- Take a new route home, making life more spontaneous so your neural pathways develop creative ways of thinking.

Would a momentum seller worry about making the investment or the $20 spent on breakfast? No! They would do what it takes – what they know through inspired action helps to create the life of their dreams. Would they flinch at taking on a marathon? Climbing a mountain? Hell no!

THE POWER OF REPETITION

Every single day for a year I want you to read nonfiction books, listen to podcasts, watch inspirational videos on YouTube, and surround yourself with the content from the masters to reprogram your mind.

The only content you should be digesting is from people who have been there and done what you want to do. Why do you think this book resonates with you? It's because I've been there and done what you want to do, creating an unstoppable wave of momentum in sales. I know exactly how it's done. I don't just think it, I know it.

Get up one hour earlier and use this time to study this material on energy. I want you to go deep on it and become so in tune that you can captivate an audience at the next dinner party you attend and be seen as an expert on the topic of energy, frequencies and changing your program.

Topics include: The law of attraction, manifesting, visualisation, affirmations, goal setting, developing your intuition, asking for divine guidance, understanding your wants and desires, deepening your awareness of how the conscious and subconscious mind works and changing habits.

It is what you must do to reach the highest levels of success in sales and in life. The ability to understand where you want to go and then put it into action is one of life's greatest skills and it comes from you developing your awareness around how to do this.

Why repetition? It's because you need to fix these principles in your subconscious mind so they become your roadmap and you can change your behaviour, identity and perception of how you see the world.

PRO TIP
Repetition

- *Study before everyone gets up in your house.*

- *Make sure it's focused study (i.e. the right environment).*

- *Combine it with an activity so that it becomes a habit (e.g. make your coffee and then write in your journal, go for a bike ride and listen to the same podcast each day).*

- *Read your mantra, life goal, gratitude list before turning out the light before bed so that it's the last thing you think about before you dream – expect ideas to come to you in your sleep, wake up and write them down.*

- *Put signs up around your house, pictures of your vision, quotes you want to meld into your mind.*

- *Buy an A2-sized board and draw out your goals, put it where you will see it every day.*

WHAT TO DO WHEN YOU'RE IN BAD ENERGETIC VIBRATION

We've spoken about energy changing forms. When you are in a bad mood it will damage your sales. I want you to be like a radiant beam of light when you are selling.

We've all been there; you're having a rubbish day. An argument with your significant other, the neighbour starts drilling the wall, your kid is screaming, a deal goes south, someone cuts you off in traffic, a bird poops on your shirt, a car splashes you with a puddle, the baby vomits right before your big pitch and your taxi is late… and all before 10am.

I get it, bad stuff is happening, and you've still got to go sell. It's like you're a walking magnet for it.

Here's where we crank it up a level so you can make it rain even when these negative nasties are coming at you from all angles.

Bad energy is bad for business. No one wants to do business with a cranky ass, uptight, pessimistic, angry dude. Ever!

Here's what you do:

Back the F away from your computer, don't answer the phone or another email and go directly to the gym, boxing ring, HIIT class, start running, get out in nature. Go now! You need to be somewhere and doing something that changes your state and to do that we've got to get you moving. Fight the urge to push through and continue working, you'll do more damage than good. You've got to change states from sluggish and deflated to radiant and light, and exercise is the number one way to do this quickly.

Next, be mindful of your thoughts and reduce your complaining. I know it feels good, but it's taking you in the wrong direction. Guard that mind!

Put your headphones in and get Level Up, Calm or Headspace

on. In this bad vibe you're going to be attracting all kinds of problems, so we want to move you off it asap.

To shift your energetic vibration even more quickly, start being extra
helpful to everyone around you (as if you weren't already), opening doors,
giving way, being extra courteous, even give away cash to someone in
need. These are all awesome practical methods of rapidly overcoming
your bad mood. Making someone else's day who is less fortunate is an
excellent way to get some perspective and begin the shift.

PERSONAL STORY
Rejection when trying to give hurts

I'm a giver, not because I know it all comes back but because
it's the right way to be. We were born to give, and also to
receive. We must learn to receive gladly. Many people understand the giving part but fall down completely when it comes
to receiving. This can be anything, compliments, gifts, ges-
tures, they don't welcome them and as a result they stop the
flow. By receiving you are also giving the other person the
opportunity to give and without your receiving there can be
no giving. Do you see what I mean?

I find that when I try to give in a big way, like I want to
donate 3,000 books worth $75,000 RRP to universities,
libraries, schools, or charities who could take the books, sell
them for $1 and make a profit, I find most just can't get their
head around it. They reject the offer outright.

I can feel it right away, as their energy is sceptical. I approached the National Library in Singapore, they said outright that they did not want to carry the books. I was surprised because these books are helping Singaporeans every day. I explained to them that universities and colleges have used my books in their courses, but this didn't do anything.

OK, so now I am frustrated. Why? Is it because I want to give, and these guys won't let me? Is it ego? I want my books to be seen by more people. Is it because my mission is to serve, and these guys are blocking my mission?

The truth is, it doesn't matter what the reason is, not everyone you want to help is going to see it as help. Everyone is on their own journey and so you can't force it.

You need to think of this as opening up the path for something even bigger. If the library doesn't want the books, that means they are meant to go somewhere else.

It's a subtle change in mindset but it's powerful because it applies to sales. Sometimes you can't for the life of you understand why a client isn't buying, when your product makes so much sense logically in your mind. What this is telling you is to keep going and look elsewhere. Not to keep battling through where it's not being received but to put your energy elsewhere and keep on going. You are destined for something greater!

This way you don't get deflated and angry, you just know you're trying to do the right thing, and everyone is on their own journey, so you shift focus. If a client can't see your value yet, you show them by working well with other clients, eventually they will come to their own realisation.

Your energy will be able to receive them when they are ready because you didn't try to force it or get angry when they rejected you. This leaves the path open. You must see yourself as a path opener, planting seeds for the future that will germinate once the soil is matured, once the elements are right. You just keep planting seeds and go where they are received.

Deflation and hurt comes because you are focusing on what could have been. It feels like a loss. What I am training you to do here is to see that nothing has been lost. Energy cannot be destroyed therefore you can take the feedback and move forward positively to your next mission. You will see when you move in this way, in this spirit, that it all comes together at the right time and life has a funny way of bringing it together so perfectly that you'll know it was planned.

I wouldn't be surprised if I end up doing a huge talk for the launch of this book across the libraries in Singapore and they end up taking all my books. **When your intention is right, nothing and no one can stop what's meant to be.**

TURNING ENERGY AROUND IN THE ROOM

Transmutation. You're about to pitch and you feel a bit nervous, there's a guy in the room and he looks angry, he's not much fun, plus it's been a while, you recently had covid, so you've been off for a couple of weeks and now you're unsure and questioning your ability. Can you remember what you've got to say in the pitch? What if I have a mind blank?

The issue is you bring this energy into the room with you. The way forward is to do whatever it takes to make yourself feel comfortable and remember that it's all good. If you're cold, buy a hoodie; if you need food, get food. In sales we can forget to look after ourselves and it comes at a cost – we aren't mentally present; we get too worried about being put on the spot or looking foolish.

What matters is you feeling like the expert, showing up in all your glory. One of the best speakers I have seen is Shivani Gopal, Founder of The Remarkable Woman. When Shivani speaks she owns the room. She does this because she's prepared energy-wise. She came with a mission and is going to show up in all her glory.

It's already within you. Muscle memory comes back quickly. When you let go and trust that you are where you are meant to be, it will flow with ease. The right people will show up to the meeting, the right questions will be asked, and you will be provided with the right words to carry you forwards. Take a deep breath and let it all go. You are light, you are joyous, you are the enthusiasm needed to create the sale. **All you need to do is get on the same frequency as the outcome you want, and it shall be.**

Authentically show that this is your superpower and, when you do, trust me, you will start getting feedback that your session was the most engaging, not like all the other boring sessions the client had to sit through. Bring that wave of energy with you.

If you get on a call and everyone is deflated, let your authenticity and imagination light the fire. It's totally fine to stop presenting at any point as you don't have to present; if the room is flat, get real with your audience and mix it up. Stop presenting and just chat to them. I do this all the time. If I feel the crowd aren't with me, I get creative.

Sometimes that's what's needed, in order to stand out, to win business, do not follow the crowd and be like everyone else.

1. PROTECTING YOUR ENERGY AND ENERGETIC STATE IS THE ULTIMATE STRATEGY

LEARNING WHEN TO SAY "NO"

Saying "no" in sales is a phenomenal skill. It might sound counter-intuitive but knowing when to say "no" is a core difference between the average and the world class. World class salespeople know that their time and energy is valuable, therefore they don't want to waste it.

They still go after plenty of opportunities, but they cut through the noise to sift out the finest sales opportunities with the most potential. This is about being strategic. Learn to get into the habit of making "no" your default answer in your mind while you assess the importance of the request.

Not all requests for proposal (RFP), meetings or quarterly business reviews (QBR) are worthy of your time. Filter the requests and protect your time so you can go after the business you want.

Ask yourself, does this align with my vision? Will doing this take me closer to it? If not, then reject.

Here's the formula:

REQUEST + PAUSE + CONSIDERATION = PROFITABLE OUTCOME

VS

REQUEST + YES = OVERWHELM + LACK OF RESULTS

The later equation plays out automatically via your habitual response. When you automatically default to "yes" without consideration of the request you devalue and disrespect your priorities.

The fact is some things just aren't *that* important. Not everything that comes across your desk requires your attention, nor does it have to go down in the way it's presented. You can push back, tighten the timeframe and influence the output so that it gets the amount of your energy that's appropriate.

The other advantage of making "no" your default is that you now have the time you need to spend on the things that matter. **When world class salespeople think about how to structure their working day, they are spending 60%+ on important non-urgent activities**.

This magical transformation takes place when the salesperson moves up a level from mediocre to advanced, these people spend more time developing relationships, thinking about strategic partnerships and ways to maximise their resources, figuring out how to do what everyone else is doing but better, differentiated and with impact.

DON'T LET DISTRACTIONS ZAP YOUR ENERGY

It's a game of levels.

Much like the advice "if you're the smartest person in the room, you need to find a new room", the sales game is no different.

In order to improve your sales so you have record breaking months, month on month, quarter on quarter, year on year, you need to get better at managing **what you focus your energy on.**

It's costing you BIG TIME!

Think about it this way, if someone or something is dominating your thoughts it's taking away precious mental and physical energy from you achieving your goals. That's why you need to significantly cut out and eliminate anything that limits your growth, confidence and desire to get after it.

When you get new ideas but don't have the time to explore them. When you hear about radical innovations, new ways to prosper and become more effective at your craft but you don't set aside time to learn about them, you are potentially missing out on millions of dollars.

This is where you really need to get honest with yourself about what matters. You need to have an image of that person you want to become in your mind. What characteristics do they have? What are they doing? How do they operate? Now compare that to what you are doing currently.

This is where you need to close the gap. Can you see the person you currently are achieving the things you wrote down in your big vision? Do you show up with vitality and an unstoppable zest for life, that won't take no for an answer? Are you constantly in pursuit of your big vision and doing everything in your power to control your energy and focus so the very best of yourself is directed towards where it counts?

You need to act like the person you want to become! That's it! Make decisions as they would, operate and live life to the full as they would. You need to project into the future and bring this person into your life now. That's how you change your habits, rituals and how you become more in life.

If you hear yourself say, "I'd love to learn more about it, but I don't have time", then you need to give yourself a slap across the face. I am guilty of this too. It can be such an easy, subtle thought process that you don't even notice it, and it can happen multiple times a day.

This type of language needs to STOP, it is limiting you and putting the brakes on game changing ideas before they've had a chance to sprout and, most of all, it damages your perception of what is possible. You need to lean into these moments and force yourself to make the time because it's never a question of not enough time. It's a question of priorities. If it was a priority to you then you would do it. This is where you level up and take responsibility for your results and act like the person you want to become. It's strange, uncomfortable and oddly exhilarating to change your mindset in this way, but it's what you must do to become more successful.

PRO TIP
Block it out

Block out time in your calendar daily to think, to follow your curiosity and to ask yourself "is what I am doing right now the best use of my time?" In order to expand, you must give yourself time to explore new ideas and be creative, to think about new strategies and moves that you can be making to expand your business.

Highly successful people design their life to be centred around their biggest priorities, they treat their energy and mental capacity as more valuable than gold.

Without a clear understanding of what you value in your life, you won't take a deeper look to see if your daily actions are in alignment with what you say you want (i.e. your goals).

Everyone has goals, even those who say they don't have goals have goals; it might just be to be lazy all day or to have a stress-free existence. That is their priority.

It's an illusion to think that you don't have priorities, or you don't know them. Take a look at what you do each day, those are your priorities. How you spend your time and energy, what your mind absorbs each day, what you think about, that's your priority, and those are your goals.

If you want new outcomes, you need to organise your life around the priorities and actions that will take you in that direction, little by little each day, like climbing a mountain.

> *"Remember that if you don't prioritise your life someone else will."*

– GREG MCKEOWN, ESSENTIALISM

The reason so many people fail to reach the goals they set each year is because they don't prioritise the actions that are required and they aren't willing to go through the level of pain and suffering, hard work and discipline to get there. They let other people's opinions shape them, they have great ideas but don't explore them because they get distracted by small talk, gossip, internet memes or just let life's endless conveyer belt of unimportant non-urgent tasks get in the way.

In reality, the truth is, they don't want it badly enough to make it back to the thought or action that they were doing before they got distracted.

That takes discipline. It's hard and it's why so few get to that level of success. It takes effort but that's the thing, it's the way you get yourself to level up, to think in higher realms of possibility and ultimately to take responsibility for the direction of your life.

When you become masterful at protecting your time, and more importantly your energy, learning to get unhooked from distraction and get back to work, you will make progress, and the more you do it, the more you will see gradual success. It builds, and momentum is ever so slightly gained, but keep doing it and you'll see it increase and the results get bigger. Discipline allows you to focus and direct the momentum you are building so that you go in the direction of your vision. You must stay on track.

MINI MOMENTUM BUILDER
1. schedule Momentum Moments and
2. capture inspiration

This is a strategic nudge towards creating the habit of sticking with ideas when they flash into your mind, learning to set time aside to develop them.

Schedule 15-minute slots throughout the day for specific tasks that you will do to drive momentum, to keep feeding the fire. Lock it in your diary now and call it "Momentum Moments" – this is where you do the things you've been thinking to do but have put off. These should be tasks that accelerate your business, like setting up an ad campaign, interviewing that virtual PA, or following up on leads with a new offer.

When you have sparks of inspiration in the night, force yourself to wake up and write them down. Thoughts like this happen for a reason, they are showing you the way and they are priceless. The mind solves problems in your sleep.

The process for capturing Flashes of Inspiration:

1. *Put a pen and paper on your bedside table.*

2. *Write down any flashes of inspiration exactly as they come to you (phone, word, journal, hand – capture the thought).*

3. *Act upon the inspirational thought with the same emotion of excitement.*

4. *If you can't get to it immediately, schedule two 15-minute windows during your day to take inspired action on your thoughts.*

5. *Commit to pushing yourself harder in this area of your life and watch miracles unfold.*

High performers understand that they must do what others aren't willing to do to go places that are extraordinary, they get that you've got to put in the work and there are things that can accelerate you along the way, such as the game-changing strategies above.

Sometimes to sustain momentum the things you do might not look like momentum. It might be rigorous planning and strategy so that you can execute with accuracy. So that the irons you are putting into the fire have the biggest pay off, with the best strategy behind them. This is where you think a few moves ahead and plant the seeds so that they grow by the time you need them.

I'll give an example. It's like when I'm at the beach with my son, he loves nothing more than to get me to dig holes in the sand so that the ocean can fill them. He puts me to work right away, directing me where to dig.

Once I've dug the first hole, if I am not strategic and I don't get back to work by digging the second hole further down the beach, he'll get bored when the ocean stops filling up his current hole.

It's about planning a few moves ahead so there's always a new hole always ready to be filled with water, and just like in sales your pipeline is always filled with top opportunities. You've got to keep moving, but in this case, using the beach analogy, doing the work might not look like momentum at the time because the result (i.e. the water filling the hole) hasn't happened yet. The payoff is in the future.

If I tried to do the work once the waves roll in, then it's too late, the opportunity is upon us. It's too difficult to dig in the wet sand once water is all around with nothing to capture it in.

The time to dig a fresh hole was before the waves came in.

It's the same in sales. You need to get ahead of the wave whilst riding the current one. You need to spin new plates whilst keeping your current plates spinning without letting them go off balance and crash. You need to stay on track whilst laying the future track ahead of you.

I need to maintain the first hole that I dug, sometimes clearing out debris and silt that has filled it up. That's maintenance and it's also momentum. It looks like time spent away from digging new opportunities but what it really is, is capturing future value by retaining repeat clients.

This is sales flow; this is momentum in sales.

PICK YOUR BATTLES: KNOW WHO IS NOT WORTH YOUR ENERGY

Is it worth getting angry at the postman, the doctor or the receptionist who makes a snarky comment or provokes you? The answer is always a resounding no, you were born for bigger and better things than this. By now you know how incredibly valuable your energy is so to expend it on pointing out and proving why these people are wrong and you are right, actually means that you lose.

I know it's hard and you want to give them an earful but it is important to know which battles are worth fighting and which are just a complete waste of time.

If you let it rip on someone that has wronged you, you'll waste your most precious resource (your energy), then you'll need to cool off, and vent and slowly come back down to normal. By that point all your creative inputs are likely to have disappeared, leaving you no further on in the quest to make more sales, or promote your services.

Battles cost you time, therefore choose to fight the ones that matter, those hurdles and challenges that are standing in the way of you and your goal. That is where to focus, not on the small inconsequential meaningless stuff. Ignore it and move on, make a joke about it, laugh it off and carry on forwards with executing your mission in a high vibe energetic state.

A couple of ways to ensure you're channelling good vibes and attracting the right situations to you are as follows:

1. Wish three people (you don't like) well. This stops you carrying that energy.

2. Do one random act of kindness each day.

I told you some things might be alien to you, but I promise you, if you are having bad thoughts about someone, this is not a vibe you want so sending them good wishes actually turns it around. The same with doing a random act of kindness for a stranger. The thought process you engage in builds your character and an incredible life.

HOW TO DEAL WITH COMPETITORS TO MINIMISE ENERGY DEPLETION

When dealing with competition, don't make the mistake of trying to one up them. It is best to make small talk but not get into business discussions that compromise your strategic ambitions or reveal sensitive information.

As a world class salesperson, you are not influenced by the competition, you have a strategy and you intend to execute it. Competitors can be friends, mind you. However, the same applies whether friends or not – the best way to handle it is to have your own plan rather than chopping and changing based on hearsay and gossip of what the competition is up to.

PRO TIP
Be civil

When meeting competition, whether waiting for a meeting at a client's office or at industry conferences or parties, be civil and friendly, treat them as you would anyone else. Don't feel pressured into answering questions that make you feel uncomfortable and, on the flipside, don't go around boasting about all your recent wins.

The best way to act is with integrity and excellence, remain neutral and, if topics for discussion start to drift into dangerous territory, excuse yourself and find someone else to talk to. This doesn't need to be awkward, simply tell the other person you need to make a phone call, attend to a message, or you spotted someone else you need to catch.

What the best of the best do is recognise where there could be an opportunity for an unlikely partnership, that benefits both parties mutually. Partnerships of this nature can, if handled correctly, provide fruit for everyone, even at the simplest level of referring each other's services or speaking highly of one another. Forming strategic alliances reduces wasted energy spent on defending your position with clients and it can even extend your coverage providing a valuable revenue stream.

Don't read the headlines. After meeting with a competitor, either by chance or intentionally, it can leave you feeling deflated because they are bragging about all the amazing business deals they are doing. However, you are a winner and as a future world class salesperson you won't let the comments or thoughts of another influence your mood or take away from the zest and energy you give out.

Remember that when people talk about what's going to happen in business it is often the most rose-tinted example, where everything goes smoothly and as perfectly as it ever could, and you are left in the dust. But as we know, that just isn't how life works.

When competitors talk about their organisations, they leave out all the pain points, the missed targets, the internal politics, their fears, the micromanagement, and they paint this perfect sunny day's picture that's rarely reflective of the current state. That's why it is best not to read anything into it and stay on your own course putting out 110% every single day.

In the book *Blue Ocean Strategy* by Renée Mauborgne and W. Chan Kim, they talk about innovating, creating new value and bringing it to the market, rather than staying in the Red Ocean, which is chasing client's dollars with similar products to your competitors, pushing prices down and eroding margins. In the Red Ocean it's a race to the bottom.

The Blue Ocean, however, can apply to how you think of your competition. That is to say, don't worry about them or the new product features they are developing. Instead, focus on creating new ways to serve your clients.

As Steve Siebold says, "average compete, world class create."

I have always felt that way – competition is a distraction. The only competition you have is with yourself. Even internal company competitions can reduce focus. Use it to motivate you by all means, but don't let it control you. The real race is with yourself and becoming the best salesperson you can become.

When you focus your energy on what the competition are doing, you are directing your momentum off track. This is a big mistake and will see you crash head on into the land of the mediocre. Focus your energy and momentum on your vision, on where you're taking your business and your goals and dreams. This is where the real battle is won.

THE POWER OF CONSISTENT ENERGY AND COMMITMENT

What are you willing to give to grow your business?

Be honest, are you all in?

Remember, in sales you don't have to be the owner of the business to think of your allocated patch or your client contact list as your own business.

To be successful, as you define it, what are you willing to give?

Really think about it. To live a life of greatness, filled with the kinds of experiences that your grandchildren will be inspired by for years to come, how much are you willing to put in?

It takes energy to attract the right energy. When you commit, you need to go all in. Your energy has to be aligned, on fire, ready for action, because you believe so deeply that you will achieve your goal that nothing can stop you.

Are you willing to get up every day with a smile on your face and think, "Today, I am so grateful that I am going to crush it. Today, huge wins are on their way to me. I am going to give my all to service my clients with excellence."

This is your legacy we are talking about; this is where you face your fears and rise, you push past the frustration, the anger, the upset, the hard, momentous, laborious, painstaking tasks, and you continue to execute on your vision day after day, hour after hour, minute after minute.

Growth comes on the other side of fear. It takes energy to rise up and to keep going, to put the negative thoughts out of your mind and fight for your dream.

I want to introduce you to a man I had the pleasure of interviewing, Iron Cowboy, James Lawrence. He's the only person on the planet to have done what everyone believed to be impossible. In 2021, he completed 100 Ironman length triathlons in 100 days.

For those not familiar with Ironman, it comprises of a 2.4 mile swim, then hopping on a bike for a casual 112 mile bike ride and finally finishing off with a full distance marathon of 26.22 miles. That's an Ironman.

Now imagine doing that, every day, for 100 days! Talk about consistency and the power of showing up!

Not only did this break his own current world record by more than 100%, but it gave inspiration to tens of thousands as to what we are truly capable of when we put our minds to it. James even saved a man from suicide based on his ability to show up and put in the work, day after day.

Energy is powerful and, when you learn to manage it and direct its focus, combined with your consistent effort and commitment, it can produce previously unfathomable results.

Imagine the levels of fatigue he must have faced waking up every day knowing he had to do it all over again, every step, the pain, the chaffing, the blackouts and mental toughness required to continue and endure this feat for 100 days in a row.

When asked, what was the most difficult part of the Conquer 100 or endurance in general? Iron Cowboy responded, "I think it's truly believing in yourself that you can do it. It's belief and conviction. It's getting to the point where you have belief and conviction, where it's impossible to fail."

This statement hit me hard, as it spoke directly to my energetic state. We must believe in our core that what we are doing is worthwhile, and that we will achieve our goal. This is what gives us energy and the stamina to continue on despite the pain, the setbacks and the questioning mind that's tempting us to give up.

In sales, when you're putting in the effort, but you aren't feeling appreciated by your clients, team or company, we can start to question things, but this is where you need to bring it back to your belief in your mission.

When asked about how to tackle fear, Iron Cowboy responded, "People need to break things down until you get to where you gain the success, you gain the momentum and by the time you get there, you're a prizefighter."

How good is this! I believe in both of these points; the power of small wins and how this relates to gaining momentum, if done consistently, will ensure that you dominate.

When you keep your commitments that you make to yourself, it builds your self-confidence. By breaking down the task to the point where it is small enough to complete and win, we can take a step towards our goals and gain momentum.

In sales, to get momentum it's the beliefs and habits you have that will help you surpass your goals. Your beliefs dictate how successful you will be because they impact how disciplined you will be around carrying out your daily tasks and habits.

Do you take time each morning to nourish your mind? Are you investing in yourself by reading, learning and constantly seeking to better yourself as a contributor?

It is the consistency piece that will see you gain strength, see your sales numbers grow beyond recognition and ultimately transform you into a sales superstar. Little things done daily over time have a powerful effect. These micro changes and small wins fuel your self-belief and give you a boost to become a high achiever.

It might sound easy to write down your goals for each day and for the week at the beginning of each week, month and year. It might sound easy to read books that build you for 30 minutes per day. It might sound easy to work out five times a week.

The good news is it is, the difficult part is consistency of action around all the little easy things that will come together to produce an extraordinary life. That's what we are after here, building an extraordinary life for yourself, reaching your goals, doing the impossible and living on that level.

Consistency is what gets you there, so that when you look back on the next five years of your life, it's unrecognisable to where you are today. It looks how you once dreamed it would look.

You have brought the vision into reality by doing the work, consistently, every day. You have made a commitment to finding out how far you can push it, to leaning into your full potential, to reaching for the stars.

If you're facing a challenge or not experiencing the success you want, you must break it down further. Take the task that is ahead of you and break it down into smaller chunks. Maybe you've been focusing on getting through the week but to experience momentum you need to focus on a shorter timeframe and work on winning every day or even every hour.

The momentum comes from the small wins and the self confidence boost comes from overcoming the objective by sticking to your commitments.

When you show up, you put runs on the board in the game of your life. Don't let fear and overwhelm stop you from achieving greatness. There's a prize fighter in there, we just have to let him loose.

When you're on a mission and in full alignment with your goals, there's a pulsating energy you give off. I don't care if it's writing a book, overachieving a sales target or building a business, when you're set on crushing it, the energy changes. When you're on fire you attract other winners.

Stallions like to run together, and when you start winning other winners take notice and migrate into your energetic field of activity.

They come into your circle, so to speak. This is where you start hitting the big time, winning multiple home runs, and things fall into place with a frequency and consistency that's uncanny.

You can almost predict success; you know it will happen and the energy you give off is magnetic. You only have to think of a sale and it's done, in the bag, on its way to you and then your phone rings, you've won the contract, the person you need is right in front of you, the email comes in and the deal is bigger than you expected.

When you evoke the power of consistency, the small wins begin to stack up, day after day, and it rains success down on you like never before. The heavens open and it just keeps pouring. You do a rain dance, and you learn to dance in the rain. You show up daily and do your thing, and everyone around you wonders how you're doing it, but you know it's belief, consistency and small wins over time that lead to greatness.

Go get yourself some of the magnetic energy today and show the world what you're made of. Don't look back, just put one foot in front of the other and keep on going.

Remember, if you're struggling to have success, you've got to break down the task into a smaller area of focus until you can win.

DON'T LET YOUR HIGH ENERGY GET INFLUENCED BY MEDIOCRE COLLEAGUES

In the same vein as combating negative clients during the discovery phase, you also need to reduce your proximity to another potential threat, average salespeople.

If you're spending time with doubters, anxious, stressed out and nervous people who are worried about hitting targets, caught up in the weeds and the minutiae of life, then you will never rise up to your full potential.

Their energy is just bad to be around. It will transfer to the interactions you have with your clients, seep into your family and home life and your mindset will become lack-oriented and limiting.

In the energy stage of the process, we are all about greasing the wheels to go faster, we are seeking freedom, we want to accelerate.

As you become more brilliant at putting these techniques to work and you start to experience greater success, stay away from the average salespeople. Mentor them if you like, but don't be led by them in sales meetings or be prepared to watch your hard-earned pipeline and high-quality leads fly away.

Let me repeat that – stay away from average salespeople, unless you are mentoring them.

The reason why this is important is because you are shifting your habits and getting around poor salespeople with bad habits will limit your growth and I want you to soar high. I want you to shine so do yourself a favour and implement this step – all in!

It is always a good idea to keep tabs on who you are spending your time with across all areas of your life. This is because your network and associations matter and you constantly want to be gravitating towards people who are lighting the world up with their brilliance. You need to be around the movers and shakers in your industry, people who are making the impossible possible, shattering sales records and putting in the work to improve themselves daily.

Keep in mind that you may also need to reevaluate your crew at all levels. This means both who you spend time with at the office and also your personal close group of friends. You want to be in a place where everyone in your circle is aiming higher and willing to push you to become better. This is how you elevate, when you get around people who are going places, the best in their field and who also help people along the way, you'll broaden your awareness and open your mind.

We are opening up and going full throttle.

Most people are trying to straddle both mediocrity and excellence. They want the recognition, status and rewards but aren't able to commit to the behaviours and habits long enough that will get them there.

Instead, they engage in gossip, belittling others, bad mouthing and worse – they waste time and energy playing politics with clients and staff. This is so typical, and it keeps you stuck in motion, with a pessimistic lack mentality focused outlook.

Listen to the conversations your co-workers, your team or your close friends are having.

Are they filled with abundance, possibility and growth?

If not, then you might consider changing your environment. Proximity is power and these folks are holding you back from your greatness. You must fiercely protect your positive energy from energy drainers. When you have a vision, you have to be cutthroat in regard to the things and people you allow in your life, you haven't got time not to be.

Another question, what happens when you share your ideas on how to generate more sales or come up with a new business idea for revenue generation? Do they contribute to it, making it better, do they see the possibility and encourage you to go bigger?

If so, you are in the right place.

If not, then this is another major red flag that it is time to spread your wings and move on. Whether it is colleagues, friends or even family members, you need to be vigilant who you spend your time with. Your subconscious mind is always picking up ideas and receiving messages in the form of energetic vibrations. Thought travels on frequency. If you spend your time with negative people then it will restrict your growth like nothing else by influencing how you think, feel and behave.

Likewise, if you seek to surround yourself with people that are crushing it, then you will rise to meet their standards. You start to expect more of yourself and you'll learn new ways to get increased outcomes.

"Stand guard at the door of your mind." – Jim Rohn

Top salespeople know that you must always be learning and expanding to keep improving and taking your sales game to new levels. Surrounding yourself with other top performers is the only way to go and keep yourself sharp. Iron sharpens iron.

If people around you have bad habits or aren't putting in the work, unfortunately, it probably won't be long until that impacts your sales figures as well. It might not be catastrophic, but it will not be helpful and certainly won't keep you at the top of your game.

The good thing is, average is not you, you are a champion.

THE POWER OF IDENTITY

Your identity plays a huge part in whether you hit sales quotas or not.

Are you someone that constantly wins?

Do you have this identity?

What if you did? Do you think it would change the trajectory of your sales career?

Your identity and how you see yourself, what you stand for, affects your behaviour. If you don't see yourself as an expert salesperson, a person of value, a leader, you'll have a difficult time making it rain.

This is because as humans we are most consistent with our identity. Come rain or shine, we will find ways to live up to our identity.

MINI MOMENTUM BUILDER
What's your identity?

I want you to spend some time today thinking about who you are and what you stand for.

1. *Are you full of energy? Do you find ways to motivate and inspire your clients to action?*

2. *Are you an innovator? Do you find ways to adapt and see opportunities that others don't?*

3. *Are you a visionary? Do you see the future and get ahead of the trends?*

4. *Do you unleash your greatness in times of crisis?*

5. *Are you resilient?*

6. *Are you confident and fun?*

7. *Do you always go the extra mile?*

8. *Are you a winner? Do you stack multiple wins, back-to-back?*

9. *Does success rain down on you?*

10. *Are you honest?*

11. *Are you giving?*

Why is this important? Well, it's because identity has EVERY-THING to do with your energy and your results. If you expect to always exceed your sales quota, then guess what, it's more than likely going to happen because this is who you are.

I realised this when I worked for a company that had a monthly bonus structure. It was awesome! Once I started making my target, for the first month it gave me a boost. In the second month, when I not only hit the target but exceeded it, it drove me even harder. Then by the third month when it happened again and I over delivered, I began to expect it from myself. **It was now my identity. I was someone who expected to exceed my quota. This identity change led me to see myself as someone who consistently overachieves on the goal and not only hits his target but crushes it.** As a result, I would go for streaks of 6 months+ where I'd hit back-to-back multiple wins, sometimes achieving over 245% to target on a monthly basis.

This identity change affected my whole sales career. I see myself as someone who overachieves on sales targets, I expect to win and as a result this is what happens more often than not. I see opportunities other people don't because it's part of who I am.

Your identity is directly related to your behaviour and your actions, this is especially important in times of crisis, when the shit is hitting the fan, when the company is in turmoil and when everyone around you is panicking and making rash decisions.

During these times, you are cool, calm and collected. This is when you make your best decisions and win, because you are a leader.

I hope the significance of what I am sharing has hit you and you spend some time thinking about this as your financial destiny and career in sales is all tied back to one thing – who you are.

YOUR INTENTION

Believe it or not, your intention also plays a part in your energy and vibration. When you intend to do good, when you intend to go out of your way for someone else, to give back, to open up doors for others, then the universe is like a mirror – it will come back to you.

What you put out; you get back. Much like with the section on gratitude and giving, you need to understand the link between your intentions and your clients. This is to say that when you intend to do your best work for them, it will be felt, when you intend to do what's right even though everyone else is taking shortcuts, it will show itself.

Your intentions are revealed in your behaviour, which is a reflection of your character. When you are clear on what your intentions are, you can start to attract new and interesting opportunities through this energy.

If you want help, help someone else out of a jam. If you need money, donate to charity. If you want a new job, help someone else find a new job. If you want an introduction, make a call and help someone else make a connection. What goes around comes around. When your intentions are honourable, you are inviting honour into your life.

This is why, as a top salesperson your integrity, intentions and energy need to be on point. When these get out of whack, you lose momentum to fear and worry. Similarly, when you intend to do right by your clients, that energy goes out into the Universe and attracts more goodwill and prosperity to you.

If you are starting out in business or you are new to sales or you've lost your way, operate with clarity around your intentions and you'll kick start an energetic alignment to receive more grace and sales in your life. Your intentions come from your thoughts, your thoughts influence your behaviour, when you think awesome thoughts, you attract and see more opportunities, your mind opens and the way is revealed.

ENERGY SUMMARY

- The sales are won or lost by the energetic vibration you put out into the world.

- All things are energy.

- Act like the person you want to become.

- Push yourself to take on new challenges.

- Saying no is a skill – not all sales are good for business.

- It's a question of priorities – is this the best use of my time and energy?

- Schedule time to explore and time to take action via Momentum Moments.

- Capture flashes of inspiration and act before it is lost in the ether.

- Focus on serving consistently.

- Use the power of small wins to boost your energy.

- Your identity, who you are, has a direct impact on your ability to win.

CHAPTER 7

Nailing the pitch – To sell more, build real relationships and have fun

"Believe it until you belong."

– JON GORDON

INTRODUCTION

As discussed in the chapter on mindset, when I started out in my career, I had a fear of pitching that was so debilitating that it caused my mind to spin and sometimes go blank. The cause was quite simple – I rarely prepared and was more concerned about how I was coming across rather than what the client needed. This is a combo set up for disaster.

I was doing it all wrong. I knew it, it was obvious, but at the time

I wasn't quite sure how to fix it.

That was, until I decided to beat this monster once and for all. When I fell in love with sales it all changed. Instead of worrying about what the client was thinking, I became their trusted guide. It became my duty to tell my clients about my awesome products. I flipped my understanding of what it means to sell. I believed in what I was selling and understood how it could help my clients, a simple shift in mindset from, *"I must nail this pitch and win this account"* and *"oh no, what are they thinking about me?"* to *"It's a privilege to be able to speak to you today and understand more about you and your business"*. I genuinely wanted to know more about my clients and their lives, and I wanted to have fun pitching.

The truth is, prior to this, I didn't realise how important it is to have FUN during the pitch. How necessary it is to inject yourself into the pitch and how much, if you focus on telling the story and bringing it to life, all of the fears, doubts and worries drift away. When you show up authentically for your clients, this is giving value.

The more I focused on my clients and not on myself or my perceived idea that everyone was judging me, the less I got caught up worrying about what others thought and the more fun I had. This is where you take your sales to the next level and get emails from clients that thank you for the most engaging session they have ever had!

When I think back to the various sales presentation training sessions I attended, my observation is that not enough focus goes into helping salespeople feel comfortable with the content – they rehearse the lines rather than own them. That is why understanding and selling the story is so powerful it allows you to adlib rather than remember a script.

Pitch training so often focuses on helping you sound polished and perfecting the delivery and, whilst this is important, it's certainly not everything. **The most important aspect in my mind is to be able to relax and enjoy the pitch process, to be able to laugh and bring your own special something to each opportunity to speak.** That's how you hold the crowd and deliver maximum impact. When you can connect the story to the audience's emotions and they feel it and they see that you truly believe in it, that's when your ability to influence and produce sales moves into overdrive. It's not about being perfect, it's about being authentically you.

I want you to know if you're starting out in your sales career and you're worried about "the pitch" that I am living proof that you can have SO much FUN pitching that it's the thing you look forward to most. It's where you can shine, and it can become your biggest strength. It starts with shifting your mindset from trying to impress to one of trying to understand and bringing your full self to the conversation.

I share this because this is where I feel a lot of salespeople go wrong and the really awesome ones have got so good because they stopped focusing on themselves **and shifted their mindset to serving their clients** and what's best for them.

When you realise that it's not all about you and your performance, your brain will stop ceasing up, ideas and jokes will flash into your mind like divine sparks of joy that you can use to light up the room. The world will seem brighter, lighter and full of potential.

WHAT IS NAILING THE PITCH?

What nailing the pitch really comes down to is bringing the energy we spoke about in the last chapter into the client presentation so that you are vibrating so highly that you are in a state of sales flow and magnetism.

When you are able to connect thoughts in such a manner that

the experience of how you are showing up in the meeting influences the client to also move into the same energetic state, it's where the magic happens.

You are able to control the pitch because you are focused on them, not you, you are able to bring the emotion of your story into the room, because you aren't worried about being judged or looking a particular way.

When you nail a pitch, you feel relaxed, you are functioning at a higher energetic vibration, you are able to communicate in a way that's right for your clients and have fun doing it. You feel calm, in control, happy, joyful. You have gratitude for the opportunity and you are at one with the moment.

Nailing the pitch is a beautiful state.

In this chapter I will show you how to:

- Be prepared (for anything)

- Begin the pitch in a way that puts the room at ease

- Increase your confidence during the pitch

- Develop a Positive Mental Attitude (PMA) that lasts

- Bring more awareness to the client's context

- Sell to a panel

- Nurture the close so you win more deals.

HOW NAILING THE PITCH HELPS YOU BUILD SALES MOMENTUM

Many sales books will focus on the fact that the pitch is your opportunity to tell the story, and it truly is, and this should not be forgotten. But there's another important aspect that I want you to grasp.

When pitching, the best of the best are also excellent at listening. Not every pitch requires you to do *all* the talking. You can turn it on and deliver a rousing speech for the audience when needed at the drop of a hat because you are prepared, but the highest form of pitching is one where you're able to help the client share as well. This requires flexibility not the rigid slide by slide format that is so widely taught. Sales masters are able to do so much more with a pitching opportunity than just present.

I want you to start today to increase the volume of opportunities to tell the story of your company and its products. Aim to conduct 90 sales meetings in the next three months.

This is a tall order but we're not here to f spiders (to borrow an Aussie phrase) and I promise you that through the process of crossing this threshold and implementing what I am about to share you will reap the rewards.

When you step out into the unknown and you feel the joy of sharing your mission with others, time and time again you learn the process of what it takes to win, rather than focusing only on winning (i.e. the end result). By doing this, you'll experience deeper confidence, more opportunities to serve and increased reciprocity. But more than that, it specifically helps you to drive momentum with your clients in the following ways.

- By showing that you care, and you are there to serve your clients, you build a trusted bond with them and they reward you with repeat long-term business.

- By treating your clients like you would a family member, word spreads increasing your referrals and your pipeline.

- By focusing on the client in front of you and giving them your all while you are in the room, you stand out from the crowd. They sense this and award you the business.

- When a client buys into your mission, they become a light that transfers your story to others and propels your business forward.

- When a client sees that you believe it, they start to buy into it as well.

Now, I'm going to show you how to own it.

1. GETTING READY: BEFORE YOU PITCH

PREPARING FOR THE PITCH

When you are preparing your materials before a presentation, make sure that they are telling a story. What I mean is, make sure you know the different content and media available to you to best make your story come alive. Don't bore them to death in Power Point if you have an actual prototype to show them or a mock-up of how it would work.

Power Point is great for providing context, but it is the words and your body language that tell the story. Anyone can go through slides; the best salespeople *are* the slides. Don't let the slides do your job because they will do it poorly. Know the sequence and have different things open on your laptop to show the client depending on where the conversation goes. In my line of work, I have examples ready to show on my phone, laptop and on USB so that the client can plug it in and away we go.

I want to make it clear that the art of the sale is a conversation that is flexible, not linear, dynamic not ridged. It is not about going in one straight line from the start to the finish of your pitch, it's an obstacle course and you are the map.

Often, salespeople can get so caught up in what they have to say they don't notice that the client isn't interested, or they have switched off completely. When this happens, if you notice (which you should because you're a master of emotional intelligence), switch it up, jump out of the Power Point deck and show them some real examples, or tell a story, or make a joke, anything to reignite their interest and stop the trainwreck. Don't soldier on because that's what you think you must do.

Be bold and take your clients on an adventure that will leave them excited and enthralled with your capabilities, blowing them away with your enthusiasm. Pitching doesn't have to be textbook, do it your way and have fun.

PERSONAL STORY
Be prepared for anything, and I mean anything!

I went to the other side of Singapore to meet with the Managing Director of an ad agency for a luxury car brand.

Due to the prestigious nature of the client, I assumed that their offices would be grand with all the latest high tech mod cons. I was wrong. Very wrong. When we arrived, it turned out that they had completely forgotten that the meeting was even taking place (I know, another one). They tried to cover it up by saying that all the meeting rooms were full, but it was obvious. I was on their doorstep and had taken them by surprise.

After an awkward ten-minute walk around their premises while they tried to recall why I was here and were searching for any nook or cranny to perch and discuss business, it was apparent it wasn't going to happen.

The client then suggested we go downstairs to the hawker centre below and grab a drink. For those that don't know, Singapore is famous for its hawker centres. They are phenomenal places where every type of dish you can imagine is on offer, and some have even been awarded Michelin stars. But it is not really the place you expect to be presenting creative ideas for a luxury high end car brand and trying to describe how your product works.

To make this new turn of events work, there were a few things I needed to have, a laptop with ample battery, cash on hand to buy my clients a cold drink (no credit card machines) and enthusiasm by the bucket load to keep my clients focused and not getting distracted by all the noise from passers-by, the interesting smells and the cooking going on.

This is where I needed to pitch my heart out in the middle of what is quite literally an open-air cafeteria. The only way you can flip from board room to bustling food hall is if you are prepared to own the situation and your pitch.

In order to maximise the opportunity, I needed to streamline the details. I needed to relish the experience and the spontaneity of it all. What I had come to talk them through was a fairly complex technology solution and, given the noise levels and high likelihood for repeated interruptions from passers-by and other diners, I needed to adapt.

This is where having fun comes in, because I am not stressed about how the pitch needs to go, and don't have expectations around the way it must go. I could bring the situation into the pitch.

It was about managing my emotions. Yes, it would have been preferable to have held the meeting in a meeting room, but that wasn't what we were doing, not today. Yes, it would be ideal if there weren't stall owners trying to flog coconuts right next to us in loud unrelenting voices, but to focus on this would have been off-putting. Instead, flip the script, enjoy the moment, focus on building a relationship with the client, and don't try to force a meeting room type pitch into a hawker centre type scenario.

The lesson is that in sales you should always be prepared for the unexpected and go with the flow. The worst thing you can do is be unprepared and get flustered when meetings and opportunities to pitch take place in a different setting to what you would expect. The pitch doesn't have to go slide by slide, be innovative and be flexible.

Rather than treat it like a pain in the ass when things change, think about the stories you will get to tell your grandkids, and the life you'll have lived working in sales.

AUTHENTICITY AND STORYTELLING

Authenticity is your superpower, this is how you connect, influence and make it happen in sales. Most salespeople are focused on saying the right thing because they believe they have to trick, convince or somehow manipulate the client to sell to them. It couldn't be further from the truth; in reality the world class focus on being themselves and sharing authentically with their clients. If you authentically share yourself with your clients, without trying to present some preconceived idea of how you think it should go, you magnetise sales to you. Sales will flow to you because you are real and not aiming to be perfect, and this is your edge.

Stories are so incredibly powerful and, if told in an authentic and heartfelt way, they can change the world. Salespeople are master storytellers.

I was at a conference and had rushed into the lecture room ahead of time to quickly send out a couple of important emails, and also in the hope of catching the speaker before they went on stage.

Yes, this was a strategy to find the only spot at the conference to maximise work and also tactically position myself for success by having a potential run in with a new client (the speaker). I wanted to meet the Executive Vice President (EVP) of Marketing for Asia's eCommerce powerhouse, Lazada. The topic of the session was on Lazada's Journey and Domination of eCommerce in South East Asia.

I didn't get a chance to speak to her before she went on stage but being one of the first people in the room was noted and bought me a little street cred.

When Michelle stood up on stage, I was first drawn in by her warm smile and confident demeanour. Then the first words out of her mouth took me by surprise. I'm recalling from memory here, but she said something like, "The title of this presentation is how Lazada has dominated eCommerce landscape in South East Asia, which I don't agree with."

I'm sorry, what? Who starts a talk to a packed room by saying they don't agree with the title of their own talk? This was going to be awesome!

Michelle continued, now having got the room's full attention, "Late last night, at 1am, when I had finished up yesterday's meetings and I was going through the slides that my team had put together for today's session, I didn't agree with this. We haven't dominated the eCommerce landscape, we're a platform focused on building ecosystems and communities that allow other businesses to flourish."

For me, this was a penny-drop moment, to see the EVP of one of the most celebrated poster child companies in Asia (Lazada secured a $1b investment from Alibaba) stand up in front of a packed room of people and have the insight and authenticity to say what she believes to be true was awesome.

We've all been there, a deck or slides are forced upon us at the last minute, and we're expected to memorise it and regurgitate it as verbatim. What happened here, and what I believe was done so well that we can all take a lesson from it, was that she made it her own, even when she didn't agree with the content. That level of honesty is the lever to a new world of sales.

Being able to own the conversation around why and how you have a different viewpoint, based on your expertise, is the exact thing your company should be paying you for. This level of authenticity in storytelling will translate to increased sales and more deeply interwoven relationships. This behaviour really indicates someone you'd want to work with.

As a side benefit, by doing this and offering this deeper insight, she really got everyone listening intently and paying attention. From the offset she had created the expectation that this talk was going to be different.

There's another lesson here for storytelling in sales; if you want to get attention, don't try to fit in. Be bold enough to stand out, to reach the objective your own way. When telling stories humans love the unexpected, the reveal, to be surprised and to let the outside world fall away for a moment while they listen with awe. It is the truest form of creativity. Capture attention and, when you can do this, you can shape the entire trajectory of what you are trying to achieve.

PRO TIP
Get there early and hang back after

Whenever you can, at conferences, try to get in early to the confer-ence rooms and hang back afterwards. You never know who you might meet and be able to network with.

BE YOURSELF AND OPEN WITH AN ANECDOTE

By bringing yourself into the picture, sharing your humour, your per-sonality and living and breathing passion for the products you are selling, you will not only have more fun and make more sales, but you'll also be a refreshing change from the conveyer belt of people your client met that day.

At the start of the meeting, whilst walking to the meeting room or before I start the pitch, I normally share with my clients a short anecdote. For example, if I am in Malaysia, I might say, "I am glad I could be here today. I nearly died in the Grab taxi ride over." And then I explain what happened. "I got into the Grab and he took off like a rocket... jumping from one lane to the next, not looking, pull-ing a massive U-turn on the highway... etc etc."

This normally gets people's attention – it prompts a laugh and creates some dialogue. This begins the exchange. In the space of a few simple sentences, the room is lighter, freer to discuss topics, ask questions and they see me as open.

The story needs to be real so don't make it up but just share a small piece of what's going on for you. It breaks the ice and says to the client, "I'm a real person. I'm here to help and I can be trusted. I am human."

The point is that by sharing yourself, you are allowing them to do the same. The law of reciprocity takes over and dictates that they will naturally be inclined to do the same. The magic cycle of opening up continues and the connection is strengthened.

MINI MOMENTUM BUILDER
Be authentically unique

Show you care by doing something profoundly unique in the first few minutes of your pitch, by this I mean present more value than they expect in the form of new insights, a tailored report that you've compiled for them, a customised offer that you've got approval on in advance just for them, or bring out something you personalised (e.g. a solution to a problem they have been having, their favourite cake, or signed book by the author they love).

This helps you stand out and makes the client pay attention. When you do the unexpected and give in this way it speaks volumes. Doing this up front, rather than later, will ensure that the client listens to what you say and recognises that you value their business.

Say something along these lines, "before we jump into it, I have a couple of things I want to bring to your attention. Firstly, here's this champagne and truffle mooncake from Raffles Hotel that I know you love and secondly, I've managed to get sign off to give you a special

10% off on any of the products we mention in today's session."

Focus on giving, not only in the physical sense but also in spirit; you are there to serve your client throughout the pitch. Give to them by delivering the pitch to the best of your abilities (every time), put your all into listening to them, be attentive, use their answers to guide you, serve them by delivering the conversation they need.

When you see the sales meeting as a privilege, the whole thing shifts. It is a privilege to be in that room, to be able to be spending this time with the client. Focus on your gratitude for the opportunity and sales will flow like water to your door.

INCREASE YOUR CONFIDENCE AROUND PITCHING

The fastest way to increase your confidence around pitching is to operate from these three principles. Positive Mental Attitude, Service Mindset and Prepare. But why is it important?

It may sound obvious, but every new level you wish to obtain requires a new you. What this means in sales is that you are always a student (remember that white-belt mentality?), looking to improve and seeking growth to be able to sell and serve more.

Aside from this continual growth strategy, you also need to believe in yourself and your ability to sell when faced with all manner of situations.

Below are 3 ways in which you can increase your confidence in pitching by planning to succeed.

1 PMA
GRATITUDE, PRESENT, FOCUSED, MORNING ROUTINE, 3 WINS END OF DAY, CREATIVE IDEAS.

2 SERVICE MINDSET
HOW CAN YOU MAKE IT EASIER FOR THEM, FLEXIBILITY.

3 PREPARE
KNOW THEIR PAIN POINTS, WHAT DO THEY CARE ABOUT, CUSTOMISE, MAKE THE EFFORT.

FIGURE 20: 3 WAYS TO INCREASE CONFIDENCE IN PITCHING

PMA (Positive Mental Attitude)

In sales your attitude is everything. You will face situations and people that will make you want to bang your head against a brick wall. There will be clients that, despite working your tail off for them, going way above and beyond, will still want more. The thing that will keep you persevering is your attitude.

Your attitude and how you respond to the frustrating events is the differentiating factor. It quite literally separates those who win from those who struggle. Clients rearrange meetings, stand you up, waste your time, over promise, aren't clear, change their mind, re-neg at the last minute, make insane requests – this is the life of a salesperson. Except those who win perceive these challenges with a different level of conscious awareness. I've flown all the way to Jakarta, Indonesia specifically to meet with one client only to be stood up with no apology, no phone call to let me know he wasn't coming. I was just left their hanging, facing complete disregard from the client. You can't get annoyed and let it take you off track.

I've been made to wait for over 45 minutes just stood around in the client's office after the meeting was supposed to start on more occasions than I can count for some trivial reason or other – like the client lost track of time or another meeting overran. No message, no email to say they were running late, nothing. I was just standing there wondering what it would be this time.

You'll have the ability to choose how you want to feel in any given situation, not just in your career, and that is the ultimate freedom.

Put a plan in place for when these things happen. There are certain markets that I cover where I know that the clients will show up anywhere from 30-60 minutes late or perhaps on occasion not at all, with no note to say sorry, just leaving me hanging.

Except, now I am not "hanging". I go to these meetings fully prepared to keep working, making phones calls, doing emails. I literally sit down in the client's reception or ask to go to the cafeteria and make it my temporary office. I set up shop. I get to know the receptionists (gatekeepers) and the baristas. I make extra phone calls and do follow up.

Business doesn't stop while I wait to see if they are going to show up. Nor do I waste time getting annoyed at how rude and unprofessional this behaviour is. I ignore it and move forward with my business. That's PMA!

Now let's talk about ways to increase PMA. The most impactful approach is gratitude. If you want to know more about this, I recommend you check out my book, *Be The Lion: How to overcome big challenges and make it happen*, which is basically a manifesto for cultivating more courage and demonstrating gratitude even in the toughest of circumstances.

PRO TIP
Test your PMA in other areas

I encourage you to also get a number of different projects/hobbies/ businesses going. This will help you in sales because it gives you more dimensions and moves your PMA into overdrive. I find that any time you are using your skills to help other people or to the best of your abilities, whether that's learning a new sport, or game, or skill, gratitude leads the way.

Whenever you find yourself frustrated, remember how grateful you need to be for even being alive and having these issues to worry about. Jot down three things you are grateful for at the moment. Whip out your note pad, or start a Word doc, and just quickly jot down the three things that spring to mind. For me, it typically looks something like this.

1. I am grateful for my incredible sons and loving wife and getting to live my life with them, to see them grow and their beautiful personalities develop, to share in love. When I am away, I thank God for the joy of having them in my life. When I am home, but out in meetings, I look forward to going home to them at night and to the fun and games we will have. I remember *why* I am doing all of this for them, to create an awesome life for them, and live to my fullest potential.

2. I am grateful for being an author and mindset coach and having books like this to share my message through. I work best when I have a number of things on the go, like an MBA, writing books, promoting my message on podcast interviews and radio shows, TV, press, working on various entrepreneurial ventures, speaking and training sales teams and entrepreneurs, and working in sales. I am grateful to have all this going on and to be moving forward each day in the life of Tim Castle. This is a constant blessing and source of abundance.

3. I am grateful for the opportunity to sell the products that I do, to have the privilege of this situation and all that it affords me, being rich in cultural learning, people, and the opportunity to develop my sales skills and hopefully make some new friends.

By turning on your gratitude, you'll attract more good vibes to you. You radiate the energy you receive and tune into, because of this you'll spot more opportunities to transform a frustrating situation into a pot of gold.

MINI MOMENTUM BUILDER
Build the system

Write down 3 things you will focus on when you are frustrated:

1.

2.

3.

When you go through life in a state of gratitude, with a positive mental attitude and a modus operandi to serve, you my friend, will be on a winning streak so big it will make your past successes look like a drop in the ocean.

Service mindset

To start having a more confident mindset that can carry you through the darker times when the sales figures are down, or your client reduces the budget and your numbers look awful, you need to reframe what it means to sell.

Switch from taking to giving; switch from what it means for you to what it means for them and you'll see a massive difference in how the world responds to you because you'll be putting out a different energy and taking service-minded action.

Whenever you go to pitch, remember you are there to serve.

Imagine this, it's 4.30pm on a Friday afternoon and your client requests a meeting at 4.45pm. Do you go or do you fob it off until next week saying that you're busy?

Answer honestly. There's no point lying, you're only hurting your own growth. What would you do, truthfully?

Do you bring your clients coffee when they are having a bad day or send them care packages? Do you reschedule the meeting again, even though this is the ninth time they've done this? Do you send them a list of every single client you work with, even though the information is on your website and you've explained that a million times? Do you listen when they talk? I mean really listen. Are you present? Do you sell with joy? Are you following up and delivering on what you said you would do? Are you reliable?

If so, you have a service mindset. You make it easy for your clients to say yes to you.

When you are pitching, this aspect of serving is how you will differentiate yourself.

What service looks like during the pitch

- Showing up early (at least ten minutes before)

- Being respectful of the client's time

- Having the right content, people and equipment to facilitate the right conversation

- Coming prepared

- Not bringing the negativity from the argument you just had with the taxi driver into the meeting room

- Being a friend, remembering significant details about them as an individual

- Caring about their life, their aspirations and goals and doing what you can to help them

- Introducing them to people in your network

- Making their day just that bit more special through your attitude

- Being a radiant light, infusing them with enthusiasm and showing authenticity in how you help when you face challenges or roadblocks together

- Going to bat for your clients internally, maybe they want cheaper rates, or more products for the same price, or need to move quicker than your SLA (service level agreement) allows. How you influence internally to help things progress smoothly shows respect, care and service to your clients

- Taking time to understand their business deeply and provide powerful competitor analysis and relevant insights and trends

What it means to service a client isn't just picking up a phone, being available or handing over information. It goes far beyond that and there are so many ways to stand out through service.

Be creative in how you weave these Momentum Moments into your pitch and show respect and you will win the hearts and minds of your clients through service.

Prepare

One simple way to increase your confidence in the pitch is to be prepared. This means putting that extra bit of something special into your sell, whether that's a customised presentation with a video from the rest of your team, a tailored prototype or mockup of their product, or just going above and beyond to show the client your business via a personalised tour.

Preparation is your homework. It's finding out the key priorities and objectives of your client before you get to the pitch. It is the groundwork you have laid before making the sale, from getting to know the receptionist (gatekeeper) and the junior level staff (door opener) that gains you access to the higher rungs of senior leadership. Become so ingrained in your client's way of life that you are part of the furniture.

It can also mean having contingencies, strategies for handling objections and just plain and simple knowledge of your own product and company. Confidence comes from knowing that whatever comes your way, you will handle it. Therefore you invest time thinking about what is likely to be of most value to your client. Even ask them during the meeting, "I know we've only got 30 minutes together, so what would be of most value to you? We can either discuss this or this?" Give them options. This shows confidence and respect.

I once went to a client's office to pitch and at the end of the meeting the client stood up and said, "That's great but can you send me the data analysis on this, this and this?" Up until that point I didn't think I had wowed her; the meeting was a solid 5/10. It was only when I said, "Well actually, I thought you might ask for that, so I already prepared it for you," and then brought up the data on screen that the whole dynamic of the meeting changed.

It showed the client that I cared, I had thought about what mattered to them and demonstrated in a powerful way that I respected and valued their time. From that point on, the meeting that was about to finish went on for another 15 minutes and the information and rapport that was built during those closing minutes solidified the next few months of sales across multiple regions.

If someone gives you a lead, a foot in the door, take it, don't be disrespectful. Prepare and overdeliver.

2. IT'S GO TIME

IN THE MEETING

This is where experience triumphs, you must have the discipline to ask the right questions and allow them the space to think. The meeting isn't a chance to impress them with everything you know, far from it, in the meeting you may feel that it is your job to convince the client, and you'd be right, but that level of influence will only be won by empathising, demonstrating determination, and enthusiasm for what you're about to build together.

PRO TIP
The meeting

LISTEN to them – *this feeds your account prioritisation process, whether a client has opportunities coming up that are warm/hot/ cold/VIP/gold/silver/bronze. This might sound super simple but even the most experienced salespeople don't always ask the right questions.*

PACKAGE – *remember, don't put them off just because you don't see the opportunity. Tell the story, frame it from the perspective of how you could work together. Sell the future potential. To move into new territory, you need to think about the next point.*

*UNCOVER **what you don't know*** *– the way to uncover more of what you don't know is to ask open questions. These begin with How, What, When, Where and Why... and do it with enthusiasm combined with transition statements, as previously discussed. "That's great news, I'm so pleased for you. Tell me, what new hotel trips do you have coming up?"*

PITCH – when you make the pitch, humanise it, bring in your own opinions and stories. The pitch should always be tailored to the specific client you are seeing. For example, the demo or big idea should be presented in a way that shows you have thought about their company using it and customised it as such. This just shows a general level of care for their business and the potential to join forces.

Underpinning all of this is empathy. Empathy is the single biggest driver of long-term relationships, the ability to put yourself in your client's shoes and understand their feelings and what matters to them. When you can speak, act and listen from this vantage point, your whole sales process shifts. It seeks to support, and out of it, new ideas, partnerships and opportunities can grow.

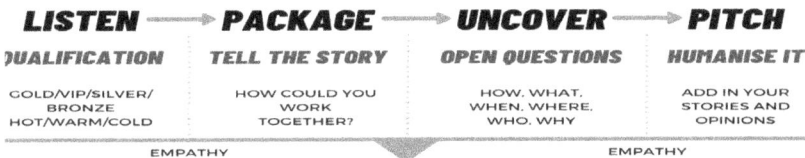

LISTEN	PACKAGE	UNCOVER	PITCH
QUALIFICATION	TELL THE STORY	OPEN QUESTIONS	HUMANISE IT
GOLD/VIP/SILVER/ BRONZE HOT/WARM/COLD	HOW COULD YOU WORK TOGETHER?	HOW, WHAT, WHEN, WHERE, WHO, WHY	ADD IN YOUR STORIES AND OPINIONS
EMPATHY			EMPATHY

FIGURE 21: THE 'GO TIME' MEETING TIPS AND ROLE OF EMPATHY

PRESENTATION CONTEXT

When preparing for a pitch, make sure you think about what the client is interested in and be keen to hear about something that is *not* the story you are looking to push. I find all too often salespeople make the mistake of thinking they need to tell the narrative from the beginning or tell the story exactly as their Power Point dictates in the set order they have prepared.

Give your clients the information they're begging for not the information you think they need to know. Give them what they need first, and then they will be more likely to listen if you have more to add. Get this the wrong way around and you could talk yourself out of a sale. And you'll know when this is happening because all of a sudden all of the energy and enthusiasm will have left the room, you will have chased it away with your need to validate your own insecurities and prove your own points.

You only need to briefly validate their reason for being curious about your company and product, don't spend the whole meeting validating, it is only likely to make them think "is this guy for real? He is wasting my time, when is he going to tell me the things I really need to know…"

And by the way, what they really want to know is:

- Which of their competitors you are working with (credibility and validates)

- The price (ballpark figures)

- How it will work (the process)

- Next steps (what needs to happen)

- What's on their agenda (their roadmap)

- Are you working with them in other markets already? (Proof of solving a need)

- How do you solve their deepest issues? (Can they justify it internally?)

PERSONAL STORY
Don't forget the client's context

This happened to me with a large banking client recently. The request came in as an in-bound lead – the bank wanted to work with us, they loved our product offering and had a strong positive feeling about the work we could do together to showcase their brand.

However, because the lead came easy (it was a referral and a slam dunk), I got excited and did two things that had the potential to derail the sale.

I forgot to prepare my pitch based on the context of the client. Due to the nature of how the meeting came about and the ease at which it seemed they were down to do business, I didn't spend the time customising the pitch. As you can imagine, this was a large global bank, with long table board rooms, multiple layers of hierarchy, and a raft of questions. Banks have formalities; they like to do things in a certain way. I should have prepared because when I rocked up, ready to do my standard pitch, it looked a little odd.

I didn't do more than five minutes' due diligence, which by anyone's rate of speed-reading is light.

Things I could have done better include:

- Finding out in more detail how much business we as a company had done previously with the bank in other locations around the world. (It sounds so obvious but because the lead came easy it distracted me from my normal preparation process.)

- Digging deeper into if there was no previous business history, what the reason was for that. Had we been in contact in other markets and, if so, why hadn't the sale moved forward?

- Broadening my understanding about the client's goals for the future, which products, services they were currently championing.

- Researching if this was the right time to be working with this particular client, given their team structure, resources and other opportunities. (Conduct a quick review of your business. Could we handle winning this client right now? In my experience, clients like banks and financial institutions want more assurances, guarantees and require more touch points than other types of clients. Therefore there was a risk/reward ratio to weigh up depending on the stage of the business, whether we could service this client to the highest standard whilst managing our other portfolio of clients.)

All of this would have helped to better inform me of the types of specialised products they might have wanted from us. It's sales 101, but the point here is when the situation leads you to believe that it's a slam dunk, that's when you have the potential to be most caught off guard. It is better to stick heavily to your pitch preparation process.

As it was, the initial meeting went well and a few months later the sale was made and we were in business together, but there is always room for improvement and in this case a fair bit.

I should have anticipated these standard questions given the context of the client. It was a bank, of course they were going to be formal, have more questions than the average client and want assurances. They were your typical compliance behavioural type, and the mistake I made was I had moseyed on up as an influencer type, without a care in the world, ready to slam dunk this puppy.

I should have found out this information beforehand. In this case, I failed to do my due diligence with enough rigour and, as a result, I knew the meeting had the potential to be much more than it was, but I failed to capitalise on it. Point noted, next time, next meeting, next opportunity, I didn't make the same mistake again.

Whoever the client is, this whole process is like a date and you need to bring your A game Mac Daddy skills. Don't be that unprepared guy, winging it with no answers and a lot of "I don't know" and "I'll need to find out". It's lame and looks terrible. If you want a second date and potentially a marriage, be the "yes, we have worked with you in London already. Here's the case study I prepared earlier, now let me take you through how we conducted business to get these impressive results." Be that salesperson!

DON'T SPEND TOO LONG SETTING THE SCENE

I see this mistake made frequently by big Fortune 500 tech companies. They go in to pitch a client and, because they have access to a huge range of products that they could potentially sell, they focus too heavily on giving the client a long overview of the market or the industry sector – for example, explaining digital transformation to their client.

The problem is that they take too long to get to the point. People move on from roles, leave companies, momentum is lost and around and around the cycle goes until a competitor swoops in and joins the party. Then, because there are now two or three potential vendors vying for the client's business, the client feels the need to launch a formal RFP in order to properly vet the goods on offer. This goes on for a few months and it becomes a race to the bottom with each competitor lowering quotes and even running at a loss to try to secure the business.

I also see the same phenomena in small companies. These companies spend too much time on painting the overall picture because they think they need to explain their right to be in the room in the first place. To justify their seat at the table.

I too have made this mistake. It's important to establish if your client actually needs a crash course in what you specialise in before you give it to them. Remember, they may have already seen your competitors, attended industry events, read the trade press and have their own internal philosophy about what you believe they so readily need to hear.

When you spend too long on the macro or justifying your reason for being there (even unconsciously by over-explaining your rationale) you are likely to bore your clients. They will start to think that maybe this guy doesn't get me, maybe he's not the mover and shaker I thought he was. They will start to question your ability to sift through their problems and get the job done. Get to the point and make an impact.

PREPARE FOR THE CULTURE AND BE PREPARED TO GO OFF SCRIPT

Think of the environment and context that your client is working in. For example, a finance client like a bank is likely to have organised a meeting room for your presentation, staff are going to dress formally, and there will be an obvious hierarchy, so respect your clients by understanding their world. Other people you are not aware of might drop into the meeting. Finance clients are going to expect you to understand their objectives, their toughest challenges. They are more likely to pepper you with questions, grill you a bit, test you, want to jump about through the presentation, stop the presentation and ask you to demo.

How you handle the change of pace, the quick-fire questions, being forced to present without being able to get into your usual rhythm or patter, this is how you become great. **Thinking on your feet, being creative, rolling with their thought processes and indulging their curiosity all whilst bringing the enthusiasm.**

Don't get flustered if senior ranking staff stand up in the meeting and announce they need to leave. This is very common at a bank. Even if they just came in five minutes ago and spent most of their time responding to texts on their phone. This is not a dis, it's their world, it's the normal way of doing business, and you should feel privileged that they showed up at all. Bring this feeling of joy into the room.

PRO TIP
Dress the part

If you're seeing a finance client, dress sharp; you need them think-ing this guy gets me and my problems, he's one of us. It doesn't have to be a complete understanding, but he understands enough for me to promote his business internally. That's the spot you must reach inside the mind of the client.

SELLING TO A PANEL

There are times in sales when you'll need to go up against a panel, this could be pitching for large accounts, in awards presentations, inter-views. Generally, panels or groups are a regular occurrence in sales.

I love a group because it offers so much opportunity to have fun and ask more questions. There is nothing better than when you get the room buzzing with excitement and energy for your product and the level of creativity is through the roof.

My suggestion with panels is to view it as the opportunity to speak to them, it's a privilege, this is your opportunity to sell with joy and enthusiasm. I say **let your curiosity ask the questions.**

Remember, it's not just a one-way street. It's not just panel vs little old you. You get to dictate the course of the conversation. By asking questions, you uncover the unknown and increase your poten-tial for making a sale. Have fun and work the room. Take control of the conversation, this is EQ, all about influencing. If you notice that one or two members of the panel are more responsive, focus on them and use them to draw out interaction from the less participatory members. Make it so those that aren't contributing will get FOMO and therefore begin to wake up and take an interest.

I do this by using eye contact to focus on specific people that are giving me the right signals, either through their attentive body language or comments. Then I build on this by acknowledging and rewarding their interest with engaging and thoughtful questions and responses to their questions.

PRO TIP
Melt the ice with laughter

If I have a problem person on the panel, someone who is either disruptive or is looking at me with daggers in their eyes because I'm taking up their valuable time, I focus on making the group laugh – there is nothing so powerful as laughter to break up a hostile takeover attempt.

Some people on the panel may not want to be there, they may be stressed out about their to-do list and other work they have to complete or even may not like other people on the panel. Therefore, it is your job, like a counselor, to try to make the group as a whole feel as at ease as possible whilst in your presence. Give them a reason to chuckle and to get out of their own head. The more present you can make the people on the panel, the more engaged they will become, and when you have a panel's full attention you can really work it to its maximum effect.

Bounce off those who are giving you the right signals, ask probing questions, like "Who here is responsible for x?", then go deeper with that person: "How so?" Use the spontaneity of your questioning to keep the panel alert. Play a game with your presentation – ask people to guess or estimate certain things, ask questions like, "How many of this product do you think we sell per year?" Or "What is the best way to impress your client?" Involve a quiz at various stages of the conversation, see who's been paying attention, give out prizes too. Whatever you need to do to keep the group with you and not end up in the same bucket as everyone else: just another boring vendor that tried to sell me something.

If you're a bit nervous, just remember to focus on the ones who give you the right signals and be grateful for the privilege and opportunity to share your message. They need to buy from someone, so make sure that it is you. Worry means you're thinking too much about yourself, so remember that it's about them, not you, their problems and needs and not yours. When you make this switch in your thinking, any nerves die down and reality kicks in.

If there's someone in the room who is unimpressed or seems to have a face made of stone, keep marching forward. Don't let someone else's attitude taint the joy you have to give. You are there for a reason; you are valuable and have much to offer. Every so often you'll come across people who, for whatever reason, take pleasure in trying to throw you off or undermine your pitch with curly questions designed to get a rise out of you.

Quash these right away by understanding that the problem they have is with themselves. Once they realise that this doesn't dim your light or the passion you have for your mission, product or service, they'll soon back down. It's easy when you are in full swing of Momentum Sales because you don't get caught up in the gossip, the need to be perfect or comparison. Instead, you are focused on delivering the best pitch you have in you, every time!

The best thing you can do with a panel or a group when presenting is to engage them, whip them up into a frenzy and let their collective energy carry the conversation forward. Give yourself a pep talk beforehand and remember all that you're grateful for, when you know why, the how shines through. Now all you need is to do it.

PITCHING TO AN INVESTOR

We've all heard of the elevator pitch, right? You've 30 seconds to articulate what's so amazing about your product or service in the hope that they are so attracted to what you're doing they stop right there and invest on the spot.

I've pitched a few investors in my time and now advise startups across the globe on how to prepare for their investor pitch days, so they can nail the pitch and secure an investment. I take advice from my mentors, as I instructed you to do earlier. Everyone has mentors.

I very much like Kevin Harrington's (the original Shark on Shark Tank) approach to pitching for investment and pitching in general, which is a three-step process. It goes like this, first you Tease, then you Please and finally you Seize.

It's simple, neat and effective. Any entrepreneur can pick this up and roll with it. Let me give you the broad outline.

1. Tease – start with an attention-grabbing problem. That is to say, make sure you're painting the full picture, get their attention.

2. Please – talk through the benefits of your product or service on how you solve the problem in a unique way. The unique part is key; you've got to show how you do it better and differently than anyone else on the market. Differentiation is life! Drop a few case studies and testimonials to further build your credibility.

Here's the rub: most people get this by the point where Kevin's three step process really kicks into gear: Step 3.

3. Seize – you've got to present an "irresistible offer" along with the problem and the unique solution. Something that is really going to motivate the investor to action and strike now!

Kevin is a big fan of Step 3 and I love it too! He suggests introducing things like an accelerated payback, whereby the investor gets to keep 100% of the profits until their initial investment is paid in full and then they still get to keep their stake in the company going forward. How could they lose, right!

The part I want you to remember is around making it irresistible. Not nearly enough salespeople understand the context of the investor, client, consumer and factor into their pitch how they are going to incentivise them to take action quickly.

A typical pitch goes like this: here's the problem, here's how we solve it, this is our pricing options and a few packages. However, it doesn't push the boat out far enough to cause serious consideration.

To get FOMO, drive urgency and gain a "I must get involved in this project" from the investor, you need to be presenting a winning formula. It must be compelling. Any big names in the field you can mention will add a huge dollop of credibility.

This aspect, combined with an irresistible offer, will make investors go nuts for your project.

3. MAXIMISING THE WINDOW OF OPPORTUNITY

THE TEST

When you're pitching, interacting with your client, in the dialogue there will be a tipping point, a crossroads, a pivotal moment where the sale hangs in the balance. How you handle this juncture will define whether you win or lose the sale.

Often when we are closest to the finish line is when we get "tested" the most. This is where you need to dig deep, summon all your resilience and strike!

When clients recognise the end of the sales process is near and it's decision time, this is when they are likely to throw a few curve balls, questions or obstacles.

The thing to take note of is a client that's asking questions is engaged, even if they sound sceptical. Don't be put off by questions that sound like challenges to what you are saying.

What I find that it is often when the client has asked one too many questions and sanity is pushed to its limits, or you find yourself going around in circles with a client on a particular sticking point you know to be arbitrary but matters deeply to them, this is where you need to influence your own mindset the most.

As insanely frustrating as it may be, if you get angry by your client's lack of understanding or for their penchant for focusing on the miniature that is largely inconsequential, you will risk putting the whole deal and all of your effort in jeopardy.

This is where you need to take a breather, get someone else to compose the email, vent, or go for a walk, do anything BUT respond.

The best way to handle the emotions is to get your gratitude up. A trick I find to do this is that I focus on my sons, my wife and my life in this moment. It helps me stay clear on why I am doing this. The bigger picture.

Remember, above all, you are the trusted guide, you are there in the room to serve your clients. While the competition is getting frustrated and letting deals slip through their fingers, you are turning up and delivering the goods.

Everything about your tone, attitude, body language and composure needs to be on point as if it were the first time you had met the client. You need to maintain the same eagerness to do business as when you started. **Any disregard, or lack of empathy towards your client, will begin to close the window of opportunity and damage your relationship.**

Clients will pick up on how you act under pressure: are you with them for the long haul? Do you get angry or short when challenged? Are you able to find solutions for them even though the end is in sight, or have you already counted it as in the bag and moved on mentally to your next sale?

Handling "the test" is an important skill to develop; it gives you the character to stick with it, to manage your emotions, keep yourself in check and deliver the result all the way to the finish line. Take "the test" as a sign you're about to win big.

Oh, and one last thing, remember before when I said this is the time to strike? This is exactly the time you need to persuade. Get super comfortable owning the tension that's created by the client's scepticism and push it back to them. Once you've got your gratitude up, your composure and emotions in check, then you can go into full on sales mode. Don't be afraid, if you believe in your products, your business and that you are giving them the best solution, then go pitch your heart out! Own it!

KNOW WHERE YOUR CLIENT'S HEAD IS AT AND DO A TEMPERATURE CHECK

Desperate salespeople chase their sales away; confident expectant sellers, however, attract the sale with a magnetism of their understanding of sales.

Maximising the opportunity is about working through the issues in the client's mind – with your client, this is also where you serve. What you don't want to do is sit on the sidelines whilst the decision is being made. You want to work collaboratively with the client. Don't make any assumptions just because you've presented to them and they understand all the information that they are making an objective decision. You've got to stay with the process, remember you live and breathe this stuff. For them, what you are selling is just a part of their overall business and they may need extra hand holding at this stage of the deal.

Your job as a salesperson is to guide the process, not to force a yes. The aim is to help them see and figure out what aligns with what they are looking for and then recognise it when it is in front of them.

When you know your client is in the process of deciding which vendor to choose, get them on a call, help them go through their questions. It doesn't need to take long, be real, upfront and open. It's these small actions compounded daily that have the biggest effects.

There are six main emotional stages the client goes through during the sales process. Pay attention to your client and don't let the opportunity go cold because you didn't know where the client's head was at.

I've summarised this in a neat table. The lesson here is that you need to know which stage your client is in, what they need and be there for them.

6 STAGES OF EMOTION DURING THE SALES PROCESS

EMOTION	CLIENT NEEDS HELP WITH
ENERGISED	UNDERSTANDING PRODUCT/CAPABILITIES
CRITICAL	THE RISK OF NOT TAKING ACTION/ FACING REALITY
WORRIED	DEALING WITH DOUBTS/ MANAGING UNCERTAINTY
INDECISIVE	MAKING A DECISION/ REDUCING OVERTHINKING
OPTIMISTIC	MAKING PEACE/TAKING ACTION/IMPLEMENTATION
JOYFUL	CELEBRATE TOGETHER/ FUTURE POSSIBILITIES

FIGURE 22: THE 6 STAGES OF EMOTION DURING THE SALES PROCESS

As an outstanding salesperson, it is your responsibility to find out exactly what the client is afraid of or wants, and then break down the barriers, either by revealing information that the client didn't know (making them feel at ease) or by working your tail off to help find a collaborative solution or Plan B to mitigate the risk.

Actions like these will help you serve your client and can lead to you closing the deal if there's a fit, which because you're incredible at qualification, there will be. The key here is to be there, lighting the path. Even if you don't win this deal, you'll be there for the next one and your clients will trust your guidance and appreciate having someone like you that they can call. By having this level of involvement, it allows your ability to forecast revenue to increase 10-fold, but ultimately if you are not willing to phone them to ask what the status is, then you'll be leaving it more to chance than you should.

The confident seller isn't afraid to ask the questions that they need to know the answers to (e.g. "When can we expect the contract?"). They also aren't afraid to ask tough questions (like "I'm sensing hesitation, what's going on for you?") then once you uncover you can seek to handle the objections and put the buyer's mind at ease.

The best thing you can do is uncover and then (because you have done your due diligence and because you are a pro and come across these types of clients and customers all the time) say, "I thought that might be the case. Well, I have adjusted for that in my pricing strategy and I am willing to give you X (product, service, time, value) free of charge and we can speed up this part of the process so you can hit your deadline. How does that sound?"

Trust yourself and push for the close, ask for it, and sell because you know it's the right solution for the client. Be empathetic and use your experience in the market to help alleviate client concerns by showing them how what you have gets them what they want. There is a reason you think that what you are selling to your client is right for them and their situation. Now is the time to back that up and show them all the ways through the maze. Remember that the client is probably experiencing some sort of disappointment, or FOMO, or wondering if they are making the right decision. As a world class seller, you are there to help them figure it out. EMPATHETICALLY.

It is in that confidence (not arrogance) that the sale is attracted; salespeople who are bold believe it can happen and expect it to happen, win!

PRO TIP
Take a temperature check

The sale is yours in your mind, therefore you never need to ask if you have won the deal, assume you have at all times. At the end of the pitch, the question you need to ask is "Which of these is closest to what you were thinking?" or "Which of these two options works for you?" This is what's known as a temp check – you are sensing if you and the client are on the same page.

If you are on the same page then, by asking this type of question, you've progressed it straight to the next level and can ask, "OK great, when can we deliver this? Tuesday at 11am or Thursday at 3pm?"

Alternatively, if the client isn't happy with either of the options you have proposed, you know you need to keep going, you aren't there yet.

If you push too hard, you get a "no". No is safe, no is where people go when they feel pressured to make a decision by the salesperson. On the flip side, when the client has already made a decision, a skilful salesperson can help them recognise it by presenting the solution in a structured and simple way in the form of a temp check question that moves the process forward with ease.

The temperature check helps you as the salesperson because it gives you new and critical information. If you are in the right area your client will say, *"I love this one because…"*

More importantly, if you are in the wrong area, they will share why what you put forward doesn't suit their needs, giving you the opportunity to objection handle or propose a better, more aligned solution based on this information.

When you have responded to a client pitch, rather than chasing to see if you have won, pose the ask as a temp check. *"What did the client like about our proposal?"* or *"Did they like example A or B better?"*

This way you keep the dialogue going through the evaluation process. The worst thing that can happen once you have responded to an RFP is it goes quiet, and you are left waiting for them to make a decision.

The reason why this is a problem is because you can't rely on your client to reach out if they have any questions. The good ones will, the invested ones will, but some, especially new clients, won't. They will make a decision based on what you put forward and assume that there is no flexibility or other ways of doing business.

This is a problem because it means that it's a binary decision: you either win or lose. If you got the brief wrong or the client changes their mind on what they want part way through the process, then you are screwed. All that work goes up in smoke and you don't even know about it. You're there forecasting $1 million when the client has already changed direction and didn't let you know.

By staying in contact, you can adapt when the client changes their mind or direction (which happens more than you think). Therefore, number one rule for maximising the opportunity is to stay in contact with your buyers, not to find out if you won, but to find out if there has been changes. You can get feedback: What is the client liking? What are they not liking? What are they not understanding? Do they need the information presented in a different way? Do they want to do a deep dive on the commercials?

A simple, "Hi Jane. Just wanted to follow up to find out if there was any feedback on the pitch" or "Hi Jane. Just checking in to see how the process was going? If you have any questions or want to go over the proposal in more detail, more than happy to jump on a call."

It takes all of 30 seconds, but very few salespeople remember to do it **for every opportunity** they are working on. This is how you keep the plates spinning.

I get that salespeople do it every now and again, but that's not enough. To be exceptional, we cannot allow any balls to be dropped. When we talk about outperforming your current results, this is also where the battle is fought.

Get yourself so ingrained with your clients that you become a valuable advisor to them when it matters. Follow through and follow up, show that you care and are there for the long haul. **This is where there's no such thing as being too proactive.**

Now let's talk about a few ways to nurture the close.

4. NURTURING THE CLOSE

You've got this far but the race isn't over, now you need to cross the finish line. We are aiming for you to be like Michael Jordan in an NBA championship game, dialled in and making it rain.

Sales is much like sports; the more experience you get, the better you become at dealing with client objections, competitors nipping at your heels, and dynamics that are often out of your control, like the economy. The best of the best know how to win in all conditions.

Remember, the main thing in your control is your attitude and how you strategically influence the situation to close the deal when you know it's right for the client.

Nurturing the close is an area that I see salespeople struggle with, mainly because they go in too hard and aggressive with a "my way or the highway" type attitude. This doesn't work, it leaves the client questioning whether they should be doing business with you and looking for alternatives.

You can't force a client to sign, and deception or manipulation are terrible levers to use. In fact, you should avoid anything that isn't right – it will haunt you and cause you to miss big opportunities. In sales, having a clear conscience and doing what's right is what builds character, respect and a legacy.

Nurturing the close goes back to what we spoke about with regards to making the offer irresistible, but this isn't your only move. Applying deadlines, creating a little urgency by producing offers that expire, creates curiosity and enables the human psyche to make decisions; however, it needs to be done in the right way, all with service in mind.

If you're applying fake deadlines left, right and centre, you'll lose the deal. If you're harsh, overly aggressive, and domineering on every call trying to force the deal through to serve your own needs, clients will not tolerate this. They will see you don't have their best interests at heart and seek to find value elsewhere.

You'd be surprised how many senior leaders get this wrong.

In my book, **you nurture the close by adding expert value they can't get anywhere else, over-delivering in how you show up for your clients and accurately understanding their goals and how to achieve them so clearly that the client knows signing is the right decision.**

We humans hate missing out on things, but you know what we hate even more? The feeling that we had the opportunity to do something about it and didn't take action.

To motivate effective decision making and put yourself ahead of the pack, remain acutely aware that time kills deals. The longer that you wait, the greater the opportunity for your competitors to build influence, markets to change, and budgets to get cut. There are too many variables to try to control them all.

If you are one of those people that thinks, "I am just going to give them a little time to think it over", you're going about it the wrong way. You haven't found what they are deeply passionate about, what their real interests are and how you can give it to them. If you had, you wouldn't be waiting, you'd be celebrating with a signed contract.

PRO TIP
Nurture the close

Use the situational facts to encourage a decision: "Do you think you'll be able to sign by the end of the year? The reason I ask is I doubt I'll be able to hold these rates in the new year, the company is reviewing all pricing."

Respond to the objection, "Sorry, we aren't looking to do this right now. We're focused on ecommerce and online sales only" with "I am surprised that you're not wanting to capture in-store purchases with the restrictions now lifted and festive season on the way". Your response is grounded in situational truths – link it to facts, plant the seed of surprise, "surprised" is a transformative word and gets the other party thinking. It's non-threatening and promotes inquiry.

Help the client discover what they want through expert questioning – "in an ideal world what would you do?", "What would need to happen to make that a reality?"

Go above and beyond, create moments for your clients and live and breathe their business goals. Use the goal as the urgency to move forward. Time waits for no one.

BEING A GOOD NEGOTIATOR HELPS YOU SELL MORE

In negotiations, you must be able to adapt to the situation in real time. This means thinking on your feet and really trying to listen and understand the other person.

PERSONAL STORY
Adaptability

I went to a client's office for what I thought was your typical meeting. I had my sales presentation, product demo and laptop ready and raring to go. I'd been trying to get this client in the diary for months, but it seemed impossible to get a response from them, then one day I got a reply. I was over the moon as it was a huge client that represented millions of dollars.

When I arrived, I walked up to the lady on reception as I normally would and told her who I was there to see. Nothing out of the ordinary (yet).

She kindly instructed me to have a seat in the lobby area and wait for them to come out. I did as instructed, sat down and started to browse through a magazine that had been neatly left out on the coffee table in front. A few people came and went, other guests were ushered through into the main part of the building where the client's meeting rooms were situated.

As I waited, I stumbled across an interesting article on Venice and vowed I needed to take my family there for a holiday soon. Just as I was imagining what it would be like to sail down the Grande Canal on a gondola, the door directly opposite me whisked open and over walked the two clients. I put down the magazine and stood up to greet them.

Then what happened next proceeded to be one of the oddest exchanges I have experienced. The client asked me to sit back down on the chairs in the reception, rather than continue through into the building like the rest of the folk had been doing, which was what I had been expecting.

"Shall we have our meeting here?" she said.

I was a little taken aback after all the meeting preparation I had done and the expectation of being able to use a big screen to "wow" them with my product demo, plus it felt slightly like a dis. But on the other hand, they were a large client, and I didn't want to lose the opportunity to speak with them as it had literally taken months to get this meeting in the diary.

This was the turning point, the moment in my mind that it all changed. As much as I felt disappointed by what felt like immediate rejection, **I decided that if this was where the meeting was going to take place then it would be the best meeting I could muster despite the circumstances.**

A swift change of mindset like this plus the ability to adapt the situation to your advantage is a key skill when it comes to using your negotiation skills to drive sales.

After the normal round of introductions and small talk, I

proceeded to pull out my laptop and begin the pitch I had been preparing to deliver. I was determined to blow them away with my enthusiasm and passion.

As passers-by came and went, I made a point to acknowledge other client contacts that happened to be walking past. This situation was ripe for sales and I wasn't going to waste it. We'd been doing business with other accounts in the building, and I wanted to highlight this.

It is extremely important to manage your emotions in this type of situation when you are trying to sell but there are constant interruptions from passers-by, other noises and conversations due to the setting being less than ideal.

The key is to embrace the spontaneity of it all and bring that energy into your presentation. Instead of focusing on how much better it would be if the meeting were held in a luxurious meeting room like you had planned, focus on what you can make of the here and now.

I also had to adapt my speaking style. After all, I was presenting in the reception area of a client's office (a more casual setting) therefore the pitch itself could be more relaxed, more friendly, more engaging on a personal level. The magic that happens when you get this informal meeting right is that you accelerate rapport and connection.

I am not sure if it was because the client wanted to look good internally or she wanted to be seen as someone who was "in the know", or the pitch in fact blew their socks off, but what happened next was an absolute sales gold mine and boy did I mine it. I went to work!

About 30 minutes into our discussion, one of the clients promptly stood up and said, "I'm going to grab Angela and Rahul from our Travel department. They need to hear about this!" She then walked back into the main office and returned a few minutes later with her two colleagues.

I began my pitch from the start and went again. Little did I know then, but this had created a buzz internally. There I was hosting a second meeting outside in the reception and people wanted to know what it was all about. The wheels of momentum were turning.

It could have been because the client that ventured into the back office to get her colleagues was an influencer and other people thought if she cared about it then it must be good. But something had changed, and a pattern had been created.

It could have been my enthusiasm and determination to make it the best pitch they had seen all week, or the fact that I was open and flexible and made my clients feel this way, whatever it was it was working.

When I finished up my second pitch (this one was shorter, about 12-15 minutes), one guy stood up and said, "Hang on, do you know Julie? I'm going to go get her, she needs to see this."

I couldn't believe my luck; here I was getting a third meeting in the space of under an hour with a client that had taken months to get on the books. Now I had three potential opportunities coming my way. And to think a little earlier I was annoyed that they weren't treating it seriously by hosting the meeting in an official meeting room.

Julie came out, accompanied by David, and meeting number three got under way. This carried on and more potential sales opportunities came. This happened for a fourth time and after just over 90 minutes at the client's offices I walked away having done four meetings and made ten new client contacts, with multiple opportunities for sales discussed. I did 3x more business that month than any other month prior, and it just goes to show the power of remaining adaptable and being able to create momentum from anything.

It may have been the combination of me saying "hi" to other clients as they walked in and so they went into the building and said, "Oh, I saw Tim out front in reception." It may have been the energy and frequency with which the clients kept returning and grabbing more folks to come see what it was all about, but whatever it was, **I had created momentum**.

When you are dealing with a difficult person that is an influencer internally, you need to figure out what they want, what motivates them, what they need (e.g. recognition). In this case the client could run back inside and be the champion that brought my super cool product to her peers, bosses and stakeholders. This would feed their need for approval and internal social recognition as being the one with their finger on the pulse.

PRO TIP
Find out what they want and then help them get it

Try tapping into the psychological drivers of a client, the underlying motivations to find out how you can help them achieve their deeper level goals. If it is a promotion, they could bring your innovative solution to the table to solve a problem and help showcase to the business why they deserve a promotion.

These are all just thoughts on how this could have transpired to create one of the best sales moments of my career. It could have been a combination of all factors, or it could have simply been to get people excited about your product and they'll go to bat for you.

I guess I'll never know, but these lessons have stayed with me ever since:

■ Don't count yourself out if things don't appear to be how you expected.

■ Always give 110%, no matter the situation.

■ Be real, have fun and allow yourself to be you.

■ Adapt to the situations you are given to gain the best possible outcome from them.

■ Go for it – there's a sale waiting to be made around every corner.

■ What stands between you and the sale is your ability to get people inspired about what you have to offer by uncovering what they want and then giving it to them.

CONDUCT A POST-MEETING REVIEW

After the meeting has come to a close and you step out into the day and head towards your next appointment, don't forget to conduct a review of the meeting.

A little introspective feedback is an important habit to get into, so ask yourself the following questions and quickly answer them.

WHAT WENT WELL?	I BUILT RAPPORT
WHAT COULD I DO MORE OF NEXT TIME?	PAUSE WHEN CLIENT LAUGHS, EXPLORE THEIR Q'S LONGER, HAVE FUN
HOW MANY REFERRALS?	6
HOW DO I THINK IT WENT?	STRENGTHENED THE RELATIONSHIP
WHAT WAS UNEXPECTED?	THEY LOST THEIR KEY ACCOUNT
WHAT DID I LIKE?	INTROS INTO OTHER OFFICES ACROSS THE REGION
WHAT WILL I IMPROVE FOR NEXT TIME?	BE MORE PRESENT, TAKE MY TIME

SCORE OUT OF 10... 9.5

FIGURE 23: POST-MEETING REVIEW TEMPLATE.
**Download the post meeting review template at
www.timjscastle.com/themomentumsalesmodel**

This process, if conducted every time, shouldn't take you long and it will help you to focus like a laser your attention on simple but effective improvements. If you want to be the best, conduct the review and sharpen your saw. After all, when you're doing 10-15 meetings a week, the feedback you give yourself and the improvements you put into action should almost instantaneously be fixed. This habit will help you keep a high standard and stay at your very BEST.

MINI MOMENTUM BUILDER
Do a post-meeting review

After the next meeting you go to, I want you to immediately send a thank you follow up note with the requested information (within 30 minutes of leaving the meeting) and then answer the questions above. Finally, give yourself a score out of 10 rated by the following criteria <5 = poor, 5-8 average, 9 very good, 10 exceptional.

Trust me, doing a post-meeting review is the way to improve and hone your skills. When you're doing a ton of meetings per week it is super interesting the small things you catch yourself saying or notice you could do better. These micro improvements, if practised consistently, add up to one amazing salesperson by the end of it.

You'll notice that you keep adapting and growing and the only way to get to this level of success is to do the work and to make these questions and the post-meeting review part of your daily habit. Even if you only have 30 seconds, it is still worthwhile and what the world-class do.

NAILING THE PITCH SUMMARY

- Anyone can go through slides; the best salespeople *are* the slides.

- Be prepared for anything.

- Develop a PMA.

- In the meeting, Listen, Package, Uncover, Pitch.

- Melt the ice with laughter.

- Pitching for investment, remember to tease, please and seize.

- Stay the course, pass "the test" with gratitude, positivity and empathy.

- Take a temp check.

- Expect to win.

- At the end of a pitch, ask for the sale: *"Which of these two options works for you?"*.

- Nurturing the close starts with your attitude.

- Pitches are won by adding expert value they can't get anywhere else in the form of revealing new insights that promote buying action.

- Post-meeting reviews help you spot areas to improve upon and track progress.

CHAPTER 8

Time Management – Get your focus right, direct your energy and win

"Your habits are driving your performance. Your rituals are creating your results."

– ROBIN SHARMA

INTRODUCTION

As a salesperson I am spinning plates – all day, every day – and, to make sure I am both growing my book of business whilst ensuring none of my precious plates fall, I have to be super disciplined with time management.

Time management is an area that salespeople get wrong... all... the... time! If you are guilty of this, listen up. If you find yourself with not enough minutes in the day, you know you are doing something wrong, and this is your chapter. Read it and re-read it until it becomes habitual.

Emails, calls and meetings that don't move the needle are the wrong focus for a salesperson. When you've got momentum, you'll realise just how much time you wasted on unimportant rubbish that sounded important and necessary but actually didn't matter at all for your business.

The quicker you can adopt the principles I outline in the Momentum Sales Model, the faster you'll be able to spot these types of inefficiencies. You want to know why some people win more than others? It's because they are able to apply focus and persistence on key targeted activities consistently, day in, day out. As a result, the payoff is massive.

In this chapter, I'll give you the hard-hitting facts of the matter so you can reconfigure your day for optimal performance.

When you want something bad enough, when you want to dominate in business or you have a big goal that's burning a fire so bright inside, you'll stop scrolling through Instagram, you'll say no to after work drinks and you'll hunker down.

When you recognise how much you can actually get done in a day, how big your potential for success actually is and that you have what it takes to live a life beyond your wildest dreams, you'll put down the damn phone, quit whining and get conscious about how you are spending your time.

All it takes is a glimpse of success, a few wins and you'll start to see how effective this sales process is at creating momentum and changing your entire life. And let me remind you, there was a reason you picked up this book and it wasn't because you are average. Something brought you to this point, brought you to me to be mentored in sales and, because of this, I know you have what it takes to be a momentum seller and to be outstanding in your field. Never lose hope, I am telling you, as you have what it takes; you can and will sell more. You were put on this earth to shine and together we're building a wave of momentum so big for your business that it will blow everyone away.

Get ready, it's about to happen for you!

WHAT IS TIME MANAGEMENT?

Time management is the ability to control what you do and when to get leverage on your day. I break my day into 30-minute windows and rely on habits and rituals to guide when I do certain activities.

I've also been in the situation where I had too much time on my hands. If you're an entrepreneur and in control of your own diary, it can turn into a productivity nightmare. I remember having all this time available every day but kept getting distracted by either working on too many items at once or letting every message, call or notification take me away.

In other words, I was *too* available, which caused me to be less productive – as a result my time was less valuable. When you are under pressure and your time is a scarce commodity it is even more valuable. Likewise, when you only have a short time period to complete a task, focus increases – I am a big fan of staying in action, keeping full throttle.

My advice – if you find yourself plateauing or drifting it's because you're too comfortable, so you need to up the pace and set more deadlines for yourself, take on new, bigger goals and get some accountability. Give yourself tighter deadlines, commit to new projects, get a mentor that forces you to do what you say you are going to do.

All of the above helps you sharpen the saw and become who you were born to be. It gives you a stronger mindset because you are again out in the wild, making it happen, testing yourself and trusting that you will find a way to make it all work.

I share this because when most people think of time management, they think about not having enough time, but I just wanted to flag that having too much time and being too available is also killer. Be aware of both – they rob you of incredible adventures.

For those of you that are like me, when I don't feel like I have enough time, I fall into the bad habit of making it an excuse and saying it aloud "I don't have time" as an answer to requests, usually to my wife. It's a bad habit – saying these words aloud gives this statement power and brings it to life in some twisted self-fulfilling prophecy.

If you do this too, I encourage you to stop saying it. It's not actually true; everything we do is a choice – you *do* have time but maybe it's not optimised well. Maybe some tasks like choosing what to wear, which location to work from, or where to go for lunch are given too much time and in the end date night gets pushed because you have to work late.

In this chapter, I will show you how to:

■ Get more done before 9am than most do in a day

■ Structure your day for sales success

■ Never get overwhelmed again

■ Eat that frog and stop procrastinating

■ Use Dead Time to your advantage

■ Implement what the wildly successful do daily.

HOW TIME MANAGEMENT BUILDS SALES MOMENTUM

Optimising your time so it is spent on high-value activities and getting a clear understanding of how valuable every minute of your day is will help you build sales momentum.

When I got this one area sorted, I went from mediocre at best to being able to dominate in a high-pressure job, write books, articles, coach others, all whilst helping to build four start-ups on the side, interview and be interviewed on podcasts and show up for my growing family. It feels so amazing to be aligned with time. It is grounded in scheduling and keeping an eye on where I am spending large chunks of my time.

It's not just what you do but how you do it. It's how present you are when you are doing the tasks that matter.

This is where you must question yourself: is my train travelling in the right direction at all moments of the day? Am I tackling the right tasks, focusing on the future, building for my legacy, growing my pipeline and harvesting the opportunities?

You've got to be aggressively optimistic with how much you think you can get done and even more savage with your scheduling. This is where you go into full-on beast mode, and you value your time like it's your money.

Let me show you how to invest that cash wisely. Grab a pen – you're going to want to take notes.

1. PLANNING YOUR DAY

HOW TO WIN THE MORNING AND GET THE MOST OUT OF THE TIME BEFORE 9AM

I can't emphasise enough just how important this is! If there's a key ingredient that closely follows enthusiasm, it's this! All superstar sellers have got this skill mastered.

Wake up early and own it. Don't let the day get a jump on you. As Jim Rohn said, "Either you run the day or the day runs you." And he was quite right.

Become the best version of yourself by living to your fullest potential. Like it or not, in sales there's work to do. However, the work isn't how you might imagine. The work you must continuously do is on yourself.

It's the inner work that helps you think more clearly and quiet the nagging inner critic that tries to pull you back from taking big bold moves. You know, it's that timid doubtful voice in your head. That's how you make fantastic decisions and orientate your life for success as you strive to be more courageous in the actions and moves you make.

Here's my method for ultimate success in sales and in life. Whatever your goal, this framework will help you execute more boldly, with an inner understanding of what you value and why you are pursuing your goals.

4.30-5.00am

Getting an early morning routine is critical to amplifying your sales pipeline. The mornings are sacred, so I begin each day not by reaching for my phone to check emails and Instagram but by setting my feet on the floor thinking about the thing I am most grateful for. It's usually my wife and sons, Levi and Rome, and then finding some place to journal, write, read, meditate and get focused on a few deeper questions.

In the process I try to drink 1.5 litres of lemon water.

Then I might read a few pages of *Think and Grow Rich*. This is a book I absorb as much as possible. It began as a commitment to read once a year but, following the steps of Bob Proctor, I now aim to read a couple of pages every day to keep developing ideas and awareness.

The mornings and how you spend them says a lot about you as a person. A person who has dreams, goals and ambitions and is so committed to seeing them through with absolute conviction will own their mornings.

Guys like ex-navy seal Jocko Willink, Mark Wahlberg, Robin Sharma, Tim Ferriss, Jack Ma all talk about how critical it is to rise early and get to work on yourself.

I use this time to journal. This helps me reflect on questions in my head. I literally write down what I want to see happen in my life, and I write it as if it has already happened.

For example:

I am a multimillionaire author, entrepreneur and coach. I have multiple thriving businesses and income streams. Everything I get involved in is a success and brings me joy, love and abundance. I love life and life loves me. I recognise and take action on an abun-

dance of opportunities daily; I don't give in to doubt or fear and push forward every day as I strive to be the best I can be. I find fulfillment in the work I do, and it is inspiring millions of people to go out and achieve their big goals, dreams and vision. Through my example, I am helping people believe it is possible and go bigger in their own lives as a result. Money flows to me in all ways and I RECEIVE it gladly. Giving more is the way to receive more in life. How can I GIVE MORE TODAY?

You get the idea; this is a conversation with myself but also with my subconscious and the Universe. I am literally telling the Universe what I will see, priming myself for opportunities and to take advantage of them when they arrive.

This is an awesome state to live in. Give it a go and see how your perception of life changes, as you will witness miraculous shifts in your ability to see light in the dark times, to connect the dots in new ways and add more value to the world.

6.30am

Around 6.30am, I hit the gym, bike or an F45 training session. When you do something enough you don't need to think about it. My legs start walking and I find myself at the gym not really aware of how I got there.

Anywhere I walk I am listening to an audiobook or podcast, always. Rarely do I not have multiple books or shows on the go, unless it is a specific walk-in-nature to reflect and recoup energy. I guard what goes into my ears and only stick to a few podcasts on rotation, like Ed Mylett, Joel Olsteen, Tom Bilyeu and Coin Bureau for investing. I am also a member of the Arete Syndicate with Andy Frisella (Founder of 1st Phrom) and Ed Mylett (Business Leader and Speaker).

What you put in; you get out. I see podcasts, audiobooks and books in general as a conversation with my mastermind group. This includes inspirational leaders like Patrick Bet-David, Ed Mylett, Tony Robbins, Jim Rohn, Bob Proctor, Napoleon Hill, and Jon Gordon. This is time to plant the seeds that will bear the fruit in the summer.

If I get out on the bike, I will do a gratitude ride. This is a technique I made up to fill me with purposeful positive energy; as I am cycling along East Coast Park in Singapore next to the ocean, I will speak out all the things that I am grateful for. It's surprising just how much comes out once you get going and it fills my consciousness with just how lucky I am and how amazing this world is. I will then get stuck into a podcast and, as ideas float into my head, I will take action on them, whether it is investing in a blockchain, emailing a contact or client or just making a note to follow up on something. The gratitude ride combined with active learning via mentors is a fantastic way to start the day, and by this point, I am already feeling amazing given how much I have experienced in the day.

8.00am

Next up, once you are done with working on *you*, get working on business development, start drafting up 9 prospecting emails to new clients that you would like to meet with. This is your 9 before 9am. Ideally this is done the night before, but everyone works differently so it's important to adapt this strategy to suit you. The main thing is, as long as these emails get sent out before 9am, you are winning. You're already starting the day with a win.

8.30am

At 8.30am on the dot, send those bad boys out. This is key, as clients are making their morning commute, some will be checking their emails and therefore be more likely to open and read your well thought out request for a meeting email.

Others will already be at work, hustling, likewise these badasses will also be more likely to open and digest your email, they too may even respond. Lastly, those that are doing neither of these will still be more prone to reading your email because it's now top of the pile.

Timing is a key driver, use it. I have used this strategy with roughly a 35%-65% success rate, every day. The beauty of this process is that you build momentum and with that many prospecting emails going out each day you stack the odds in your favour of having a consistent pipeline of interactions with your clients.

HOW TO STRUCTURE YOUR DAY FOR SALES MASTERY

MASSIVE TOPIC ALERT, one by the way, that most mediocre salespeople get wrong.

Watch the best in class and you'll observe that they get a lot done with what seems to be a productive yet effortless aura about them. They're busy, don't get me wrong, but focused on the right things, at the right time. They know where to direct their energy.

How do these guys know what to do? Are they some sort of Jedi master? Did they go to a secret training camp?

No, they learned how to structure their day to maximise output and hustle by having discipline around what they direct their energy at during specific parts of the day. These go-getters are too busy making it rain to get sucked into office politics, or aimlessly watch social media. They're all guns blazing, all day, every day, to keep their plates spinning and serving their clients with excellence.

Be one of them by following this simple yet effective method of structuring your day.

Here it goes. Put this time into your diary, actually schedule it in there, don't expect yourself to remember until it becomes automatic. That way you'll get into a habit of remembering to do it and suddenly it will become second nature.

Bucket your day into three parts.

Morning 5am - 10am – Explorer – spend your early morning on personal development and the latter part on your most important (not urgent) tasks. This is where you brainstorm new ways to expand your sales pipeline. You're going to get more done in this time than you ever thought possible – this is about expansion, growth and acceleration. Use your creative energies to chart new territories and prospect, prospect, prospect and remember your 9 before 9am.

11am – have a client meeting.

Lunch 12pm - 2pm – Entrepreneur – plan your weekly lead generation activities, merchandise, competitions with prizes, partnerships (all according to your budget). It doesn't matter if you've got $50 or $5,000, use what you've got to create maximum momentum. It doesn't have to cost a bomb. Stand out, do what no one else is doing.

Afternoon 2pm - 4pm – Servant Leader – More meetings. This is where you're with clients and you are putting your strategies and plans into motion.

Using this structure, it allows you to get three client meetings whilst building the business. Most average salespeople just focus on meetings without treating their sales patch like a business.

Every business is different, so you need to run it the way that makes sense for you. The way I do this might change depending on my schedule, but I make sure that I hit each one of these three themes during each day.

In my past sales roles, I focused on doing business development (Explorer) in the hours of 6am-8.30am, and then jumped into sales meetings 9am until 3pm (Servant Leader) before finally finishing the day with a bit of client retention and servicing (Entrepreneur).

I also do Explorer activities on Saturday mornings or Sunday evenings, as you know. This structure doesn't need to be rigid; you can adapt it to suit your needs. However, this comes with a warning – don't slack off here, get into a rhythm.

If you wake up in the night and can't sleep, do some Entrepreneur type activities. How can you surprise your clients in new and unexpected ways? How can you not only retain them but consistently overdeliver on their expectations, so they have no need to go looking elsewhere?

Make this plan work for you and allow it to take your business to new heights of success.

DO THE HARD TASKS FIRST – EAT THAT FROG

"If the first thing you do each morning is to eat a live frog, you can go through the day with the satisfaction of knowing that it is probably the worst thing that is going to happen to you all day long."

– MARK TWAIN

Brian Tracy wrote a book on the topic called *Eat That Frog*. It goes into detail on why successful people are the ones who waste little time on doing the most important and hard things first and are able to focus on it without procrastinating until they get the job done.

In sales, you are required to manage competing priorities; whether you work in a team of one or 15, there is always a never-ending cycle of requests.

It can be FULL ON! The way to manage your time when you have multiple tasks you need to get done is to go straight at the harder more complex tasks first. You know, the ones that you want to ignore, to leave until last. These don't just have to be hard in terms of mental power that they require, they can also be hard emotionally and hence that is why you are avoiding them.

Hard can be having an uncomfortable conversation with your boss, making the case for new budgets to be unlocked, or it could be preparing the sales figures and forecasting for a particular client vertical or region.

As a rule of thumb, if you're avoiding it, then there is something inside your brain which thinks it is difficult, and by flipping the switch and going for it first you uncover any new information, challenges and problems that might be lurking in the background. By dealing with these first, you save them from becoming urgent problems that need your full focus and attention, taking you away from other important matters.

When you build the habit of doing the hard stuff first, you experience more success. I sat down to interview legendary YouTuber Evan Carmichael and in that impactful conversation I was thrilled to hear his motto is "I do difficult things". Having this type of attitude and showing up for yourself and the life you want to create is badass! This impresses me no end and the payoff is huge for two reasons.

Firstly, you gain more self-confidence when you walk courageously forward through things that scare you, and secondly, you respect yourself as a result of doing difficult things.

Hard stuff in sales can also include writing that new presentation deck for the big pitch you have coming up in a couple of weeks (preparing in advance), so don't leave it until the last minute. You need to get started and dig into it, that way you are more likely to produce outstanding work and overcome any hurdles and blockers standing in your way. It can be sharing a new idea at the team meeting, or volunteering to speak at an event. It can even be something as simple as committing to overachieving the target by 20% this month, which means you need to pull numbers on the weekend to figure out a new sales strategy.

When you get into the habit of tackling hard stuff first, ticking it off your list, it leaves you free and easy to blast through the more pleasurable stuff that you enjoy and are good at. This is the sweet spot in sales. It also feels good, and we like good – good helps drive momentum and helps you become a fuller, more expressive version of your highest self.

2. EFFICIENCY BUILDS MOMENTUM

TIME MANAGEMENT IN MEETINGS

The sales meeting is your ship to sale, your journey to guide, and the recipients of your meetings are in your care. If you only have 45 minutes for the meeting, state this up front rather than rushing through your pitch and firing out questions.

Give the client the opportunity to understand what is going on for you and turn it into a positive. When pushed for time, I begin meetings by explaining that I only have about 30 minutes and encourage the clients to ask questions throughout.

By providing the context, for example, "My flight is leaving in just under three hours' time but I really wanted to see you guys", the clients quickly understood that I had prioritised them and this meeting and that I was willing to risk not making my flight for them. This goes down really well, so don't let the opportunity to express how much your clients mean to you pass you by.

This showed that I valued their potential business. This also showed that I was willing to go far for my clients and that I don't let problems or challenges stand in the way of doing business.

These are qualities that are brilliant to highlight to clients in a subtle way.

If you are in a rush, slow your actions down. Know when to move fast and when to move slower. Funnily enough, as I was hustling from the Kwun Tong ferry port back to my hotel to collect my suitcase, I saw a beautiful butterfly flutter by serenely and I was reminded of the famous Muhammad Ali saying, "Float like a butterfly and sting like a bee."

This is what I mean by slowing your actions down. All that energy and action, if focused in the wrong direction, won't allow you to sting like a bee. It is better to pause momentarily and think clearly so that you may get it right. If you're moving at speed and haste to try to make a meeting, for example, ensure that you have the simple stuff right, like are you actually going to the right address, or did the client recently move offices? (Yes, learn from my mistake.) Call ahead to give them warning you might be a few minutes late. All simple yet effective strategies for allowing you to perform to your best in sales.

This also goes for meetings and presentations. If you find yourself tumbling over your words and rushing to make a point, try to catch yourself, slow it down, regroup your energy and then control the pace. Not only will your clients feel more at ease, but you'll also improve the quality of commutation and perceptiveness. The way to do this is to breathe.

Ask the client a question and then just take a moment when they are speaking to inhale slowly and deeply through your nose and then back out. After taking a beat to recalibrate, smoothly begin letting the words flow out of your mouth as you continue to exercise control of your breathing. In and out, four seconds in, four seconds out. You are physically controlling your physiological response and calming yourself. Literally controlling the flow to produce the rhythm.

In sales, controlling the flow also means knowing what matters most to your clients and putting that above all else. Being on time for your meetings is an excellent trait to have, don't be the sucker who is late. It reeks of shark behaviour and suggests you value your time more than theirs. Even just a few minutes isn't great.

If dialling in on a video call, make it a point to jump on two minutes before everyone else. Make it part of what you do, your operating principles. I find that I often get the most time to bond with people in the small talk before everyone else joins the call and the meeting begins.

It is hard to claw back that first image and being late only shows that you don't have yourself together, that you prioritise your time more highly than theirs and that you aren't someone serious to do business with. If you're late for the meeting, it begs the question, what else do you take shortcuts with?

Control the flow of the meeting, give signals as to the timeline as you work your way through the content (e.g. "We have ten minutes left, while we are together what's the most important thing we need to discuss?").

This invites the client to share valuable information and get right to the heart of the problem. As a superstar salesperson, one strategy for actually uncovering more valuable information is to only give meetings a 30-minute timeframe upfront. That way the most important information has a way of finding its way to the top.

Remember, you are the guide for your clients, and it is your job to manage the timeframe appropriately. Great salespeople know how to take their clients on a journey, giving them the exact pieces of information they need to make a decision, all whilst telling the story that has them enthralled.

Learning to control the flow is about becoming a leader and taking responsibility for the things you can control, being authentic and composed when things go wrong and actually leading your clients towards making the best decision for themselves. Walk tall, my momentum maker, and go take your patch by storm.

SALES EFFICIENCY VS EFFECTIVENESS

*"Efficiency is doing things right; effectiveness
is doing the right things."*

– PETER DRUCKER

Efficiency has to do with speed whereas effectiveness is about quality. Like firing an arrow from a bow, how fast it travels is efficiency, but hitting the target is effectiveness. The balance of these two variables will see you become a remarkable salesperson.

When you think about your current sales process and its productivity, you need to think about the time you spend creating vs the time you spend doing or, in other words, your input and output. Your input might be time spent creating promotional materials, new decks, crafting the story, case studies and your output is the number of calls, meetings, engagements, appointments you have each week.

The company may set targets around the optimal amount of output they think you should be doing. For example, at the end of each week you may be required to submit a report to the company detailing the number of client meetings conducted, revenue made and RFPs received.

It's all fairly standard, but what they don't tell you is that in order to be a high performer, you need to minimize the time you spend in input mode (i.e. how long it takes you to prepare for your core selling activities and how long it takes you to find the information you need).

The best organisations that I have worked for that were geared for sales structured the flow of information in a transparent nature. They had systems in place to ensure that their salespeople were armed with the latest and greatest information at all times. If an opportunity came in, it would only take a matter of seconds to locate the necessary information to provide an effective response.

The other area these outstanding organisations had nailed was providing timely updates to sales staff on the content and pitches that they found to be resonating in the market with clients.

Why is that a big deal?

Well, because it helps you become more effective, and massively saves time. If you can take the learnings from hundreds of pitches and streamline that into useful data, you can see what lands well with clients, what is turning the key and locking in the sales. By arming their salespeople with the best practices, it meant that valuable opportunities don't go to waste by providing ineffective responses to pitches or by sending out incoherent messages across the globe as an organisation.

Imagine you are walking into battle, if you all move as one, like an organism, the enemy will have a harder time breaking your spirit and your advances. Whereas, if the ranks of troops are all responding sporadically, in a random fashion, the enemy will be able to pick off and target groups, thereby breaking through your defences.

Companies that do this well regularly take the time to update all their salespeople on what is working (weekly). They take an interest in how their salespeople perform and where the magic is happening, and then they arm their sales team with the facts. They are not afraid to make adjustments to their pitch, even re-writing it if they find a formula for success. They keep innovating and tweaking to continually improve. It is this commitment to excellence that gives their sales teams no reason not to sell well.

In doing so, the company is actually saving their employees hundreds of hours across the year. If you can streamline your sales process, you increase your efficiency, and if this is optimised as you go forward, you are on to a winning set of rules to play by.

DEALING WITH OVERWHELM

Picture this, dawn breaks and a new day begins…the sun is rising, the birds are singing, and the sky is that clear blue, a new day is on the way. And then, the alarm clock goes off, your baby wakes up and begins to cry for milk because he's hungry, you check your phone and you see a stream of Slack messages pouring in one after the other, then WhatsApp starts kicking off as well, one message, two messages, pop, pop, pop, six, nine. *Oh my gosh, can this day just behave already.*

Then you open your Gmail and a block of unread emails beckon. You notice that little red dot on LinkedIn pop into view provocatively signalling that someone you don't know has sent you a direct message and is quite probably trying to flog you their financial services expertise or offer you another lead gen automation tool, but you aren't sure and can't resist checking.

End scene…

If you're anything like me, living in the 21st century, and you have a phone, a baby and a high-pressure job with responsibilities, then there's a heck of a lot to get your head around in terms of demands for your attention, time and all of the above. Before we know it, our days can get off to a pretty hectic start. Life in the 21st century is full on if we don't learn how to control it.

Working out what is important and what is simply a cry for attention can be quite difficult. In short, it can, at times, become very overwhelming.

If you're anything like I used to be, I hear you.

It wasn't until I decided enough was enough and came up with a system to deal with overwhelm and the constant stream of life's demands that I really started to be able to take back control of my day and get the most important tasks done.

My system allowed me to feel more fulfilled, spend more time on the important tasks and be more creative. If you want to become the top performer at work, you've got to get smart about how you organise, value and prioritise your time.

To overcome overwhelm and have a system for operating life, I developed my 4C's Framework for living every day in charge and with purpose. This helped me achieve my main goal which was to get the most out of my fullest potential. The 4C's are Creation, Conditioning, Certainty and Connection. If you're interested, you can find out more about my 4C's Framework in my book, *Be The Lion: How to Overcome Big Challenges and Make It Happen.*

I guarantee you, if you spend your days in reaction mode just dealing with things as they appear in view, putting out fires, dealing with urgent requests, it will leave you frazzled, overstressed and in a state of panic. You will lose your motivation. It will be difficult for you to hit your stride and get the most out of your fullest potential to be a top performer.

The way to think of it is, if you are always suffering from a lack of time, stretched and busy, then you never get the time to spend on the things that will actually move the needle, the things that matter and can actually be a game changer for your business and sales numbers.

It comes down to one thing! **Effectiveness.**

But to be effective, first you need to know what is worth spending your time on. As salespeople we are often pulled in multiple different directions, across an array of competing priorities. I want to show you a neat little tool that can help you quickly understand where you should be focusing your time.

Introducing the Eisenhower Decision Matrix, in this neat little table it holds the key to becoming a master of effectiveness and decision making. This tool will help you structure your day and get more done than ever before.

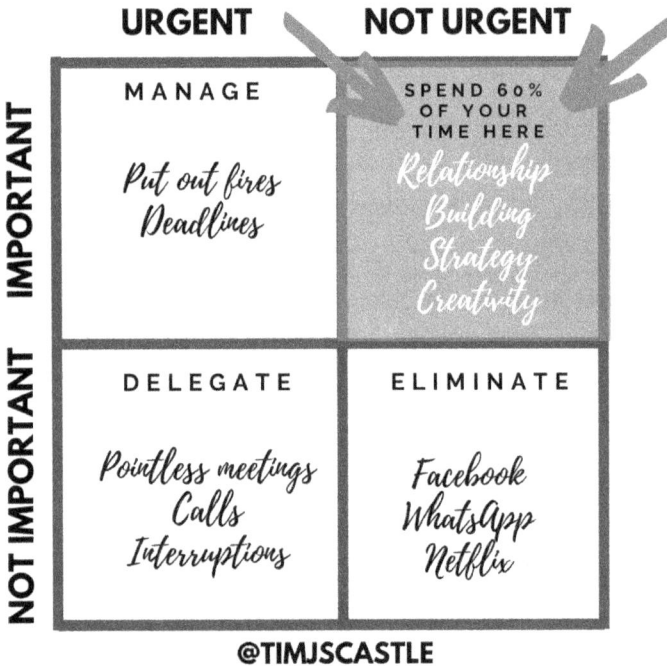

FIGURE 24: THE EISENHOWER DECISION MATRIX

To get straight to the point, the goal is to spend at least 60% of your time in the Not Urgent/Important quadrant (highlighted in the top right-hand corner).

If you are spending time in this space, doing activities and tasks that are important but not yet urgent you are working on what matters most, building relationships, being creative, planning, strategy, exercise, doing the work of developing a business pipeline, planting the seeds for the future and nurturing what is already there. 60% or more of your day needs to be spent here.

THIS IS WHERE YOU NEED TO FOCUS YOUR EFFORTS!

If, however, you are spending your time in the Urgent and Important quadrant (top left) as most overwhelmed folk do, this means you are always up against it, you're putting out fires as they happen, reacting to the world around you, you never have enough time, you are busy dealing with deadlines and barely making it through each day with any or no time to dedicate to your craft.

It is the biggest misconception to think that busy equals effective. We think we are a high performer because our day is full, but in reality, we aren't able to put in the groundwork that will help us produce results, retain business, build sustainable growth and develop the relationships that could transform our lives.

If this is you then believe me, I understand, the constant pressure and bombardment of fires to fight is unquestionably difficult in this day and age. But it has to stop. If you are going to become a person who operates at your highest potential and live the life of your dreams by becoming a top salesperson, whether that's opening up that online fashion store or selling that multimillion-dollar pad in New York then you must get serious about how you organise your time so that you can pursue your dreams. Sales masters take their time seriously.

By contrast, what spending time in the Important but Not Urgent category does is it allows you to be proactive, to scale, to expand, to build the base that will support your bigger vision.

Just to talk quickly about the other two quadrants so that you may also avoid them, the Not Important and Urgent quadrant is even worse, this means you are literally wasting your time doing things that not only won't move the needle, but they will be stressful, annoying and frustrating, making you a hot mess in the process.

If there are tasks that you can delegate in your daily business to a colleague like attending hour-long meetings, or sitting on conference calls, or a place you can go where you won't be interrupted whilst you are doing your best work then make it happen.

Likewise, at home, if there are tasks that need to get done but are sucking up your time, like cleaning your apartment, or walking your dog, then DELEGATE IT! Your time is valuable.

This is how you reclaim your time so that you can spend 60%+ of your day in the Not Urgent but Important quadrant. Not all tasks are created equal so spending a little extra cash to automate, outsource and delegate some of the not important tasks to free up your day has remarkable value.

Now that you've delegated the not important tasks (e.g. cooking, cleaning, meetings that you don't need to attend, con calls that are not relevant) it is vital you also get rid and free yourself from distraction – otherwise known as the Not Important and Not Urgent quadrant.

If you spend time here then this is where you are literally watching your dreams die, and your sales numbers fall off a cliff. To get an idea of how you are performing in this one area, just track how long you are spending on social media (Facebook, Instagram, TikTok) procrastinating per day. iPhone does this automatically under the screen time option in settings.

Now, I know many of you will say I need to do Instagram for my business or to get sales leads, and I get that, I agree, but it should not be at the detriment of your other work. Social media is there as a tool to propel your business and grow your audience if used correctly, it can also be a distraction if you allow it. It's configured and optimised to keep you scrolling.

Take a deeper look and get accountable at what you are doing when you are on social media, if you are indulging mindless scrolling then you need to eliminate this. Bye bye Netflix, YouTube, computer games – THIS IS ALL TIME THAT YOU NEED TO REALLO-CATE to things that can move the needle.

How badly do you want it? If you aren't willing to significantly reduce the amount of time you spend unwinding, relaxing, watching TV, and instead work on your business, your performance, your goals, your future, then life will pass you by and the opportunity will move to someone who goes after it.

A trick I learned for maximising time and moving away from distraction was something I called "dead time", which I will go into in more detail in the next section.

In dead time, we normally divert our attention to social media for a distraction, to kill the time and also get that hit of dopamine when we see something funny, or that someone has liked our photo, or our favourite influencer has released a new clothing line.

You get one life, don't leave anything on the table. Go for it with all you've got. Eliminate the activities that are holding you back.

PRO TIP
Bulk task

For example, you know those 10 new business prospecting emails I recommend you find time to write on Sunday night? It is more efficient to write them all at the same time, this reduces the chances of any overwhelm and by getting focused bulking tasks means you can move faster. You will achieve synergies because you are in the right mindset, rather than write one email, then going for a pizza, then writing another and stopping to watch the news. Get into the habit of bulking tasks into 30-minute blocks of time, by giving yourself a deadline you will achieve more.

Top salespeople figure out a plan for how they are going to spend their time and what they will be doing for each half hour block of time.

For instance, today I am going to follow up on all my meetings from the previous day and I might section off 30 minutes at 4pm to respond to all my recent briefs.

Or if I have identified cold calling as a strategy I want to investigate, I will block out 30 minutes at 9.30am to do all my cold calling in one go. The point is by bulking tasks together you will be more effective, learn from trends easier (because you will spot them) and actually get more done with the time.

I'll say it again, learn to value your time.

When you say you are going to do something you follow through and do it. If it's writing a blog post, you do it, you don't start to write whilst listening to a podcast and getting interrupted by pings on your phone. Shut off the phone, cut off all the distractions and get focused on the single objective at hand.

Get into your creative flow and get the work done. You will find that it is a habit and the incredible thing about habits is the more you do it the better and deeper ingrained it will become.

Like building any muscle, learning to be focused on the task at hand will see you achieve more and, because you are using the Eisenhower Decision Matrix framework above, you will have identified that the task is actually valuable, it will be worth your time and so it becomes a virtuous circle.

You actually have to do less but achieve more, and as the quality of what you are focusing on improves so does the quality of your output also increase.

I promise you, if you implement the steps highlighted above and reorganise your daily schedule so that you are spending more time on the things that matter, you will not only reduce overwhelm, but you'll also become a top sales performer in the process.

LEARN TO USE DEAD TIME TO GAIN MOMENTUM

You're an ambitious person, you have dreams, a vision of your ideal life and your goals mapped out. You have it all figured out; you know where you want to be yet for some reason you're stuck.

What's going wrong?

In a nutshell, gaining momentum has to do with two things:

1. Initiative

2. Persistence

Taking initiative when you're stuck and being persistent in the face of challenges are the ingredients required to gain massive momentum in the direction of your goals, dreams and desires, especially in sales.

So, what is Dead Time?

Dead Time is any time you spend waiting. This could be for a person, a train, a plane, a boat, a bus, doctor, dentist, an appointment, a movie to start or stuck in traffic. It is when you would normally be reaching for your phone, scrolling through social media to distract you from the monotony of waiting or watching Netflix or checking email. This is Dead Time.

Whenever you find yourself browsing aimlessly on your phone, or at a loss for something to do, get to it and blast out a few prospecting emails, make some calls, or plan how to go bigger than last week.

Action Time needs to become your best friend. Using Action Time to make that very important call to a potential new client, or pitch your idea to an investor, or email that radio station asking to be a guest on their show, or write that book, record that podcast. It's all going to help you gain momentum in sales, the bigger your platform and the more value you can add, the more it gives you credibility in the market. You are a brand.

This is what makes the difference. I need to pull back the curtain here. It's those moments when you're on an 18-hour flight and you decide to write and plan instead of watch movies. It's getting up at 3am and reorganising your thoughts into a coherent vision for the next five years of your life. It's making the effort to put your dreams front and centre of your life. Sales can make this happen for you because when you reach this level of commitment, you reach Sales Flow, you build momentum, you cultivate resilience. It all works together.

The key is getting out of Dead Time and into Action Time. When you notice yourself reaching for your phone, try to get into the habit of questioning whether this is the best use of your time.

What could you be doing right now, using what is around you to propel your business forwards?

It's a simple equation:

DEAD TIME + INITIATIVE + PERSISTENCE = ACTION TIME.

The next stage of Action Time that will really help you to gain momentum so that you are constantly hitting your sales goals is ensuring that you have enough opportunities in the air. You need to be like a juggler, constantly throwing balls up and catching others, always keeping them in motion.

By this I mean you need to be taking action whenever you have Dead Time and get into the habit of thinking creatively about what you can do to move forward.

The more you get used to be taking action and asking the question "What is the next right action I can complete to help me to achieve XYZ?", the more opportunities will come your way in abundance.

This is where initiative and persistence come into their own. You will flourish and become an inspired action-taking machine. Opportunities are going to flow towards you and, because you have this new way of thinking, this open, motivated and creative mindset, you're ready for them! This is your time to shine!

PERSONAL STORY
How to use dead time

I discovered this powerful combination at Changi Airport, Singapore. I had just published my first book *The Art of Negotiation* and was filled with emotion, enthusiasm and hope. I walked into WHSmith's in Changi Airport whilst waiting for my flight and my life has never been the same again.

I had about an hour to kill before my flight to Hong Kong was due for take-off. I was going away for business and I remembered I had packed a copy of my new shiny book in my hand luggage. I had some dead time on my hands, so I decided to give myself a little challenge. I gave myself 30 minutes to go into WHSmith's bookstore and convince them to carry my new title in their stores.

This is a big feat considering I was not a well-known author at this point; I didn't have millions of copies flying off the shelves, all I had was a copy of my book and time on my hands.

I strode into the store, stood in the queue at the counter and when my turn came, I proceeded to make my pitch to the woman serving me. After hearing what I had to say, she sent me to another store to see the manager on the other side of the terminal.

Unperturbed, I marched on, I found the other WHSmith's store and asked to see the manager. When she came out, I made my pitch and left a copy of the book for her. I only asked one thing, that she would please pass my book along to the book buyer, then I flew off to Hong Kong hoping that wheels were in motion and this challenge I had set myself would come to fruition.

The manager of the store gave me some crucial information, telling me which distributors I should contact in order to have any shot of making this happen. I knew that this was something I needed to follow up on; before landing in Hong Kong I had already sent out a few emails explaining my situation and what I thought the opportunity might be.

A few weeks and a lot of emails and calls later to distributors and local printers and miraculously it happened – WHSmith's liked my books and agreed to carry them. We did a deal. Of course, this took the grace of a number of key people, from the book buyer seeing the potential of the book to help people and generate sales revenue, the store manager making good on her promise to pass the book along and give me critical information, the distributor being open and having the mindset of possibility to go for it. By taking initiative and persisting, you can start to put yourself and your goals in position for success and this comes from making use of every opportunity.

The BIG lesson here was I discovered the ability we all have to transform "Dead Time" into "Action Time".

WHY MOST SALESPEOPLE FAIL

Remember Momentum is won or lost on your ability to take more action in the right direction consistently every day. Most can't sustain the discipline it requires to keep the top priority the main priority until it has been completed. Consequently, they can be doing all the right things but missing this ingredient which causes them to wonder why they aren't making sales.

Most underestimate how time management plays a part in your results. If you're too busy trying to do it all, you don't achieve much. If you learn to focus on the tasks and clients it could significantly move the needle, change the face of your business forever, upgrade your life and the life of your family, build a legacy and a brand as the top salesperson someone has ever come across. If you're not getting the results and outcomes you want, take a look at how you are spending your time.

The 80/20 rule is a rule for a reason. Take a look at where most of your revenue comes from – how many clients bring in 80% of the revenue? These are game changers, lose one of these and you'll be struggling, find more of these and you'll be on your way to momentum.

Now think about your time, do you spend 80% of your time serving these clients that bring in 80% of your revenue? Do you mine them for new opportunities, or do you take them for granted? Would they call you an excellent salesperson, on the ball, bringing them new insights and opportunities? Do you challenge them to think differently about the future of their business and work to ensure their success? Or are you focused on the next shiny thing?

As a salesperson who is leading the pack, you've got to be able to find a balance between managing your existing client base whilst growing your new business pipeline. This is especially true if you're the founder of a business – it's hard, but it's got to be done. New opportunities for expansion could be right under your nose except you're too focused on everything else to see them.

I have given you the tools to dominate at your business and bring in sales like never before. You will open the flood gates if you implement the Momentum Sales process with rigour. By spending the appropriate amount of time with your top customers, you learn new things about them, you spot trends, and this feeds your strategy for how you approach new business.

It might sound harsh but average salespeople fail because they are too busy doing nothing that matters. They're busy, but not impactful. If you think about where you want your business to be in six months' time, which clients do you want to attract? Who do you want in your network and on your team? These are much more productive questions that prompt you to take action in the right direction.

Focus on the big money, it might even be right in front of your face. It's tough because all these distractions, issues and people want our attention, they even shout for it – "hey can you look at this", "can I just get your thoughts on…" You've got to be able to deal with the request and get right back on track. I don't mean you have to be unhelpful, being a positive team player is a large part of how you dominate, but you've got to keep the top priority your focus and that's where the discipline comes in. How quickly can you reset after an interruption? How fast can you get back to serving your biggest focus after needing to attend to a call, email or message?

YOU HAVE UNLIMITED POTENTIAL!

The question is what will you do with it? Average salespeople listen to the opinions of others, and they buy into their negativity ("oh, the market's not hot right now", "that client will never spend" or "don't waste your time on them").

Those that are wildly successful in sales know to follow their own unlimited view of the world, and they know how to keep themselves focused on the golden opportunities that surround them. Like a sniper they lock in and execute.

Average salespeople talk the talk, get distracted and then talk the excuse. Outstanding salespeople, however, know that it's down to them and how they direct their time. No excuses, no self-limiting beliefs, just pure and simple laser focus.

Once you understand the power of time management (which is really code for attention management), you control what you allow into your life, what you let influence you and what you get done each day. Once you truly understand how much is within your control and your full potential, you will be so successful it will take you by surprise.

DO THIS ONE THING TO LEVEL UP

As part of the chapter on time management it would be a failure on my part not to share this one strategy that will help you become wildly successful in sales and life.

I want you to commit to spending 15 minutes a day brainstorming ideas on how to achieve your mission. I want you to aim to come up with 20 ideas that could help you to improve your service. If you are running a business, an entrepreneur or working in sales, write down your overarching mission and then list out your ideas as they come into your head.

I want to increase my new business sales pipeline:

1. Get featured in large publications and industry press

2. Do interviews on well-known podcasts

3. Write op-ed pieces and submit and upload to my blog/LinkedIn

4. Hire an intern to do marketing and BD

5. Create a future industry trends playbook and send to network

Earl Shoaf (Jim Rohn's mentor) came up with this strategy for advancing one's mission. However, back then he asked for a one hour a day commitment, so I am going easy on you!

In conclusion, how you spend your time has everything to do with your commitment to your goal. It is not acceptable to say you don't have time, you don't prioritise it. Eat the frog, structure your day for success, expect to win and you'll be off to the races.

Millionaires and billionaires did this when they started out, and they still do it, daily. It is the strategy to maximising time and moving with momentum.

TIME MANAGEMENT SUMMARY

- Structure your day in 30-minute increments

- Use Finder, Keeper, Doer to guide your time

- Eat that frog and attack the hardest most important tasks first

- Spend 60% of your day doing Important Not Urgent Tasks (Networking, Strategy, Creative Thinking)

- Dead Time + Initiative + Persistence = Action Time

- Spend 15 minutes a day thinking about how to achieve your goal

CHAPTER 9

Understanding – Demonstrate empathy with your clients

"Everything happens for us, not to us."

– ED MYLETT

INTRODUCTION

Huge quote there from my man Ed Mylett. I suggest you get into his podcast if you've not already discovered a bit of his world, just phenomenal, glorious conversions that add a ton of value!

When it comes to sales, boy oh boy, we put in the work, we hustle and grind to get the sale over the line and it can feel devastating when you invest so much energy and time on a client and then they decide not to go forward.

Man, it sucks – but here's the kicker. The client is also going on their own emotional rollercoaster, they too have their own journey with the sale and, more importantly, with YOU!

Therefore, considering how you deal with losses is key, how you deal with where your client is at in terms of their mindset, their annoying, insane questions that always need to be answered in a flash at the most inappropriate times and feels like a repeat of the information you've already provided 60 gazillion times.

This, this right here, is where you need to activate your empathy and understanding. If you can become a master at knowing when you are more likely to blow a sale and when empathy is most needed you will become very rich indeed.

In this chapter I will show you how to:

- Develop emotional awareness and take personal responsibility

- Understand who you are dealing with using DiSC behavioural profiles

- Speak their language (Visual, Auditory, Kinaesthetic)

- Make it so easy for clients to do business with you that they keep on coming back

WHAT IS UNDERSTANDING?

It's showing you care, and you can put yourself in your clients' shoes, you are there for them.

You will help them through the six emotions they will experience during the sales process, you will adapt your sales style to how they want to be sold to and you help them become so much more than just an advocate of your products and services.

Understanding is about falling in love with your clients and spreading the joy. When you adopt this attitude, you can change the world. If you move through your day with the intention of spreading love, abundance and joy, you will experience success. This is because your client servicing will go through the roof, and you will pay more attention to them. In return they will feel this, they will offer you opportunities no one else will get a chance to look at.

Your attitude affects your emotions and your energy, work will become lighter, easier, and seem to effortlessly flow from one amazing thing to the next. Your actions will be impacted as you move through your day, inspired by positivity, courage and love. You will be motivated to go bigger, not giving in to fear and doubt.

Understanding is your intention to raise your game, to care and attend to your clients like no one else and to be the very best. When this is your intention, you can't help but make a difference and touch more lives. The more lives you touch, the greater your wealth. When you choose to serve and to lead in this manner all things become possible.

Growth and contribution are what it all comes down to, this is where the meaning and fulfilment is found, when you can change your clients' lives by what you do as a salesperson. Think about this for a second: you're becoming an expert salesperson, you are going to impact others around you, whether it's your clients or people in your team. You will have a direct, positive effect on the trajectory of their lives!

HOW DOES UNDERSTANDING BUILD SALES MOMENTUM?

Your ability to read the room, to know your clients' tells, to hear what they are saying and adapt to help them are key. If you want to be a top salesperson you must develop your ability to be able to communicate, this is what humanises the relationship, the experience, and allows transformation to occur.

Just like the story of the carrot, the egg and the coffee bean. If you put a carrot in boiling water, it gets weak; if you put an egg into boiling water, it gets hard; and if you drop a coffee bean into boiling water, it transforms it – **be like the coffee bean**.

I love this metaphor of the coffee bean – remember this the next time you are facing a difficult client and remember it is your job to figure it out for them. How you respond affects what happens next.

You can take that anger, rage, resentment, pissed off attitude and carry it around with you for the day or a few days. This will annoy your colleagues, your wife or husband, your kids, the person that serves you at the supermarket. It will basically make you a walking crap magnet where anything and everything of a lower abundance state is tangled up with you.

Or you can do as I suggest and control your own response and mindset towards the situation and resolve it with empathy.

When I talk about delivering empathy and understanding this comes from a place of being an expert in communication. It's the one skill that you need to be able to handle any situation you are presented. This, combined with the focus of delivering huge value to your clients, will have a magnificent effect on your sales that is so vast that you'll be changed forever.

I know you're reading this book because you want to win, you want to dream, you want to achieve and contribute – trust me, all of this will happen every day when you choose to empathise and teach others how to model this behaviour so that it spreads throughout the world.

When you want your dreams bad enough, you understand that they become realised through giving, through sharing your gifts, talents and lessons with others. When you have that penny drop moment, the next time you are with a client and you choose to empathise and communicate with them with skill rather than focusing on what it means to you, there will be a shift.

When that shift occurs and you notice an aura, a flow, an energy of sales momentum moves into your life and it gets smoother, please do me a favour and share the experience with someone. Tell them about it, tell them how you chose to see the situation – your client's demands, their impatience, their lack of clarity – with another perspective responding instead with love and grace.

When this happens, you will have become the master salesperson and have begun the continuous improvement journey of the expert communicator.

Part of becoming world class in sales is mentoring and helping others. By bringing them with you, together we raise the global consciousness of empathy and understand the role these elements play.

This chapter explores empathetic relationships with both external clients and also internal stakeholders. Let's not forget how you handle internal situations impacts your success and your bank account.

1. EMOTIONAL INTELLIGENCE

PERSONAL STORY
Take personal responsibility

I'll give you an example on taking personal responsibility – twice I have landed a new job, created momentum, handed in my notice and worked my notice, then moved into my new role at a new company. As you'd expect in sales there's often some unpaid bonuses that, depending on the company policy, you either lose or you get paid. However, here's the twist, in sales it seems that when you leave (depending on the company), they may or may not want to add in a few caveats to *when* you get that payout – this is especially common in smaller private companies. Both times I was asked to chase existing debtors and chase up outstanding payments before the companies would pay me my final bonus cheque.

Now the timing of this is never great – 15 weeks out from the birth of my second son Rome, I had been banking on getting this bonus payment to take care of the cost of the birth and the pregnancy. To then find out that the company wasn't going to pay up until I cleared their debts with clients was a kick in the teeth. It was completely my fault – I hadn't seen it coming, blindsided again, although I'd kicked ass and smashed my targets to ensure my family would be protected through this period. It hurt to think this company would do this to me, but you've got to remember – that is victim speak.

I could have done a number of things to prevent this. Firstly, I could have asked more questions about the bonus payments during my notice period and got ahead of it. Just because the company doesn't communicate to you in a timely manner doesn't mean that they won't change the goal posts upon exit – this is business.

Secondly, I could have read the fine print in the contract and pre-empted this outcome with a conversation months earlier.

Thirdly, I could have built a stronger relationship with the finance team and done more to proactively chase clients for payment. I could have made this a priority earlier on my own steam.

Instead of being pissed off and threatening lawyers, or kicking off, talking bad about them in the market, I knew the only way forward was to let it go. By let it go, I mean play the game; you have to do what you can to take action and, in this case, it meant responding with empathy. They are a business and these clients should have paid them. Although not formally part of my remit, they were accounts that I had won and therefore they were linked to me.

The money is rightfully theirs and just because I fundamentally didn't agree with the action they were taking because I had worked tooth and nail, and dedicated most weekends to the business for six months to a year (I had even spent my own money on flights to go see customers to drive new business and hit the numbers I did), that doesn't mean that responding with anger or frustration would yield the best results. It was my decision to invest my own money into the business to win sales. The company didn't know about this, nor did they ask for it, but I needed to move fast so didn't want to wait for approvals.

This was a big lesson in taking responsibility for my own actions and now I had to face the potential that was always there. I was working for someone else, not my own business, yet I had treated it as my own, and ironically, if it was my own, I wouldn't be getting paid my bonus either because the money was still an outstanding debt to be collected.

The reason I wanted to share this example is because when it's all on the line, when you think you've done everything you can to execute at the highest level of your ability, something or someone can still pull the rug from beneath your feet.

Here is where I needed to become the ultimate coffee bean, respond with empathy and transform the situation in a manner that healed my resentment and ill-feeling whilst solving the problem and building trusted relationships.

This takes strength. On the surface it might look like you're a sucker, not sticking up for yourself or telling them why they are wrong, and it was disgraceful because it didn't fit into my plan and I had done my part – I had sold, and they had contracts anyway so they would get paid.

However, that does not build influence – the way to build influence is through transformation, seeking to understand, bringing and delivering value, and this is where you can then get understanding for your side of it. Only at this point.

If you want something, first you must give it.

So, what did I do? I didn't respond right away (never respond when you're angry). I took the weekend to collect my thoughts and then I got to work. I called every client on the list on top of working a full time job. I didn't waste time complaining about the ordeal or the extra work, I rolled my sleeves up, and got stuck in – after all, my baby was coming in a matter of weeks and I promised myself and my wife finances would not be an issue. I was going to keep that promise – I doubled down my efforts in my new job and doubled down outside of work.

By the time the baby came, I had a large bonus from my new job to pay the bills, but God had other plans. It was all magically taken care of by a new insurance policy update on my wife's side, and I also had the good fortune of knowing the wheels were in motion for the old bonus payment and it would be on the way.

Sometimes things work out better than we can imagine, and we are rewarded in ways beyond our control. By taking personal responsibility for every situation, we put ourselves in the position to prosper.

I used empathy as a transformation agent to get what I wanted whilst building other people and situations up.

Be like the coffee bean – note this down, look at it every time you need it. Remember empathy and expert communication allow you to humanise, build influence and rise.

Abundance and faith sit above the trivial details of who did what. You must believe that the sales are on their way and that, as long as you operate in consistency with your highest principles and values and follow this process, it will happen in greater ways than you can imagine. Keep that tank full and your head held high no matter what you're facing.

Situations like the one I just described are an opportunity to grow. Help someone else out of their stress, give your skills as an incredible salesperson to help solve a problem and in turn solve your own.

When you do this, you can release anger and built-up resentment and walk lighter, you can actually forgive the other person, the company and not feel pissed off. This is where you want to be, holding yourself to a higher standard, living in a state of abundance and gratitude, forgiveness, empathy and the realisation that you are powerful beyond belief when you get your mind right. You want to hold yourself to these values and be above the level of the needy, limiting, restricting situation that you are presented and go beyond it – you have the skills, capacity and are strong enough to forgive and move forward with grace.

EMOTIONAL AWARENESS MATTERS

Think about how you want to be served at a restaurant. Depending on what the situation is, you'll want different things. If you're in a rush, you'll value speed and efficiency over entertainment and culinary details. If you're on a first date, you'll perhaps value camaraderie and laughter to help break the ice or being left alone to talk with privacy. Each situation is unique and requires a different type of service. It's the same in sales.

Using the restaurant example again, it's the waiter or waitress who can adapt on the fly, that has it completely together, the one who can memorise your order effortlessly and gets it right, that transforms your experience.

Not to mention their ability to be attentive yet not overbearing, offering that light touch that facilitates the meal and helps it move along giving you exactly the experience you were looking for.

Expert waiters or waitresses understand the importance of analysing and responding appropriately to the meal's purpose – if they want a repeat customer that is. Bad waiting staff rush in, do their thing, and go through a systematised process on autopilot without bothering to understand what the situation really needs. They are oblivious or don't care enough to learn that there is another way.

By contrast, you can spot an amazing waitress. She takes careful assessment of each situation as it changes throughout the meal, adapting her service as required. It's as if she seems to know if the date is going well, whether the important business meeting on table 12 is reaching a deal or if the couple at the bar have cleared the air and are now looking for reconnection. Limoncello anyone?!

This type of behaviour is highly prevalent in high-end restaurants; if you're there on a business lunch, the staff don't walk over and serve the food right as you're delivering the pivotal hook of your sales pitch, or when you're all intently focused on one person speaking and the concentration level is high.

In essence they don't push their agenda over yours. How about the waiter that understands and can read the situation to know that things are tense, and you might need swift uncomplicated service so as not to add fuel to the fire?

It comes down to emotional intelligence (EQ), which is the ability to have empathy for the situation at hand and to be able to read what's going on for the other person. This way you can put yourself in their shoes and respond accordingly, as you would like to be treated.

Empathy, and how you use it in sales makes a huge difference to the types of relationships that flourish. Sales leaders with high emotional intelligence will always outperform those with only a limited grasp.

Remember, people buy with their hearts not their heads so learning to understand a person's emotional state is key.

TUNE IN

When you are plugged in, you are in the zone, you have absolute clarity on what your clients are saying, and you are both energised by the feeling of being on the same page. If you find that this is happening, go for it, tune in to it and ride the flow of positive energy that is being created between you.

When you are both in sync, it is the perfect time for innovative and fresh ideas to be bounced around. There is an environment of psychological safety which protects both parties from feeling awkward or vulnerable about sharing out of the box ideas and, also, if you are perceptive, allows you to gain a deeper understanding as to what is really motivating your clients. **It's like the curtain has opened, giving you a glimpse of what's going on inside.** If you get to this stage with your clients, you know you're on to a winner.

There was an episode of the Gary Vee podcast where Chase Jarvis, Founder of Creative Live had joined to be interviewed[4]. At one stage in the podcast, they get callers to dial in with their questions and this one guy asked about using creativity as a muscle and if you should rest it and, if so, for how long.

I bring this conversation to your attention because I want you to witness how tuned in Chase and Gary are to each other, and to the points they are each making. They are so on the same wavelength and, even hearing this back and forth between them as they answer this guy's question, it made me smile and realise that when you're in the moment and you're locked into each other's way of thinking sparks of genius fly.

The guy on the end of the line wasn't quite getting it, saying phrases like "I'm getting *started* with my podcast" and "I've got the *right* kit" but Gary and Chase both wouldn't let him off the hook.

---

4 https://www.chasejarvis.com/project/chase-jarvis-live-podcast/

They knew the only way to help someone is to help them, to get right into the thick of it and call them out when you know they just won't make it with their current level of thought.

This podcast episode is fantastic at highlighting how something can be clear as day for two people and they can riff on the topic building for days, developing and building on each other's points like some sort of relay race and then there's the guy that isn't quite getting it but wants to.

This might happen to you with your clients in the room. There may be someone that you are just hitting it off with, where you are matching each other thought for thought, getting so in the zone together. This is fantastic when this happens, and I would obviously encourage you to maximise this.

The question is, though, what about the other people in the room?

A world class salesperson knows how to bring everyone else along or at least give them something to work with. They are able to catch the stragglers and break it down in a way they can relate to, so they understand and are a part of the journey.

As in the example above, it would have been easy for Gary and Chase to go, well, we know we're right and keep on going without stopping to check in and make sure the guy whose question they are solving actually got what they were putting down.

The same goes for you and your client interactions: clients need salespeople that have the skill and emotional intelligence to pick up on when others in the room are lost, or not following at 100%.

The skilful seller is able to weave this into the narrative without losing the pace, energy and excitement generated from the ideas that have been created. It's about bringing everyone along together and, if you do this, your clients will appreciate you even more.

It is human nature to want to understand, but we don't like to be made to look stupid so this must be carefully handled. The way you do this is demonstrated by your intention, you are checking in with your clients because you want to help them, not make them feel like an idiot in front of their peers. The is a subtle but major difference and if you get it wrong, you'll be ushered out of the room and the meeting will be over before you've had a chance to even smell the money. Goodbye, case closed, that guy's a douchebag. Don't be that guy.

When your intention is to help (rather than to say, "Look at how clever I am! I understand this stuff and you don't."), then you're offering to lift someone up, to bring them into your circle, not undermine or disrespect them.

PRO TIP
How to tune in in your sales meetings

Pick up on non-verbal behaviours. Are they yawning, distracted, over it? If so, you need to change the energy.

Are you focused on them? When a client is repeating details that you should have picked up the first time, it shows you were not paying full attention.

Remain open and polite. Instead of rolling into your sales patter, keep in mind that each customer has unique life experiences, preferences and hopes – learn to tap into these through questions.

Get the client talking about something they love – passion infuses conversations with possibility.

Be aware of your surroundings. Does your client look flustered, upset, tired? Light up their day and help lift them up. Build your clients up, give them that boost.

Again, opportunities like this are golden because, if done right, you can create magic moments where everyone in the room feels safer, more secure, and confident enough to ask questions... which if you haven't got it already, is what you want.

When clients are asking questions and delving deeper into your offering and capabilities, it is positive for a number of reasons. Mainly because it also gives you the opportunity to ask well-structured questions back, meaning you get vital information whilst the questions do their work of making people feel good about themselves. Whether answering or asking, they are providing value and psychologically this gives them a boost. We all like to feel a sense of purpose, and engagement in meetings is one of the ways in which we can make this contribution for ourselves, our teammates and our companies. Get clients talking and you're on to a winner, where more ideas get thrown about and, ultimately, more progress is made.

UNDERSTAND WHO YOU ARE DEALING WITH

I'd like to introduce you to a tool that will help you no end in hitting the spot with all your clients. The key premise is that you shouldn't sell to your client how you'd like to be sold to, but rather, how they'd like to be sold to. What do I mean by this?

We each have a behavioural profile. If you spread everyone out on earth and put us in order from insanely outgoing to reserved, we would fall on a spectrum. At one end you'd have the most outgoing person on earth and on the other the most reserved and everyone else would be ordered in between based on their profile.

The big penny drop here is…

If you want to consistently win deals, you can't sell how *you'd* like to be sold to.

Therefore you must understand who you are dealing with. Do you need to feed their ego? Are they new to business, so do they need handholding? The goal is to understand the other side's interests and let them feel heard. If you want to consistently win deals, you must adapt to the buyer's communication style and behavioural preference.

Learn behavioural profiling so that, when you're sitting with a potential or existing client, you know how to approach them. In fact, let's go through this right now.

I want to introduce you to the DiSC behaviour profiles, first proposed by William Moulton Marston in 1928, these are Dominance, Influence, Steadiness and Compliance and they will help you place people into different behaviour categories. They are simple yet very effective for helping you adjust your sales style to suit their needs. Let's dive in and take a look at each of these profiles in order.

The first question you need to ask yourself when you are profiling a client is: are they more outgoing or more reserved? It doesn't matter if you are communicating over the phone, or in person or even on text. You can tell what they are likely to be by the kind of language they use to express themselves, if they're first to say "hi" when you join the call, whether they have camera on or camera off, what they got up to on the weekend and how they chose to spend their free time. It all signals something about them to you.

As you practise this, you become more aware so don't worry if you don't feel that proficient at first, you will improve, and it will become easier to stop major tell-tale signs.

The second question to note is: are they more people oriented or more task focused? Do they want to build a relationship or are they on a mission to get the job done?

Once you have this information, you can start to place them into the quadrants more readily.

FIGURE 25: DISC BEHAVIOURAL PROFILES

Let's look at the four buying styles in detail.

D – Dominance

This is your direct, uber competitive, impatient, decisive, to the point, knows what they want (and they wanted it yesterday) kind of person. They are easy to spot. They likely have all the coolest, latest stuff. You will have met this type of person, they don't need to build a relationship with you to buy, they are in the zone and focused on moving forward, they are all about taking action and getting to the bottom of things.

Therefore, if you are selling to someone of this nature, who is completely task-focused and outgoing, my recommendation is: don't frustrate them by spending too long on non-essential trivial items such as small talk or visions of the future. Hit them with the good stuff right out of the gate, pitch the best points up front, get to the point and give them the bottom line (any cost savings, revenue increase, profit advantages). Be respectful of their power, acknowledge it even, stroke their ego and make sure you stay on mission. Treat these clients with a results-oriented focus, like you are under a deadline, so don't waste their time. Help them make a decision by presenting the main points fast. This sale will be swift and efficient if you recognise their dominant preference and handle it well. Sell them on your ability to deliver the best products to them that will help them win.

I – Influence

These guys buy from people they like. Full stop! The Influence type wants to build a relationship with you, and they want to get to know you, in depth. Make sure you wine and dine them, listen to their stories about their latest holiday in Cancun and how they had a frat party in college that got way out of hand. Indulge their outgoing and friendly spirit. You'll spot these types because they are the life of the party, talkative, sociable and bubbly, with a tendency to be spontaneous and follow their emotions.

Sell them on you because these are the type of clients who need to like you in order to give you the sale. It might sound simple but to get in with this type of client you will need to turn up your people-oriented behaviours and sell to the part of them that responds well. If you can get on this level with this type of client, the sale becomes the natural course of behaviour. You need to give these clients your time and invest deeply in meaningful relationships with them if you want to work together.

S – Steadiness

If clients in this group were an animal, they would be an elephant – intelligent, considerate, no need to be rushed, they want guarantees and consistency, they like to take time to think things through. They are caring and patient and could even be described as laid-back. The way to sell to this group is still via the personal connection but it is much more centred around providing the same service or product as last time, or what they have experienced in the past from another vendor. It's not about getting too crazy but maintaining the status quo, repeating the excellent high-quality service and output, so deliver consistency and stability and you will win.

C – Compliance

You've seen these guys before; they come at you with 50,000 questions ready to go. They've even read the small print before your meeting, the T&Cs, studied your company website and they want answers.

This behavioural type is methodical, analytical and systematic. WOW them by delivering the goods, give them that juicy extra detail they so desperately need, get into the weeds and don't hold back. If a high-compliance person thinks you're hiding something, the deal won't progress.

This is your chance to play it cool, provide them with the information they need, don't be too talkative and give them the space they need to make a decision. The key trait for this type of sale to go well is preparation – put yourself in their shoes and really think about what questions they might have before you enter the meeting room.

PUTTING DiSC INTO ACTION

The key here is to remember that you can't sell to someone else how you want to be sold. You need to adapt and morph into the salesperson of their dreams. In effect, **speak their language and show you understand them.**

For example, if you do the assessment on yourself and it turns out you're a Compliance-behavioural-type profile and say you're going to meet a Dominant-behavioural-type client, you are aware of this up front (side note: we're all on a spectrum – some of us are ultra-dominant and others are a fairly equal mix of steadiness and compliance, so remember to factor this into your assessment and calibrate for the subtleties). In this example, let's say your client is bold, direct and all business.

Before you go into the meeting, arrive a few minutes early, go to the bathroom and give yourself a pep talk. Remember, the DiSC profiles diagram and focus on selling to them how the clients want to be sold to. This will require you to strip the pitch down, eliminate your need to go into the details and desire to explain all parts of how your solution or product works (compliance type). Instead, stay high level, big picture, help them understand what it means for their profits, KPIs and business growth. Give them the facts of the matter, the bottom line, and don't dilly dally.

At first, as a compliance type, this might feel uncomfortable, but if you want the sale then you need to give it to them straight, stay away from the mission, away from any of the small talk, and use your ability to know your product inside out as an advantage. Allow your super skill to be the very best tool you own and match their energy so that they feel connection, answer the client's questions, and literally blow their mind. I must point out, this is not about being inauthentic, it's about selling and giving to your clients the bespoke experience that helps them understand and get excited by what you are pitching to them.

Similarly, if you would categorise yourself as an influencer type (high up on the outgoing and people-oriented scale), and you're selling to a dominant type, you've got to resist the temptation to make this all about building a relationship and realise that closing the sale relies more on your ability to help your client make the decision by giving them what they need.

In this case, your challenge will be controlling the amount of you talk during the interaction, especially with the small talk and controlling your emotional response, not getting overly offended if the client ignores your invitation for drinks, staying focused on the task at hand. Once your dominant client sees that you came to do business, it will be on like Donkey Kong. Be adaptable and flexible, meet your client's needs. This is where the skill, the art and the experience all come into play and the sky really is the limit once you start learning how to be a master of recognising what each situation needs and giving it.

Let's do another example, just to make sure it's clear. If you're a seriously Dominant type and you're selling to a seriously Steady type, don't go in there with all the latest flashy stuff that's going to scream "untested beta project". The way to sell to this crew is to stick to your most tried and tested products, focus on stability, consistency and long-term delivery of projects. Don't rush this type of client, or pressure them for action, these guys want to have the time to mull it over and then decide.

Whether you're a D, an I, an S or a C, you have got to figure out what your client is and then sell to them in the manner that they understand. You'll know when you've got it right because there will be a sudden outburst on their part where you can tell they get what you mean. **It's in this energy of shared understanding that deals get done. When you hit the jackpot in this way, and your client feels heard, you can accomplish so much more.** The sales process is accelerated, and you can work together to creatively solve any challenges that pop up along the way.

This is much more than the art of learning how to form a bond with someone, this is the ability to recognise *who* you are dealing with, pivot and adapt to become your best self for that situation and that client.

It's not being disingenuous or inauthentic, the thing I want you to note here is you're still being yourself; you're just focusing in on the things that matter to your client, **in your way.** You don't need to morph into some quadruple personality, one minute you're a direct, ultra-competitive, spare me the details dominant style and the next a bubbly, life of the party socialite. No. The key is you recognise what your client needs and then pitch to them in a way that they will understand whilst still being totally you and real. When you can do this, you are well on your way to selling more and broadening your network.

In addition to this, there are two critical elements of expanding your business and your sales pipeline. The first is, when you understand who you are dealing with it becomes easier to show them that you understand their pain points and can offer them a solution.

In sales, you need to be able to get along with a range of personalities and very quickly understand what the situation needs. It is likely that you can have multiple behavioural types in the same room, and it is likely that you'll need to be entertaining them over a lunch or a dinner or hosting them at a formal event.

This strategy gives you the tools to work the room, to get more meaningful information and momentum from your entertaining opportunities and to sell using your personality in a more strategic way.

We are all somewhere on the spectrum for outgoing and reserved, and task oriented and people oriented, and this can change multiple times in a day based on the situation we find ourselves in.

What top salespeople are able to do is they are able to turn it on even when they don't feel like it. They are able to entertain and listen to their clients even when they have had no sleep due to the baby crying and they would much rather be at home tucked up in bed with a hot cup of cocoa. They understand that the opportunity that is right in front of them can go one of two ways and that they value themselves enough to make the most of it.

Victim salespeople on the other hand find excuses, they don't even try to adapt or present the information in the way their clients would like. They take umbrage at clients who are different to them and only see problems.

These are the type that leave an event having failed to make the most of the opportunity. They might even spend the whole time talking to colleagues who they see every day in the office rather than trying to form a deeper bond with their clients.

You can easily spot these types of subpar salespeople. They have an excuse for everything, and it is easily highlighted "that client just doesn't get it", "they're not interested", "they're so boring", "they're annoying and rude and I don't like them".

To deal with this, if you are managing a team and you have a "victim salesperson" that you are coaching, just ask them what they think the top seller in your organisation would do in that situation. When they in their own words compare the two behaviours it is as different as night and day, and it shows in the results. They will try to over-justify their position and make excuses as to why it is different for them, but deep down they will know the truth of the matter and a shift will start to occur. If they really have a motivation to become a superstar salesperson, then they will see that all salespeople need to deal with all types and find the opportunity in amongst the difficulty.

If this is hitting home right now, or you are a salesperson who wants to lift their game, I can't impress on you enough the fact that you need to find it within yourself to keep going, to bring your 'A game', especially when you don't feel like it, to find the opportunity in the adversity and push yourself to be a professional. You can do it.

This doesn't mean you have to turn yourself into something that you are not or hangout with clients that you don't like for extended periods of time, but it does mean that you bring more of yourself to the job at hand and you are always looking for ways to make your client's lives easier. You are in the business of people.

Victim salespeople only see the wins, they are closed minded and operate from a taker's mentality. They don't see the consistency of process, the follow up, the hours spent finessing the delivery. What these sales types will never realise, until they make a commitment to take responsibility for their own sales, is that sales are easier if you work them and harder if you don't.

When your numbers aren't coming in, management is all over you to explain them. They micromanage and pick at details until it becomes unbearable. Usually these types leave the business and, if not, they end up bringing the whole team's performance down due to their negative attitude. This is not where you want to be. This is a place of fear and lack. Not a place of accountability and professionalism.

Rant over, but you get the point. It is all about how you look at things as to whether you see a problem or an opportunity. This relates to putting the DiSC profiles into action: you can either choose to learn how to sell to different profiles or not. Those that learn how to speak Influencer type even though they are a Steady type will go far; victims will stay ignorant, not understanding why clients aren't buying from them.

DOMINANCE OUTGOING INFLUENCE

Character
Competitive, Direct, Results Focused
Independent, Demanding

To Get Their Best
Focus on the result. Get to the point.
Give feedback fast

Avoid
Talking about non-essentials
Reducing their power and inhibiting
their desire to take action

Character
Friendly, Optimistic, Enthusiastic,
Sponteneous, Energtic, Emotional

To Get Their Best
Make it fun, Focus on positive at all
times. Laugh. Let them talk

Avoid
Being negative. Don't focus too much
on the details or bring down their
high energy.

TASK ORIENTED ━━━━━━━━━━━━━━━━━ **PEOPLE ORIENTED**

Character
Exact, Contemplative, Cautious, Formal,
Accurate, Systematic, Disciplined

To Get Their Best
Answer their questions fully. Provide all
the detail. Be patient.

Avoid
Keeping information to yourself.
Don't be too chatty.

Character
Laid back, Patient, Calm, Modest,
Sincere, Caring, Careful.

To Get Their Best
Don't rush them. Slow it down. Provide
guarantees. Give them time

Avoid
Pressuring them into a decision or
making any sudden changes. Do
what you say you will.

COMPLIANCE RESERVED STEADINESS

**FIGURE 26: HOW TO GET THEIR BEST
AND WHAT TO AVOID FOR EACH PROFILE**

SPEAK THEIR LANGUAGE (VAK)

According to Neuro-Linguistic Programming (NLP) there are three types of learning modalities, these are Visual, Auditory and Kinaesthetic.

A person who is a visual learner wants to see the product, they want neat graphics and demonstrations that blow their socks off. They are likely to appreciate videos, images and the visually appealing qualities of your product. You can tell these types of people because they have pictures of friends and family all over their desk, it's tidy, everything has its place and they enjoy the visual aesthetics of life. A person of this nature will often say things like "Did you see her ring? It was stunning, you must see it" or "I see what you're saying."

An auditory learner (i.e. someone who prefers communicating via speaking) is likely to be a talker (normally on the phone or needs to make a phone call), has the best quality when it comes to surround sound, gadgets for listening and playing music, has the bluetooth connected to the car and at home has all the kit for recording voice. They say things like, "You have to hear it, it's the bomb", "I heard that it was like that" or "I hear what you are saying."

A kinaesthetic person is all about the way something feels ("It didn't feel good, so we didn't do the deal" or "It just felt right"). They are all about comfort, aesthetics, they have the best super comfortable chairs, they care about their pillow and the mattress, they love a pillow menu in a hotel. "I feel you, this is spot on" or "It feels like this is a good deal to me" or "it just feels right".

The important thing here to note is when you are aware of how someone sees the world, you can take the time and care to offer them your information in that way and tailor how you deliver that information to suit their preferences.

For example, if pitching to an auditory person, you might have testimonials read out or base much of the sales pitch around having a chat rather than slides. These guys like to talk, so why wouldn't you let them?

For the visual learner, you might get stuck into demonstrating the product and bring examples with you so that they can see it. You might not say as much, but the visuals might speak for you. You could even bring a video testimonial to play so they can see the happy customer.

For a kinaesthetic person, you would focus on the feeling and the energy of the room, the pitch and the ambience. You would offer them a drink and take care to make the experience of the meeting as pleasant and rewarding as possible. You would tailor it to them. You know how ad agencies try to win clients by turning the office into that client's brand, it's that kind of thing. This client needs to feel like you get them, like it feels good to do business with you and that the experience was one of satisfaction. It's less about what's said, but how it is said, less about what is shown, but how it is shown.

Like going to a spa, the service and the ambience is as much a part of the experience as the treatment, it is an all-encompassing event from start to finish. When you walk in you are greeted by a friendly host or hostess at the reception who speaks in soft, calming tones, you are offered a drink and a fresh towel to cool your face and this ritual transforms you from being in the outside world to being in a new world of complete tranquility. It is the association of these events happening with being in a spa type experience. If they didn't happen then it would take away from your overall experience of the spa. The little details matter, the cleanliness, the lighting, the floral arrangement and the air temperature. I'm not saying you need to turn your meeting room into the Mandarin Oriental but to get the most out of a sit down with a kinaesthetically oriented individual the small touches make a difference, even if you don't end up doing business together, they will leave with a glowing recollection of you and the way you conduct your operation.

THE QUESTION ALL CLIENTS WANT TO KNOW THE ANSWER TO DEEP DOWN

In the opening scenes of *The Hummingbird Project*, a little known 2019 movie based on Michael Lewis's book *Flash Boys*, which is about two traders in the game of high frequency trading, the camera pans to Jesse Eisenberg who is in the middle of trying to convince a client into signing what seems to be a huge contract. The millionaire client turns to Jesse and asks the crucial question, "Why should I trust you?" and Jesse calmly but confidently answers with a story. "Ever since I was a little boy..."

Not all clients will be as direct as in this example, but deep down this is what they are all thinking. "Why should I trust you?"

If you get lucky enough to be asked this question, answer with a story about *why* you do what you do and why you believe in what you are selling. This is a golden opportunity to open up to your client and solidify the relationship. Being vulnerable and honest in this moment is key, vulnerability is actually the purest act of courage there is and that is what helps you land clients.

PRO TIP
Insider intel

This is where your inside man or woman comes in handy. Be the investigator (subtlety) and then give it to them how they like it. This is your opportunity to find out what was missing from the previous vendor's pitch and feed it to them how they want it. How did the other competitor's pitch go? What did the client like or not like? Call ahead and get the extra details, refine your pitch and then go for it!

ULTIMATELY, IT COMES DOWN TO TRUST

Trust is a valuable commodity; a client is ultimately buying into you and your ability to work on their behalf, to help them navigate challenges and problem solve on their behalf.

When the covid pandemic hit, a wave of panicked buyers called my phone, they needed flexibility to postpone bookings until they understood how the crisis was going to impact their business. I could have been hard-nosed and purely revenue focused but this was an opportunity to show up for my clients, to serve them in their hour of need and find a way through the maze together.

- Do they trust you?

- Do they trust you to make them look awesome?

- Will you stick around and take their call once the sale is closed?

- Do they like you as a person?

- Can they relate to you and your mission, and can you show them you understand theirs?

- Do they think you really care about their specific needs or are you just trying to make a sale to hit target?

That last one is a killer. It catches average salespeople out… all… the… time! Depending on the sales incentive structure of your business, you might be inclined to make short-sighted moves that aren't in the best interest of your clients to make some big money on the accelerator.

I get it, those accelerators tend to ramp up after you go beyond 150% to target. I know this means you can pay for that 10-day full board Maldives vacation in the upgraded overwater villa with jacuzzi and still have plenty left for a down payment.

I know you want to be a baller, but you know what's actually baller? What's going to put more dollars in your pocket than taking the quick road? Yes, you guessed it, actually working the Momentum Sales Model and ignoring all those ads from Luxury Escapes tempting you to hike the rates, pressure the client and lock them into the longest contract so you can book a trip (it's like they know).

I know you watched movies like *Wolf of Wall Street* and part of you enjoyed the chase, the hustle, the idea of making so much money you can pull up in a Ferrari outside the club and splash the cash.

I get it!

Ferraris, AP watches, sunset pool villa vacations, it's all possible, but let's talk facts. It's insanely better to build a client base on your reputation of being there for your clients, your ability to serve and to surprise and delight them in the process.

Speaking of surprising and delighting, top performing salespeople know how to gain trust with clients, and what makes it all the more special is that they put their own unique spin on it. Whether you join a new company, or you're tasked with selling a new product, getting to grips with the dynamics involved in trust building is what matters.

That means you are authentic, and you can get behind your company and its products fully, if you know they are the right choice for your clients. In my mind there can be no greater hook than someone who is willing to go to the ends of the earth to solve your problems and who passionately believes in the mission and product they are selling.

People buy on an emotional level, guided by their hearts. They may have all the logical reasons under the sun, but they still go with the choice that got to them on an emotional level.

When explaining complex ideas, you want to humanise, bring some relatable examples into the conversation, break it down for them, be real. Not only does it make you more relatable, but it gives your clients a confidence boost when they are able to explain your complex solution to colleagues.

People want to feel valued, intelligent and needed, as humans in society we crave significance and recognition. If your client gets a dopamine hit because they can articulate your solution at their next all hands meeting in front of their boss, it reflects well on you too.

The fact is people remember stories not statistics, 63% remember stories and only 5% remember statistics! Say what?! But clients love statistics, don't they? Yes, it's true clients *adore le stat*, a juicy case study gives them confidence, but it is the overall message that is remembered long after the deal has been done.

You've sold them on yourself and your ability to stay with them through the process, to be there when they are feeling doubtful, frustrated and finally happy.

Facts and figures are just indicators of credibility that nudge the sales along. What matters in the long run is how you make people feel. It is your attitude, your energy, and the ability to allow your clients to express themselves and feel heard that makes the difference.

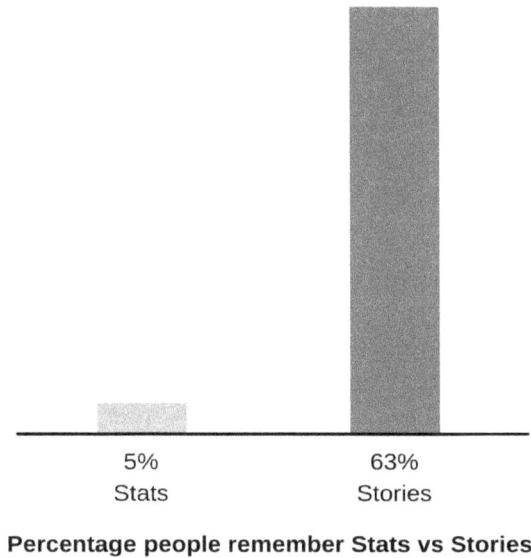

5%   63%
Stats   Stories

Percentage people remember Stats vs Stories

**FIGURE 27: PERCENTAGE OF PEOPLE
WHO REMEMBER STATS VS STORIES**

High calibre salespeople understand how to let their clients vent, especially when they have messed up. Becoming a top salesperson requires grit and stamina, it takes a lot of courage and determination, but if you can allow your clients the freedom to feel heard and to take on board and entertain what they are saying rather than continually pushing your message or dropping knowledge bombs on them it will transform your sales numbers, believe me.

Remember you aren't there to impress the client with how much you know about a certain topic or area, you're there to work with them collaboratively to solve their problems. You can start any meeting by saying this, "I'm not here to impress you with how much I know about guerrilla marketing in (insert your industry), my job is to add as much value as possible so please feel free to ask questions and make this a collaborative two-way session." It's a better way to encourage a dialogue and set the tone of the relationship.

MINI MOMENTUM BUILDER
Find the top presenter

My Momentum Sales tip for anyone joining a new company is to take the company sales deck and ask the number one salesperson in the organisation to take you through it, record the conversation on your phone and then listen to it on repeat. Over and over until the salient points stick in your mind. You aren't looking to repeat it word for word – it's not a script, it is about permeating your brain so that all those points are soaked up and can be pulled out whenever you need them.

Better yet, ask to shadow the best salesperson in the company to a client meeting and then record that interaction on your phone. That way you'll get to hear how they handle the objections, rejections and keep the conversation moving forward. This is a sure-fire strategy to get up to speed fast and learn from the best. Respect yourself enough to aim for the best, to be associated with them and to form relationships with them from the start.

What you'll find is, because you've got it on recording from the number one salesperson, you'll actually relax about learning it word for word. What top salespeople do is take the best elements that stand out to them and reconfigure the rest to suit their style.

Offer to take best in the business to lunch once a month, use this time to elevate your thinking, exchange ideas and get coached. Never be too big, or too great to make time to learn, everyone's got a mentor, even if it hasn't been labelled. We all take inspiration from someone.

You are going to make an incredible amount of sales if you can **own** the presentation and the company story as if it were yours. What I recommend is to tell clients why you joined the company, how you heard about the company and what matters to you. This is more real; it speaks to who you are as a person. Clients can relate to their own mission and why they joined their company and what they aspire to accomplish.

After all, the products you are selling are part of your brand and if you don't believe in them, you're going to have a hard time convincing anyone else they are valuable too.

Say things like, "This is literally the reason why I joined the company, this product here..."

PRO TIP
Don't stop believin'

You must believe in the product or service you are selling to sell to your greatest potential. If you join a company and find out the product isn't actually what it said on the tin or the company culture doesn't float your boat, leave and don't look back. This is not a failure on your part, this is a lesson in what aspects of work you don't want.

2. SERVE YOUR CLIENT

MAKE IT EASY FOR CLIENTS

I say this ALL the time, but it is worth repeating as I still see people making this mistake. Sales is a service, therefore even when you are sending something as direct as an email, you need to make it super easy for the client to see what it is about and grasp the message in two seconds. It's not clear, it's not easy, and you will lose their attention. There is literally no point sending out hundreds of boring emails with nothing to hook your clients.

Here's an awesome example of a world class email.

Hi George,

I hope you had a fantastic weekend.

Hope the family and kids are well. I saw this Harry Potter exhibition was in town and thought of you.

Adding something personal shows you actually care and sets the tone as a conversation.

I know we haven't had a chance to meet since I've been at **XYZ Company** *[Insert Company Name] but I'd love to catch up regarding* **your paid media strategy** *[Insert reason/client/specific reason], if you have time next week.*

By signalling the intention of the email early, it helps George quickly scan his mind for solutions whilst he continues reading. This also helps in case he gets distracted or suddenly pulled into another conversation – you have planted the seed.

Now that we have the **super galactic technology** *[Insert new update, something that has changed your company for the better, this could be an acquisition, a new product or partnership] integrated for* **your media buying needs** *[insert specific department or product or service it impacts] we have greater scale in Indonesia and Philippines, meaning* **we can now reach KPOP fans with your advertising** *[state the broader benefit].*

I wanted to share with you these incredible ads [insert the name of what it is you're selling] we have just done for Intercontinental Hotels [*Use an appropriate competitor client, e.g. Intercontinental

Hotels (highlighting the other clients is a credibility fact check for George, in his head he makes the link and knows you are legit)]. as they are a superb example of how we can maximise both engagement and sales. [This was off the charts!*Insert the specific benefit and the WIIFM – why should George care?]

- www.Example 1.com

- www.Example 2.com

- www.Example 3.com

Add 1-3 url links to examples or insert into the body of the email because this increases the chance you have to hook George with something AMAZING! The content in these links should WOW him.

*Also, please see below the best-in-class **case studies** from the **Auto vertical** from last quarter. **[Insert relevant case study, document, proof that you are working with the best of the best.]***

- Case Study

- Visual

Insert GIF/Attachment/Visual/Infographic – the hook to get George to look twice – this is literally a case of help me, help you! Get his attention. Make him want to meet with you so bad that he picks up the phone immediately and calls you instead.

Would you be available for a catch-up next week on Wednesday 18th December at 10am or 3.30pm?

Make the request to meet again, this time be more specific to drive home urgency and relevance, by stating the day and time. We want George to actually check his calendar to see if he can make the time proposed.

It would be brilliant to see you again,

Best,
Tim

Once you take away all the bold text from my commentary, what you are left with is a very neat, succinct, and simple easy-to-digest email with a specific request and the reason *why* George really should think about taking the meeting with you.

Download the world class email template at:

www.timjscastle.com/themomentumsalesmodel

It's not pushy, it's not rude, nor is it desperate, it's collaborative and sexy. Yes, I said it, emails can be sexy, and what's sexy about it is what you're not saying. The allure is created by dangling a few tantalising examples of your best-in-class work in a short but "I know my value" type of way and "I'd like to see if you feel the same way".

Rather than sending the client everything you have on a specific topic and overwhelming them or, worse, still getting your message deleted. The key is to provide a short overview stating the benefits and making a simple request (twice).

I like to make the request twice in my prospecting emails, the first early on so the client knows my intention and can then be thinking *Do I want to meet this person?* rather than *Where are they going with this, what do they want?* Every email should only have one call to action, one specific thing that you want to get out of it – in this case it was a meeting.

By flagging it early the client can then move on to their next question which is *What's in it for me (WIIFM)*, which is the driver of whether you'll actually get the meeting or not. If you've answered this question correctly then the client will be inclined to check their calendar and respond to you.

This email framework is constructed in a way to speak to the questions that are going on in the client's mind at a deeper level.

- Who is this person?

- Do I know them?

- What do they want?

- What's in it for me?

- Do they genuinely care about me?

- Do they work with anyone I know?

- When do they want to meet?

It's a psychological game that's being played by pre-empting what's on the client's mind and then answering their question in your next sentence, making it easier for them to say yes to your request, because they have all the information they need in a succinct manner to make a decision or at least connect you with the right person.

Think about it this way, if you're in a bar and you are being hit on, why is it that the people that go after everyone don't feel attractive? It's because they aren't putting any effort into their pitch, they are rushing the process and not answering your questions in the right order.

They are going straight to the close when what you really want is the build-up. They aren't making you feel special and, even if they are in the moment, on a deeper level you know these one liners and compliments have been used a million times before and they are playing a numbers game to complete their own mission.

It's the same in sales.

It's precisely where there's no build up, no passion, no patience, that deals don't even have a chance of getting started. When salespeople treat clients like a commodity, like they're only in it for a brief moment and then on to the next one, it fails to impress on a deeper level. We as humans reject this behaviour. We feel it.

The same applies if your emails, phone calls, or texts feel automated, or reek of being copy and pasted and altered slightly. The client wants to know that you care about them, about their problems, and that you have thought about what motivates them. That's why you must add your own flare. It's a balance between being efficient and caring about them as an individual.

In dating, what's attractive and forms sparks is knowing your value (but not arrogantly) and yet not overwhelming the person you are trying to form a relationship with. You are present, aware of what you have to offer and yet confident in exploring the possibilities. It's in this exploration that the fun is found, where bonds are formed and testing and getting to know you occurs.

You know what I am going to say... it's the same in sales.

Don't rush the getting to know you process and miss out on all the fun. Well-constructed emails do the same thing for clients, providing a reprieve from the clutter, the demands and the constant barrage of information. By presenting requests simply and not overwhelming clients with information, you'll get cut through.

This is what you need to think of yourself as, a sales superstar, you are a reprieve, a sanctuary, a welcome break from the mundane for your clients – trusted, present, confident and world class.

Let this high standard guide your emails, calls, meeting preparation the next time you sit down to reach out to your clients.

In conclusion, the Momentum Sales Model is anchored in its values of understanding, empathy and service. By keeping understanding front and centre of your mission to serve, the understanding salesperson is able to spot more opportunities for action. This is primarily because they are tuned into the client's issues, they have developed a heightened sense of awareness and through this wisdom they create rivers of gold.

Understanding doesn't mean weakness, far from it, an understanding salesperson is able to get to the heart of the issue, get past the layers of fear, doubt and disconnection and forge unions that last.

The misconception here is that "understanding" translates to push over, when in reality if you are following all steps of the Momentum Sales Model it will allow you to be more like a sniper. Outsiders won't be able to comprehend how you've done it, they'll constantly ask you questions to try to uncover how you've got such killer sales numbers, like there's some magic shortcut they can steal.

In truth, this process will set you free. It takes work, massive amounts of work, but it also brings with it huge rewards and financial freedom. If you want to sell and be able to build skills that you can take anywhere, this is where you need to start. Ingrain this sales process into your values as a person and live on your terms.

UNDERSTANDING SUMMARY

- Take personal responsibility

- Never respond while angry

- Tune in during meetings

- Think about DiSC before every email, meeting or call

- Ask yourself, is the client a Visual, Auditory or Kinaesthetic learner?

- Adapt and sell to clients how *they* want to be sold to

- Building trust is core

- Focus on stories over stats

- Make it easy for clients to say "yes"

- World class emails get replies

- Your goal is to serve

CHAPTER 10

More – Always go the extra mile, give it your all and separate from the pack

"Do what is easy and your life will be hard. Do what is hard and your life will become easy."

– LES BROWN

INTRODUCTION

Right now, it's 8.24am on a Friday, it's a public holiday for Chinese New Year and I am sitting in my office, alone. Sounds shit, doesn't it?

Wrong – I am moving my dreams forward and setting up for a successful week ahead. I am providing for my family and, rather than feeling stressed out with all the things I need to do, I am getting it done!

This is how you dominate. The point is – I am the only one here out of hundreds that could be.

Therefore, I need to make it as enjoyable as possible. Maybe that's remembering or planning a fun activity in with my sons, Levi and Rome, to do later and focusing on that. Maybe it's making friends with the barista at the local coffee shop and suddenly I end up getting a free oat latte and an advocate for my message and products.

Remember you are in it together, the door guy, the security, cleaning people, so make their day just a bit better and that positive effect will ripple back to you. What you put out comes right on back. It's not about just going the extra mile for yourself or your family, it's spreading that generosity out far and wide.

I have worked public holidays for the last seven years to move my businesses and projects forward. Rarely do I see another soul in the office, but when I do I know their light is shining brightly, their fire of ambition is burning, and they are turning up the heat on themselves and their goals and dreams.

If you're not going to do it for yourself, how can you expect to do it for your clients? Again, this comes right back to doing what others aren't willing to do to get ahead. The bold moves are made when others are still sleeping, the battles are won in the preparation, the confidence, the ideas that form as a result of being so deeply interwoven in your passion.

Make sure you don't die with the fire still left inside. If you have an idea, however crazy, however far-fetched, if you think it can advance your business and increase your momentum, you've got to go for it.

That is what this chapter is about, those crazy, out of the box moments that move the needle in an irreversible way and change your identity forever. You become a person who goes the extra mile for your clients, yourself and the privilege to serve others.

My books have been featured in British prime ministers' offices, celebrated by TV stars and found their way into the curriculums of top colleges and universities around the world. The good you put out comes back multiplied. This is just the tip of the iceberg of some of the awe-inspiring things that have happened.

Astound yourself today and take inspired action on that spark of an idea that's been niggling away. As I said at the start of the book, I want this book to truly impact you, to become a manual for learning how to create momentum in your sales activity and in life so that you may never fear what's ahead.

From my sales seminars and training sessions, I have seen first-hand how people rarely go as far as is needed for as long as is required to make the impact that will change their stars. They get stuck at the idea phase. Really, that just means we need to get you some better ideas, ones that excite you and could literally transform the size of your sales pipeline and business.

Here's a mini momentum builder to get you started.

MINI MOMENTUM BUILDER
Ideas and action

Pick up a pad of post-it notes and spread them out on the table.

Now I want you to fill each one with an idea that you could do to take your business into the stratosphere and then stick them on the wall. Now there might only be 100 or so of these ideas, but just imagine if you took action on one of them daily until you completed all of them. How much better off would your business be after going on a mission like that?

This exercise must be completed daily for it to work, you have to become a person who is focused on one goal with everything they have got and persists. The payoff comes after not before. You don't just read this book and you're full of momentum – you are better off that's for sure, you have learned proven strategies that will help your sales to explode, but you have got to stick with it.

For example, as an author I am always looking for ways to get my books into the hands of new readers.

My post-it note wall could look like this:

1. Stand outside vaccination halls and give books to people waiting in line.

2. Send books to every radio host in my country/state/city.

3. Schedule 100 podcast interviews.

4. Send books to top TV hosts, sports trainers and celebrities in the hopes they will tell their friends about it.

5. Run a giveaway with the best influencers in key markets.

6. Secure promotional billboards at co-working spaces to reach entrepreneurs.

7. Host a free negotiation/sales workshop.

And so on... think about it like this, to become a person who has momentum, who embodies it and is constantly taking daily action towards their big goal, you need to become a different person and do what people who have success in sales do. I am telling you that these strategies, like going the extra mile and doing one thing from the list of ideas daily, will help you transform not only your business but yourself.

In a conference, millionaire speaker and sales leader Brain Tracy said something that struck me as vital to understand and it relates to this point nicely.

When talking about how to become a self-made millionaire, he said:

"One of the things that I learned by the way is becoming a self-made millionaire is not the important thing. What is really important is the person you have to become to become a self-made millionaire. You have to become a totally different human being. One of my friends says in order to achieve something you've never achieved before, you have to become someone you've never been before."

– BRIAN TRACY

It's the exact same thing with developing momentum; it's the person you become when you develop the characteristics and qualities of a person that is an expert at creating momentum in any business that is valuable.

You change on the inside, there's an inner knowing and understanding. You have tried and learned from the results enough times that you get hyper aware of opportunities. You know they are going to work out before they do, and you are so in tune with the decision making and discipline that you need to have to make it happen.

WHAT IS THE EXTRA MILE?

The extra mile is "extra" because it is beyond what everyone else is doing – not just the masses but even the high performers and pretty damn good people. This place is reserved for absolute weapons.

To own a place here, you need a mindset of resilience that is focused only on one thing – doing whatever it takes to make your dream a reality, and in sales that means making it rain, selling!

This place is reserved for the few – but I know you have what it takes.

It's a place beyond everyone else, so only a select few will ever be there. It's the remembering your client's favourite type of cake, their daughter's birthday, which band they adore and surprising them.

It's making a sales pitch fun and memorable by including a quiz with prizes customised to your clients' preferences or renting a boat and inviting clients to go wakeboarding for the afternoon to let some steam off.

Going the extra mile means working on the bank holiday to get ahead. When you're building a business, you'll be so passionate about what you are creating that you'll wake up earlier, your brain filled with ideas and possibilities.

It also means going into the office when you don't feel like it as well. A little voice in your head might say, "but it's a public holiday, you need to spend time with your kids." However, you know that if you get up early and get ahead your can be done by 12pm and enjoy a quality afternoon with your family having dominated at work.

Don't give in to the voice; it's a trick and it holds you back from greatness. It can feel lonely on the road to success – after all, you'll be doing what others won't, but that's why you must make it as fun as possible.

In this chapter I will show you how to:

- Normalise doing more

- Review your year and ask the right questions

- Conduct a Sunday night prospecting ritual

- Get creative when going the extra mile

- Execute my Friday night ritual for success

- Use doubters as a driver to do more.

HOW DOES DOING MORE AND GOING THE EXTRA MILE BUILD SALES MOMENTUM?

It starts with a mindset, once your mind is tuned into doing more and the potential you have within you to push yourself, you'll break through the barriers, self-limiting beliefs and start to witness yourself going harder.

Your body can do it. It's your mind that needs training, and the way we do this is incrementally. By adding in the rituals and strategies I will share with you in this chapter, you can make a remarkable difference to your sales numbers and the health of your business.

What people won't tell you is, in order to be successful at their craft, they got their ass to work. More is more, if you do one more of everything, think how much further you would go, think how much resilience, courage and fortitude this would foster as a strategy in life.

More is about keeping your train fully locked and loaded. We're running at full speed and now we want to maintain it with fine-tuned tactics that have leverage. More isn't about burnout, working your-self to the bone. More is about putting your strategy and network to work. It's about executing on what matters; it's about doing the stuff that everyone else forgets, but not you.

I'm not going to lie, it can be lonely at the top, doing the work that no one else around you is willing to do, but this is what it takes and trust me, when you get around others who think like you (mas-termind), you'll feel a fire so strong inside that your whole outlook will change.

This is where I take you to a whole new level.

1. NORMALISING DOING MORE THAN EXPECTED AND GOING THE EXTRA MILE

PERSONAL STORY
Sometimes you've just got to make it happen

You'll find that many of my stories begin with me rushing across one large Asian city or another, dashing from meeting, meeting, meeting, meeting to plane, new country and then meeting, meeting, meeting, back to plane and onwards to the next country. This is because in sales there are times when you simply need to make it all happen without focusing on the "what if?".

In sales, taking initiative and being resourceful are the two biggest skills you can possess. I'll say that again, **taking initiative and using your resourcefulness are the key to success in sales**.

What I mean by this is that these two skills, combined with persistence, enthusiasm, solid decision making and the ability to build relationships will keep you firmly on the road to success.

That is why when the opportunity to pitch in Malaysia came up, I went at a moment's notice. When the client got excited and the session overran by 48 minutes, leaving me only 1 hour and 40 minutes to catch a Grab taxi and a train to get to the airport to fly to my next destination, I didn't fret. I smiled calmly onwards, enjoying their excitement for our solutions and asking questions. If you've ever been to Kuala Lumpur, you'll know that crossing the city at 4.30pm is complete gridlock, I mean wall to wall bumpers for as far as you can see, and you need at least an hour and a half to comfortably drive to the airport. I took the risk anyway and prayed that my flight would be delayed.

Was it inconvenient that when I left the meeting (already about to miss my flight) I then bumped into another vendor (semi-competitor) who said he could introduce me to an important stakeholder at the client and to just hold on for five minutes? Yes, it was. Did I wait? Yes, of course.

There are moments in sales when timing and luck and everything in between is working for you; however, if you are so fixated on your own agenda and not willing to take the risk (in this case missing my flight) then you'll never get anywhere.

If I had shown anxiety in the pitch as the minutes ticked away or had let the thought of missing my flight cause me to lose focus or not stay present, then I wouldn't be doing my team or myself justice.

Therefore, in these moments of opportunity, **I would encourage you to say "yes", to go for it,** to trust that you will figure out how to coordinate the pieces so that a workable solution will appear. Life is willing to help those who have fun with it. There have been countless times where remaining flexible, open to the situation and present have provided huge rewards.

If you find yourself in a situation where you have a looming deadline like a flight and you aren't able to risk it (e.g. another meeting, a family emergency, another commitment) then the expert salesperson manages expectations throughout.

If you risk it, don't stress, relax into the uncertainty and adventure of it all. Maybe you'll make your flight, maybe you won't, and you'll have to get the early morning flight back and end up sitting next to an important client that gives you your next sale.

Of course, there are times when trying to do it all is a bad idea. The skill is weighing up what is worth it. In this example, winning this pitch would have covered my entire month's or possibly year's target if it went well.

WHATEVER IT TAKES

Sales is a service profession; therefore, it is your job to make it easy for your clients to work with you. This means attending meetings when it is inconvenient, sending information at odd hours, hustling to get the job done and being there for your clients. Sales isn't 9-5, it's 24/7, and, if you want to be at the top, you need to focus on making the process seamless for your clients.

"If you're interested, you'll do what's convenient. If you're committed you'll do whatever it takes."

– JOHN ASSARAF

As a sales professional, you are a problem solver, you find ways to make things happen every day, not just with your products and solutions but with logistics – having the right equipment, having a spare laptop charger, pen, converter, it is your responsibility to be prepared for all eventualities. Making sure that you're ready to go, your devices are charged, you're fed and watered, and you look presentable.

When the client arrives at the meeting you should be engaged, business cards in hand, ready to make a solid first impression. Mediocre salespeople miss this point and can be found slumped in the corner on their phone or, even worse, talking on the phone as the client arrives. Far out, that's bad. This is not the way to do things.

Clients are looking for superstars to work with and it is your job to be one. Take pride in your appearance, bring a little something for the client to brighten their day, go the extra mile, bring cupcakes. This will set you apart from the average salespeople, but you'll still have to fight harder than this to make it to the top.

The difference between good and great and exceptional salespeople is those that can move meetings around in their diary to be there when the client needs them, who can manage multiple stakeholders internally to get special approval, and more than anything, be flexible. This is what "wows" clients and it's where you want to play.

This type of action will also build your reputation. Your reputation is your brand, you'll carry it wherever you go and by caring for your clients in this way, showing them respect and making it happen you'll be rewarded handsomely.

GO THE EXTRA MILE FOR YOUR CLIENTS AND FOR YOURSELF

What is the "extra mile" in 2022?

In today's day and age, relationship building and sales have reached new heights of competition but, armed with your people strategy and caring attitude, you are set to dominate.

Dinners, lunches, drinks, are all standard and don't scream top seller. In 2022 it's all about personalisation, go the extra mile and get something custom made. The extra mile is in the detail, it's in doing it anyway even though most meetings are over Zoom or video call. The fact that you follow up and send prizes from the quiz you ran in the presentation shows extra effort. Previously, when you could just mail gifts and prizes to the client's office, now you've got to go extra to find out their personal address and mail them out individually.

PRO TIP
Small gestures lead to big results

Remembering your client's birthday and sending a handwritten note and some flowers or remembering that they love lavender as a fragrance and sending them a luxury candle after a big win. It's something that says, I care, I remember, and I am here to be of service when you need.

The question you are really answering here is how can you stand out in a meaningful way to your clients?

The way you stand out in 2022 is really simple.

It's putting your clients first, being present and not checking your phone. It's coming prepared with a well-thought-out leave behind and doing your follow up. It's answering WhatsApp at 9pm at night when they are stressed and need some numbers. The way to stand out is to be a superior operator. To have it together and to hand hold your clients through the process. These are rules for life as a salesperson not just this year.

The other aspect of this is to go the extra mile for yourself, put yourself in a position to win by doing the work. As I write this it's 2.18am on 25th December, Christmas morning, my baby son has woken up and finally gone back to sleep after searching the living room high and low for his favourite two toy cars.

Here I am now fully awake and deciding to complete a review of the year by asking some tough questions and analysis of my sales revenue data. This will help me go harder in the coming year and be more strategic (added note: writing this from the future, looking back, I can tell you 2020 was a bumper year despite all the crazy challenges it brought). This review and strategic planning helped me navigate 2020 because I had momentum and knew how to adapt and generate more of it when shit got real. Some of the clients that helped me over-achieve (upwards of 220% to my targets) in 2020 came from referrals from other clients who were friends with them due to my positive upbeat nature, efficiency in always responding to requests before deadlines and generally trying to make it work for my clients. I didn't find this out until later, but sometimes miracles are working for you in the background – your reputation and dedication to over-delivering works wonders, opening new doors and relationships. Remember this: sometimes when you are dealing with a client and they have no money to spend or a sale gets pulled due to a global pandemic, how you deal with them and your commitment to excellence even when it seems like the world is going under, matters. It can literally be your way forward to your best year yet and this compounds too. Imagine if every client you deal with recommends you to their other friends in the business, how much would your business grow? Exponentially.

I'm asking myself questions like:

Where are the most sales coming from?

Which market are we most reliant on?

Where could we do better?

Yes, it's Christmas Day, but I am passionate about my business and understanding the drivers and the assumptions that produced the results over the last year. I'm going the extra mile. I am putting myself in a position to win by arming myself with the data and analysis to make decisions going forward.

Success in sales doesn't always look pretty when you realise what "doing the work" really looks like, most people only see the champagne and commission checks and wonder *"why not me?"* without looking under the hood at the hard graft, the sacrifices and the drive that has gone into it.

Be your own champion, be inquisitive and do things without asking. The more you act on curiosity, the better you will become at sales. After conducting this review, now I know where my biggest clients are, where we need to try harder and where the biggest opportunities are.

Download the year-end review sheet at

www.timjscastle.com/themomentumsalesmodel

In the heat of the daily grind, the weeks fly by, and it can be hard to stop the daily barrage of demands for your time, but you must. Give yourself the gift of analysing the data, spend time with the questions that matter. Here are some examples of questions that matter:

- Where are the majority of sales coming from?

- How can I diversify?

- Where am I exposed?

- Which clients are most profitable?

- Where should I double down?

- What happens if I maximise my effort?

- How can I work smarter and harder?

- Where am I wasting time?

- Which clients didn't end in a sale?

- What is the order of revenue priority by market/region/state/vertical/client?

- Where can I do better?

- What is the biggest opportunity going forward?

- If I went all out and could only spend 20% of my time on one client, vertical, market where would I choose?

- What am I selling when I have the most fun and to whom?

- Why did I win/lose the sale? Are there any themes?

- Where is there an apparent 80/20 relationship occurring?

- Which 20% of our clients produce 80% of revenue or profits?

Sales is full on, and the more you can get into the habit of not relying on chance, the more you can arm yourself with the data, you will be set to make waves. **My friend, just by having the initiative to pick up this book and invest in yourself, I know you are going to do amazing things.**

SUNDAY NIGHT PROSPECTING RITUAL

Every Sunday I have this routine that sets me up for success. I review the week ahead and think strategically about potential leads I should be prospecting. All up, I invest 30 minutes of my time into this ritual, but the results I get from this process are magnified and vastly greater than the time it takes me to do the thinking and pull together the emails.

This is the process I go through.

Do this between 3-6pm

1. What's going well right now? Which clients, verticals, are selling well?

2. Compared to that information, what are the biggest accounts in these sectors I would like to have but don't yet?

3. Identify ten clients that have slipped through the net or haven't been in touch for a while.

4.   Compose ten well-structured, tailored emails that inform clients on what we've been doing, add some competitive analysis, show case results and, most importantly, request a catch up.

5.   Save emails in drafts ready to send out at 8.30am on Monday.

Obviously, you could take this strategy and maximise it, what if you drafted up 25 emails, or 50, or 100? How much extra business could that generate for you? How much momentum would that set in motion? Would you have an issue with your pipeline or qualified list of prospects if you spent the next five hours drafting well thought out, tailored emails ready to send? Remember, creating momentum is all about waves, so you set the pace – if you want more waves of new business following into your sales pipeline increase your activity. It all starts here, in the nitty gritty, the tasks that no one else (only top sellers and founders) does.

Make sure you have a catchy headline on the email and infuse your personality and energy into your emails. If you are not seeing results in the form of responses, it's likely this could be a problem, or you just aren't sending out enough emails and meeting enough potential clients to create a big enough wave of momentum.

If I ever felt that I wasn't getting enough emails or calls flowing into my business, I would sit down for an afternoon and hammer out a ton of emails, tweaking my approach to see what worked. Try sending 40-50 emails a day until it changes and you see what I mean ;) . You get to spot trends that work, like the time of day that works best for you in your business for sending emails out that actually get a response – for me, as you know, that's 8.30am. Remember, it could just be the way you are explaining something that makes all the difference. Try a casual approach, maybe you're being too formal, send a series of "jolt emails" to kick start old conversations, play around with the email subject or move to WhatsApp to spark interest. All it takes is one email, one phone call, one meeting to change and transform everything. Never lose hope because it's always all to play for.

If you're experiencing a lull, this is when you need to sell yourself even harder on what it is you're doing. Everyone goes through this, it's completely natural, but the best of the best find a way to persist regardless and pull themselves through it. Sell yourself on your purpose and your mission, how your product or service is helping people, truly helping them. Find meaning in your work and you will awaken a light inside you that will only get brighter the more you pour meaning into it. Like a self-fulfilling prophecy, you'll see your sales pipeline skyrocket back up again.

Top sellers get in early and they do the work. They aren't afraid to put in the time (where it matters) to land the bigger fish. By working a couple of extra hours on the weekend it can set you light years ahead and it is a world class habit to get into. Once you find this regular cadence with this process, you won't even notice, and you'll find that you're using dead time to do even more prospecting. Get into the habit of maximising dead time. Dead time is your biggest ally when it comes to driving momentum. When I do this, I literally can't wait to send the emails out. I know they're carefully crafted and going to encourage a response. I am buzzing to get to work on making my clients happy and seeing what we can create together. Make it a part of who you are – you are a person that knows how to create momentum!

These are some of the key rituals and habits that drop away after six months in a new job or even an old job, for that matter. We get complacent, we expect the sales to keep coming in and for what's happening now to always stay the same.

Average salespeople stay at mediocre levels because they never really experience the level of groundwork you need to put in on a daily basis to get big results. They lack the discipline of following a process, making the extra calls or sending messages to clients to check they are OK, demonstrating they care through their actions and consistent effort towards producing top notch work. Momentum sellers do all this whilst being available when it matters, responding in a timely manner, offering outstanding levels of service. If you've overachieved targets before, you'll know that this is groundwork that got you the results in the first place, so don't let your standards drop even when business is rolling in.

What is vital is that you are consistent in your prospecting, you have a healthy pipeline and you take action every single day. If you do this, I guarantee you'll have more business than ever before.

I'll repeat that again, never stop prospecting! Keep the momentum up on the front end whilst managing outstanding levels of service at all stages of the customer sales funnel and, like an oak tree coming from an acorn, your business will become mighty in ways you never could have envisaged.

As a salesperson you are an entrepreneur of sorts, creating your own business patch, overcoming hurdles and finding the pathway through. To some extent, much like an entrepreneur, this means you never really stop applying mental power to your sales book of business.

In this way, don't limit yourself to the 9-5, open yourself up and get creative. Don't limit yourself only to email, there are many different pathways to the result you're after.

Go hang out in the coffee shop outside your biggest client's office, or better yet, work from their reception area and "randomly" bump into them. In sales, you need to think out of the box to meet new clients and put yourself in a position to win. The way to do this is sometimes by physically putting yourself in front of them. If you are seen and you can get their attention, you'll be five steps closer than just hoping. **Action always beats intention every time.** This means you can intend to do something but unless you get out there and execute relentlessly, you're doing yourself a disservice.

Remember there are so many incredible tools at your disposal to win, Instagram DMs, LinkedIn, WhatsApp, the gym, events, referrals and when you go the extra mile in this area you put yourself and your business front and centre to win.

HOW TO WIN IN SALES BY GOING THE EXTRA MILE

I'll say this again, in case it isn't clear, but it has been implied through every single lesson and paragraph throughout this book, **the way you win in sales is to add incredible amounts of value, yes, going the extra mile.** The way to win the fight is to go above and beyond, to do more than is required, to stand out, to go against the grain of whatever the other sales guy or girl is doing and be different. The difference comes from how committed you are to how you develop the relationship throughout the length of it, and by the way, it's never over.

Use the following structure for your email outreach – I called it Never Give Up Email Outreach Sequence – it's a game and it isn't stopping until we have a victory! This is a roadmap to a combination of emails that you can send in order to create massive amounts of momentum with your prospects. When you are not getting a response from a client, move to the next step in the chain.

Below is a list of the 8 Powerful Steps you need to follow to complete this email outreach sequence.

1. The Intro email – *Hi Sammy, I just joined award-winning XYZ company....*

Three days later...

2. Send the Jolt Email – shorter, to the point: *Hi Sammy, just following up on the above...*this quickly jolts them into action; vary the time of day you send it. Don't send it at the same time as you sent the intro email as that didn't get a response.

Three days later...

3. Add Value – invite your client to a fun event/relevant webinar/ lunch/sporting event. This is a chance for you to catch up in a less formal setting out of the office.

Three days later...

4. Send an additional competitor specific Case Study 1 – this is sent to remind them you are doing business with their competitors and that it is worth their time meeting with you. Remember, you are only trying to sell them one meeting with you at this stage, not fully buying the service or product you offer.

Three days later...

5. Send a vertical specific Case Study 2 – this is sent to remind them that you are creating insane results for big clients in the same context and therefore it would be advantageous for them to look into this.

Three days later...

6. Add Value 2 – send a new article/vertical specific information – this could be infographics, expert opinions, whitepapers, research, customer insights, industry trends data, M&A activity.

Three days later…

7. Mix It Up – be spontaneously in the area, want to grab coffee?

Three days later…

8. Repeat the sequence – remember, Never Give Up! Some of the biggest deals I've done have been after 15+ follow-ups with no response. Can you imagine how much more business you would get if you implemented the "never give up email sequence" across your outreach efforts! Imagine that wave of energy you put out coming back to you ten-fold!

PRO TIP
Get creative in how you demonstrate going the extra mile with clients

When implementing a process like the one above it can be easy to slip into a monotonous, robotic pattern and come across as automated. This is where I WANT YOU TO PAY CAREFUL CLOSE ATTENTION – each email must be tweaked and hand crafted to add proper value to your clients. If this is going to work properly they NEED to feel that you care about them and their wants. This is about going the extra mile, after all.

Therefore, you have to infuse each email with the energy of joy, enthusiasm and positivity. I've given you the recipe but now you need to add your own secret special sauce to make it yours. That's where you win, that's what creates the value and that can never be taken away from you.

Imagine for a second the client that hasn't done business with you for 18 months. How about if you sent them a hamper to their office and reminded them of who you are. You aren't just someone who's chasing the commission cheque, you're building relationships for the long term. Surprise them, make their day! Help them feel a little better, add a note with the hamper that says, "I haven't forgotten you. I know you're busy, but I'd love to take you out for a coffee when you next get a moment".

I talk about this in the section called Get a People Strategy and it's true, to increase my sales when I was starting out in the programmatic media world, I literally planned out clients' full holiday itineraries, packed with hand crafted recommendations on where to stay, what to do, where to eat. I took what I knew about travel and turned it into a way to add value in a huge way. I made a difference to someone's life and, as a result, I built a tighter relationship with my client and that made hundreds of thousands of dollars for the company. What you put out, you get back. When you help your clients win, both personally and in business, it comes back in mysterious ways, maybe not as you imagined, but that positive energy that you put out into the world magnifies and, as the world is really a mirror that reflects back to you what you put out, enormous amounts of good energy, wins and success come your way.

PERSONAL STORY
Use what you've got to create
value for your clients

As I sat down for coffee with my client, Sebastian, I was a little apprehensive. This was my first time meeting face to face with him and he seemed a little stressed. Over the course of the next half an hour Sebastian dropped some key information. He said he was planning a trip to Thailand next year (well, trying to) but he had a lot on his plate as he was also angling to get a promotion to Senior Manager and manage some very demanding clients in the process – *"Hello, ding ding ding, let's jump all over this. Now you're talking my language,"* I thought.

To me this smelled like an opportunity, here I had a clearly stressed out but ambitious individual who needed a break but wasn't getting the time he needed to properly devote his attention to planning a trip that would allow him to relax. I showed enthusiasm (not only because Thailand's my favourite country in the world) but because I wanted to help. After asking him more questions to get a deeper sense of the kind of trip he wanted, and also understanding more about the kinds of projects he was working on at work, I uncovered even more about Sebastian. He was one of the key people within the company that the leadership relied on for recommendations about who to work with and the latest innovation in the market. From a people strategy perspective, Sebastian was an influencer, he was well-connected internally and was considered a rising star.

As the meeting drew to a natural close, I knew two things: 1) I wanted to help him, 2) I knew how I could. I promised I would send him some information and tips on where to go and left the meeting.

Now here's what I did that made all the difference. I wasn't just saying those things and listening in the meeting to be kind or because it was my job, I did it because I knew I was going to follow up on my promises to him. This is what will make you stand out from 99% of sales people. Doing what you say you will, in a timeframe that blows their expectations out of the water when you follow up and overdeliver, puts you into a league only the best salespeople reach, but it surprises the client on a deeper level. You become someone they can trust, and guess what? That's not the only benefit, as you become someone that can be trusted and that is an unshakable level of confidence to reach.

Self-confidence is called *self*-confidence for a reason. It's because it comes from you doing what you said you would.

I did it. I followed up with the information, and I delivered on what I said I would. It might have taken me a few hours to pull together, but I was adding value to my client and helping him have a wonderful holiday.

For example, if you're in Bangkok you must do the Co Van Kessel[5] three-hour night bike tour. Not only will this mean you're cycling in the cooler evening air, but this special tour takes you through the backstreets of the city. By doing this tour, you get to see a completely different side to Bang-

5 http://www.covankessel.com/tour/co-by-night-3-hour-bicycle-tour/

kok, a calmer, more real side than the throngs of the tourist hotspots. You'll even get to try some local Thai food and see the famous flower market.

At the same time and in the same email, I also added value by sharing some of the innovations my company had coming up in beta and suggested, if he was keen, we could catch up for a second meeting next week to discuss it further. These new features could help him get that promotion he wanted by being first to market for his clients. It wouldn't hurt for him to win for his clients and for himself. I had planted the seed. I was helping him get what he wanted and showing a way to get there.

The key lesson here is use what you know to help you add incredible value to others. It doesn't need to be related to the product or service you are pushing, add value to your clients in this way and it will change the nature of your relationship over time. Small shifts in the relationship over time, add up and when they compound, the relationship transforms. You will be privy to information and ideas that are off the table for others, reserved only for the trusted few.

The second lesson here is, even if you don't know about a topic or subject, it doesn't stop you from doing some research or trying to find someone who does and asking them critical questions and summarising what you learned or putting them directly in touch. By going the extra mile here, you stand out but more than that you create a mentality within yourself of someone who creates value. This is a super powerful habit to build for yourself.

This is how you win in sales; you aren't looking for the commission cheque, you're looking to add huge value and develop the relationship. From here, you can close the deal, but it takes **patience**.

You can't chase the sale, or else you'll chase it away. You must help the sale by giving it things to grow off and the way you do that is to differentiate yourself by the type and amount of value you give.

You must have seen this: don't chase the cat, attract the cat!

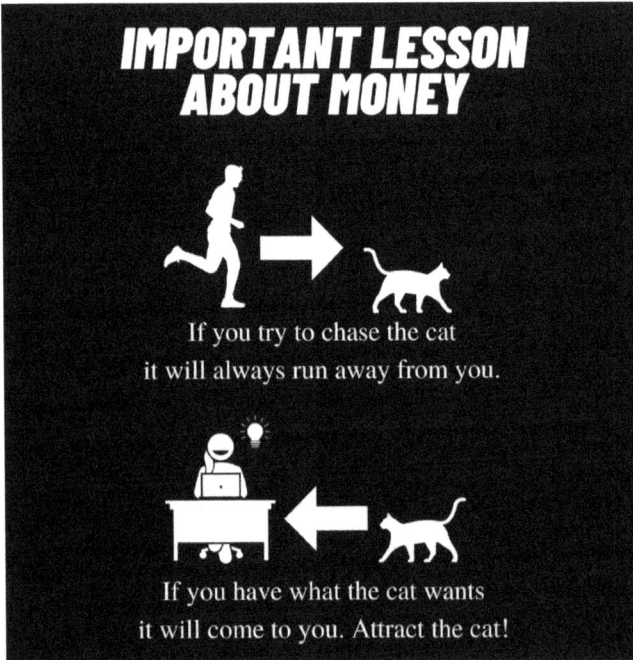

FIGURE 28: ATTRACTING THE CAT

Too many salespeople go in too strong right up front, they want it all without first giving value. This is a mistake. You might close a few sales this way by making clients feel pressured into buying, but you are leaving infinitely more money on the table and not developing any relationships to build a sustainable business on top of. The first moment they have, these clients will drop you for someone they know, like and trust and I don't blame them.

There are far too many business leaders who promote the wrong way of selling, "go in strong, make them work for you, they don't deserve our business." These ideas are all fuelled with negativity and a lack mentality. It makes me feel gross even just writing them out.

In addition to the glut of "bad bosses" out there, mainstream blockbuster movies do an excellent job of highlighting the wrong skills that are actually used by exceptional salespeople to close business. It's not a case of he who shouts the loudest or forces the client to act wins, it's the ones who confidently offer value, go the extra mile in the spirit of service and also get the job done that win. And by "job" I mean offering the solution to the client's problem that is of greater value than its price. We've chatted about this earlier; there's no need to rip clients off. It undermines them and you!

Another example of this is, if everyone's sending thanksgiving gifts to their clients, how about you remember their individual birthdays, work anniversaries and key celebrations too?

PRO TIP
It's all an opportunity, bad week, good week, sad week, happy week

If your client tells you they've had a hard week, take them to lunch, or send them a care package when you know they are working late, or better yet, send them some vouchers so they can take their partner out for dinner. No doubt, if they've been working late in the office, they won't have seen much of each other so, by you giving them this gesture, you are helping your client stay on top for their home life. Movie tickets, Uber Eats, chocolates, theatre tickets, spa days, it's all there to differentiate you. The question is, will you notice when it's needed?

MY FRIDAY NIGHT RITUAL FOR SUCCESS

Each Friday evening, right before I go to bed, I have a quick browse through the last 300 emails or so. This is to catch anything I have missed, any prospect that didn't respond or I got an Out Of Office message from. I then quickly draft a reply, only a couple of words, "Hi Tom", then save it to my drafts folder.

Why do I do this? I do this because when I come to work the next day, or on Monday, and sit down at my desk, I have instantly got ten or so emails in my drafts folder that I can write and send out to follow up on meeting requests. It's a great way to ensure that nothing slips through the cracks, and it will build your persistence.

When it's all on the line, when you are fighting through the jungle as an entrepreneur in the business of sales, every inch counts.

I am reminded of my friend and mentor Patrick Bet David. He took a big risk in 2009 and started his own insurance company. He put his life savings into it: $500k! He backed himself, and what's crazy is he went bigger than he needed and began by signing a $2m lease for an office.

A couple of years later, in the summer of 2011, things were not looking as rosy. At the time he had just lost his number one client, he was down to his last $13k and no one knew, not his wife, not his employees, not anyone. He came home one night around midnight and found his wife in tears; she had just had a miscarriage. After talking for a while, they decided to go for a walk. It was 1.30am and on that walk Pat was asking God, "Why am I going through this? I'm giving my best. I'm working hard. I'm loyal to the vision. I need your help. I need a miracle."

The very next week into his account a $100k bonus slides on in. His only client, AIG, had given him a bonus he'd forgotten about.

Pat likes to quote Churchill and refers to this statement, "When you're going through hell, keep going."

The lesson here is when you are truly in it for the right reasons, you're working your butt off and you're doing the right thing, you can't help but win. You've got to have a grand vision and stay loyal to it, doing more even at times when it feels like the world is falling down around you. If you do, great things will happen. Treat people with respect, have faith in your vision and speak it into existence. Say it out loud. Ask for a miracle.

I know at times in sales it can feel like the world is against you, that big client you were hoping to land suddenly disappears off the face of the earth and you're left in the dust, but if you focus on always doing *more* than expected for your clients and yourself, you will rise up and experience amazing success.

It's the little things like the Friday night ritual that add up over time, taking the risk to go all out and really believe in your business. When you do more, clients notice, they respect that type of commitment and that you believe in your vision. It is real and it pays off.

Getting 1% better each day has a reward at the end of the year. Just focus on bettering yourself, staying true to your vision despite the external circumstances and give love to your clients by showing you came to deliver.

MORE MINDSET, MORE POTENTIAL, MORE YOU (AUTHENTICITY), MORE FUN

Just like joining Evolve MMA to promote change in my life, we all need to evolve. If you have got this far and you're questioning your sales career, trajectory and what's possible for you, maybe it is time to make a change.

Towards the end of writing this book, I moved jobs. It might seem like a strange move considering I was hitting targets, life was incredible, and the business was, in the words of one of my clients, like "my baby".

I had worked more weekends than I can remember for months, put my own money in to speed things up when expenses were slow, and given myself fully to this role, but I knew if I didn't change I wouldn't be pushing the boat out for what is truly possible.

I was so comfortable and I loved it and that was the problem.

When you are comfortable you stop planning for the future, you start to take shortcuts because you can do it with your eyes closed and you stop raising your aspirations. In order to get that fight back you need to change.

You can be taken down at any time, so it's important to be ready and have that sharpness, that zest for life, that expansion in your blood, that hunger for sales, to build something even bigger, to accelerate your life and jump onboard a bigger rocket ship.

Whether that is starting your own business or taking a new role, in order to force yourself to grow it must be done. It is the way. Change and grow to make it to the next level, or else you'll get left behind as mediocrity slowly creeps in and saturates your life. You won't see it happening, but the years roll by fast and that dream of starting your own business or taking the helm becomes dust.

This is where you need to go the extra mile for yourself and what you are truly capable of. It is knowing that you can have it comfortable, or you can push yourself and create more adventure, more fun and more money. It's all out there for you to discover.

I wasn't sure how I would be able to do it all – a new job, the articles, books, speaking, courses, start-ups, investments and coaching – but that's exactly why I needed to make the change, so I could figure it out and make it happen. The only way to make it happen is by taking the opportunities that life throws your way and getting started.

If this speaks to you, take ownership of the situation and make a change. You'll go through some big uncomfortable unknowns that when you've travelled through them you will have expanded. Keep it fresh!

Change seems hard until you look back and realise it was necessary to keep moving up and forward. Attach yourself to the biggest rocket ship possible, your future potential, and keep making moves.

USE THE DOUBTERS AS A DRIVER

This is where your desire to win and commitment to your vision comes in. You can use it to your advantage to push yourself harder to go the extra mile and deliver excellence. If you've got people around you that are always focused on what could go wrong, not overdoing it, telling you to slow down, you can use this as motivation to fuel yourself to go harder. Use their negativity and self-limiting beliefs to prove them wrong. Limit contact with these types as much as possible, but when the self-limiting text comes through turn it into a catalyst for action and delivering more value on a daily basis.

You are only in competition with yourself, if you get 1% better daily you will become exponentially better. Think about this in the context of delivering more to your clients: if you get exponentially 1% better at this Momentum Sales process, at your prospecting email, cold calls, closing, how much more business do you think you would be doing by the end of the year? You are your only limit, and the game is there to be won. Don't celebrate the finish line if you didn't really cross it; if you set a goal make sure you dominate and then celebrate.

People around you will try to make you conform to their standards. They will pat you getting 80% of the way their rather than crossing the finish line and completing the job, this makes you weaker and compromises your standards, don't go there. You want to run with the bulls, this is how we do it. We are *all* in and ready to win the day, every day!

Pay close attention to those around you, especially when you are going the extra mile for your business. This could mean working Saturdays, sending care packages, making one more call, sending one more email, being meticulous and prepared for every meeting, thinking about the DiSC behavioural profile and calibrating your pitch to suit their needs. Whatever it is, when you are doing it, there will be some that, through no fault of their own, will try to hold you back. They won't get it. This is because they haven't developed the awareness that you have, they can't see the bigger picture, they don't have your perspective. Therefore, don't pay attention or get caught up in responding to their limiting comments, instead use it to go even harder. I'm not kidding when I say it is ALL possible, but if you want to experience what others haven't, you're going to have to do things differently to the expectations of others. It makes sense, right? Like making your first 100k, it seems hard at first then, once you break through, the rest follows. It's the same all the way up: $1m, $10m, etc. It is just down to awareness and knowing what it means to deliver MORE.

I hope that you have supportive people around you that don't question your vision, that is the ideal, but stay alert.

People's opinions that you can use to drive you to do more include:

- Your parents

- Your siblings

- Your husband/wife

- Your in-laws

- Your boss

- Your colleagues

- Your friends

- The annoying removal guy who turns up late with an attitude that stinks

- Literally anyone that's trying to hold you back with their limited view of the world and what's possible – use it to drive momentum.

Use the fact that they don't understand as a driver and a tool to gain an edge. When someone annoys you with their lack of belief or comments that undermine what you are trying to do, this is where you need to use it as a trigger to focus on your own game. Rather than getting uptight and pouring your energy into their negativity, which ultimately brings you down and takes you away from your goals. Instead, step back and think to yourself, "What do I need to do now to win? How can I serve my team, my clients and the people that depend on me better?" Having this elevated level of awareness turns you into a servant leader. This is the level we play at; we don't have time to have a problem with everyone that's got a problem with us, we're going places.

At the end of the day, you've got to be able to find the ability to deliver more for yourself, your legacy, your family, your future, from within. What most sales books aren't telling you is that it takes commitment, discipline, and a heck of a lot of work! Don't underestimate the work part of this.

That's not to say that life is not for living. What I hope you are getting is that the Momentum Sales process is a way to weave having fun and your personality into the day to day of sales whilst over-achieving.

It is worth it! For sure it's worth it, when you sit back and look at the empire that you and your team built, it will be so rewarding.

We only live once, why not go for it? Why not do everything you were designed to do? Fulfil your destiny, what do you have to lose?

It's about expecting MORE from yourself to be relentless. Don't get embarrassed or worry about what clients might think when you're emailing them for the fourth time. The best know it's a numbers game and you have such value to offer your clients. Flip that switch, you're not annoying, you're turning up the volume on the solutions you can provide. It is a fight and sometimes the loudest voice wins. So, are you in this fight? You're not bugging, you're helping, you're prepared, offering unique insights, adding a tonne of value and you're pretty fun to hang out with on a call or meeting for 30 minutes. Worst case, your client is at least going to have a better day from meeting you!

Don't let pride or the fear of looking stupid stop you taking action. You've got to be in motion. Many salespeople who could be outstanding never get that far because they worry about what everyone else will think. They try to be perfect, wait until they have all the answers, never step outside of the lines and, as a result, it restricts them to a life of mediocrity.

"Don't let your ego get in the way of your effectiveness."

– ANDY FRISELLA, FOUNDER 1ST PHORM

Fear is the number one reason that holds most back, you've got to find a way to push past your fears and do it anyway. When you do, you'll be free, think about what motivates you to win. (And by win, I mean reach your client, not sell to them at any cost. I know most will get it but there's always one who's still not clear.)

You don't want to look back at your life on your death bed and think I could have done more. You want to lay there thinking I left it all on the table. I had some remarkable experiences, I made memories with some great people, I lived life to the best of my ability, and I fulfilled what I was designed for.

I believe this is the meaning of life, to help others through our own unique talents and gifts, to seek the truest expression of ourselves and exist in that bright flame of momentum doing what we love. You can see it in musicians when they are performing, in sports people when they are competing, and you can see it in yourself when you're selling at the highest level of your ability.

Face everything and rise, look for the signs, do more than expected. Invest in your relationships, do more, go harder, thinking bigger, and focus on what matters.

This world is yours for the taking; you can do anything you want in this life.

To wrap up this chapter, think back to the chapter on energy, we spent some time exploring the fact that everything is vibration, which is energy and energy functions on frequencies.

You have a choice to control the thoughts you accept into your conscious mind and your attitude. You can literally program yourself to see things in a more positive manner, to give out more kindness to the world, to respond with love and turn situations around. It stems from your thoughts and shows up externally in your attitude.

The world needs more kindness in it, division has set in all over the place. However, you have the power to change all that through how you show up for business.

Remember to do more around this subject of programming yourself to have the life you want. Write down what you want and look at it every day so that you can see the image of what you want in your mind. The more you do this, you'll impress the life you want onto your subconscious mind and the more you'll attract what you need to make it happen.

When you repeatedly show your conscious mind the result you want and it turns into a burning desire inside, that's good because desire seeks expression. When you get on the right frequency then it has to happen.

Your subconscious influences your feelings, which dictate your actions and then your results. The more awareness you bring to what's

going on inside, and filter what you let in, the bigger and brighter you can shine.

More is all encompassing, it relates to your clients, yourself and your life. More time spent learning and growing, more thoughtful approaches to sales, more understanding around who your client is and how to get the best out of them. More in terms of work, focus, commitment and doing what's right. More runs through every aspect of the Momentum Sales process.

MORE SUMMARY

- Complete the post-it note exercise, this is what it takes, you constantly want to be looking for ways to expand your business and integrate them into your strategy.

- Normalise doing more and going the extra mile. Make it your standard.

- There's a difference between being interested and being committed.

- Use Sunday nights (30-minute block) to get a jump start on the week ahead with the Sunday night prospecting ritual.

- Never lose hope because it's always all to play for.

- Get creative when you add value, aim to stand out and be memorable.

- Don't chase the cat!

- Play the infinite game, aim to get 1% better each day.

- Channel the doubters and use that energy to propel you forward through the road blocks, let it fuel you to do more.

- Doing more becomes your norm, when you set daily high priority tasks and you accomplish them you activate the achiever mindset. Success and winning becomes expected.

CHAPTER 11

The final word

SALES FLOW

What I am aiming for here is for you to reach the top of the pyramid, a place I like to call "sales flow". Here you are mining opportunities, you have increased the momentum to a point where sales flow directly to you and you spend your days stoking the fire, picking off the best ones, and acting from a place of abundance, consistently operating at the highest pinnacle of success.

In sales flow, you can maximise your ROI, opportunities are flowing in through all available avenues, and you are in a position to act on them. Every action you take drives even more momentum. You are operating in a high energy state, and life is amazing.

How you get to this point is everything we have been discussing, and the pyramid is built in layers as per the diagram below. I have only revealed this to you at this moment because I wanted you to understand what is packed into each layer and what is required.

FIGURE 29: THE SALES FLOW PYRAMID

This is what it takes to have success in sales; all of these elements combine to build momentum and create the next layer of success whilst operating from principles of a commitment to do your best at everything you do and listen to your inner wisdom. It is the hallmark of a sales superstar.

You'll know when you've reached a state of sales flow because opportunities will surround you. Don't mistake sales flow for meaning it will be easy, because it will still require you to put in 100% effort and there will still be challenges (remember the jungle, it's still there). What's different in this state is how you will operate, your attitude to challenges and hurdles and how you will feel about each opportunity.

Reaching and experiencing sales flow is important for every salesperson because once you know how it feels you will never look back. If you have never felt sales flow, you must have faith that it exists. The trick is putting in the effort, day after day, and recognising sales flow when it happens so that you can maintain it for as long as possible and then replicate the steps to get there. Speaking of which, make sure you remember to go back and take note of the *Hitting Targets Formula* previously discussed and write down the steps you need to take for hitting any sales target.

Real selling comes from the heart. Your clients can feel it, your team can feel it and deep down you can feel it. If you are not 100% fully into the purpose of your product or service, you are leaving energy on the table.

What I hope you have grasped in the time that we've spent together is that becoming an expert in sales is a combination of factors, it can't be faked (well, not for long). You must live it, love it and own it.

To create momentum, it truly comes from within. What I have given you is a secret formula to success in sales; it's a system and if you follow it you will win. But I want to end this book with a final point, and it is all about your customer. If you fail to remember this, no matter how many sales you make, no matter how well the systems and frameworks I have provided work for you, you will be leaving your full potential on the table.

The customer is where your heart needs to focus, merely following the process without falling in love with your customer won't get you to your full potential as a salesperson. When you can find out what your customer wants deeply and cares about and help them get it, you've cracked the code.

Never forget that it is a privilege to be a salesperson for the products, services and companies you represent. It is your duty to inform your customers about it and help them through the process.

Leave your ego at the door; keep asking them "why?"; when you face rejection, hold tight; get used to asking these words "can I ask *why* you chose to go with the other vendor?"; and use silence.

You have now unlocked within yourself a new sense of mastery around the subject of sales, go out into the world and practise creating momentum with every ounce of your being, lean into it so greatly that it becomes a part of who you are. Embrace the energy, after all, everything is ENERGY!

You may not have been born to do this, but now you are prepared and when you have taken the journey you've just been on, you are more than ready. Put it into action, step boldly into the biggest vision you have for your life and GO FOR IT!

This is your time!

Know that I will be cheering for you from the side lines, urging you to be the best salesperson that you are capable of being, and help train other salespeople with what you have learned. I am only ever an email or message away.

Your friend,
Tim Castle

No explanation needed for this fly wheel, you got this!

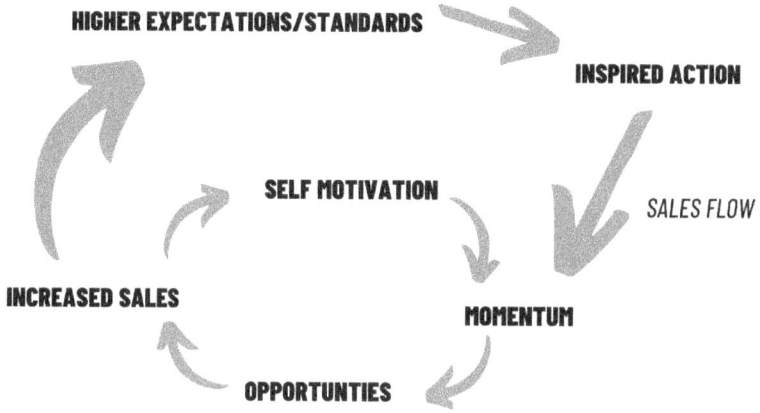

FIGURE 30: THE SALES FLOW FLY WHEEL

You're ready!

A momentum building sales superstar is born. You are ready to go give your greatness to the world.

I hope that this book has served you, given you the tools to go out and sell with joy and helped you see where you were going off track so that you can achieve your biggest vision.

Everything in life is about awareness. People don't do better because they are ignorant, salespeople are just the same. If you know someone who's struggling in sales, pass them a copy and give them a leg up.

Sales is the most thrilling game and, if you stick with it, put these skills to work, you will see your confidence, mindset and life change as a result. Once you shift your habits and identity, your world will become abundant and filled with meaning. You have now made that shift and I believe in you.

This is by no means everything that you need to know in sales, but it's the fundamental base that will allow you to build on these impactful skills in the real world and deliver meaningful work. By getting out there every day, giving it another shot and owning your light, you will sell more and make a difference to the lives you touch.

With respect, deep gratitude and thanks,

Tim

Recommended reading

Shoe Dog – Phil Knight, Creator of Nike

Think and Grow Rich – Napoleon Hill

You Were Born Rich – Bob Proctor

Sell it Like Serhant – Ryan Serhant

The Third Door – Alex Banyan

When I Stop Talking You'll Know I'm Dead – Jerry Weintraub

Max Out – Ed Mylett

Thank yous & requests

This book was written with one goal in mind, to help you enjoy the process of sales, give more and (as a result) sell more. A world filled with skilled salespeople is a better world.

It would not have been possible without the help of those who have mentored me during my sales career and entrepreneurial journey. Thank you.

It takes a team to write a book, thank you firstly to my incredible wife, my constant inspiration, drive and sounding board. I feel so lucky to be living this shared vision we have together. Thank you to my two boys, for reminding me to take breaks and that joy is all around us. You're the love of my life and I am blessed.

To Leila, Ali and the team at Known Publishing, thanks for keeping me on track, helping me deliver my best and going on this adventure again. You always go the extra mile, and I am grateful to be on this journey with you.

I would like to express my deep gratitude and thanks to Bob Proctor, Ryan Serhant, Richard Branson, the folk at Playground XYZ, WHSmiths, Leslie Lim, Pansing, Misfaiza Abdul, Bob Burg, Steve Seibold, Glen Sanford, Evan Carmichael, Iron Cowboy, Robin Sharma, Phil Knight, Ed Mylett, Jon Gordon, Joel Olsteen and Tom Bilyeu for your mentorship, guidance and message. You are all truly incredible!

Do You Want Free Bonuses?

Thank you for buying my latest book!

To celebrate the journeys, you have just taken, I am giving away a number of free bonuses with this book, including:

- Excel worksheets and PDFs to accelerate and track your sales momentum activity

- A private Facebook Group where you can meet like-minded souls and other momentum sellers

- Entry for prizes and to win 1:1 coaching time with me.

To get the bonuses, just send me an email with a photo of you holding your copy to **tim@timjscastle.com**

Thank you once again for your incredible support and for sharing this message. Let's help create a world of better salespeople and bring more light into the world.

Much gratitude,

Tim

A final quote:

"Any idea that is held in the mind, that is either feared or revered, will begin at once to clothe itself in the most convenient and appropriate physical forms available."

– ANDREW CARNEGIE

PLEASE RATE AND REVIEW THIS BOOK ON AMAZON, IT WOULD MEAN THE WORLD TO ME AND HELP CREATE MOMENTUM.

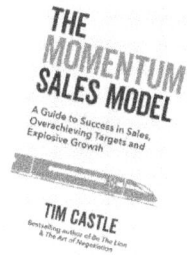

★★★★★

amazon

THE
MOMENTUM
SALES MODEL

A Guide to Success in Sales,
Overachieving Targets and
Explosive Growth

TIM CASTLE
Bestselling author of Be The Lion
& The Art of Negotiation

www.ingramcontent.com/pod-product-compliance
Lightning Source LLC
Chambersburg PA
CBHW030449210326
41597CB00013B/597